Aubrey De Vere

Antar and Zara

An Eastern Romance

Aubrey De Vere

Antar and Zara
An Eastern Romance

ISBN/EAN: 9783744794695

Printed in Europe, USA, Canada, Australia, Japan

Cover: Foto ©Thomas Meinert / pixelio.de

More available books at **www.hansebooks.com**

ANTAR AND ZARA

AN EASTERN ROMANCE

INISFAIL

AND OTHER

POEMS MEDITATIVE AND LYRICAL

BY

AUBREY DE VERE

HENRY S. KING & CO., LONDON

1877

ADVERTISEMENT.

THE first poem in this volume, 'Antar and Zara,' will be new to the reader. 'Inisfail' reappears in a revised and enlarged form, realising more nearly than before, and perhaps rendering plainer to others, the original scope and meaning of a poem which was, on its first appearance, in some instances misconceived. The subsequent poems are, for the most part, republications, except those in the last forty pages, few of which have appeared among the author's previous works.

I have been permitted to enrich this volume with a series of sonnets by my kinsman, and earliest friend, the late Stephen Spring Rice. To those who knew him well their beauty will be no surprise, though they lacked his last corrections. Friends less intimate will be pleased at discovering how compatible is the poetic power—imaginative emotion, refined thought, and delicate expression—with habits of business, and the most ardent practical energies directed to their most generous and dutiful ends.

Within a short time this volume will be followed by another, uniform with it, including 'The Fall of Rora,' 'The Search after Proserpine,' 'Psyche,' &c. These two volumes will together comprise, in a corrected form, the author's secular poetry previous to the 'Legends of St. Patrick' (1872), together with many poems composed before that date, though not published. His religious poems will be collected later in a separate volume.

A. DE V.

CURRAGH CHASE : *March* 17, 1877.

PREFACE.

' INISFAIL,' the most considerable poem in this volume, is an attempt to represent, as in a picture, the most stormy, but the most poetic period of Irish History. In simpler days than ours, when even rude feelings were tender, and when thought had not separated itself from action, poetry and history were more akin than they have been in recent times. In England and in Spain a series of ballads had early grown up, out of which rose the later literature of each country, ballads that recorded many a precious passage of old times, and embodied the genius, as well as the manners, of the past. Irish History no longer stands thus related to letters. Nowhere in Ireland can we move without being challenged by the monuments of the past ; yet, for many of her sons, and those who ought to be the best instructed, and for the traveller from afar, there exists no Alfred, and no Wallace. For the English-speaking part of the population nearly the whole of the old bardic literature has perished, and with it much of a history admirable for the manner in which it exhibits the finer, together with the more barbaric, traits of a society the spiritual civilisation of which had been early developed, and the civil early checked. Yet for centuries the bards occupied a more important position in Ireland

than in any other part of the West: their dignity
was next to the regal; their influence over the
people unbounded; and they possessed all the secular
learning then in the land. The Gael required that
even the precepts of the law should be delivered to
him in verse, as well as that the lines of the Princes
and Chiefs should be thus traced. The influence of
the priest alone equalled that of the bard, and between these two orders a rivalry often existed. We
have the testimony of Spenser as to the merit and
power of the latter so late as the sixteenth century.
He admired them and he feared them. The love of
the bard for his country was a lover's passion. To
him of course his Erin was in some degree an Ideal
Erin. He could see the crimes of individuals, and
denounce judgment on them; but beneath the accidents of the hour he ever recognised in his Land the
child of a divine predilection. The closer the hunters
beset her, the more thickly the 'winged wounds'
came about her, the more vehemently he hailed
her as one 'doomed to death, yet fated not to die.'
The name 'Inisfail' signified the 'Isle of Destiny.'

In Ireland the alliance between poetry and love
of country was, perhaps, closer than elsewhere. For
ages her History was but a record of calamity; and
to every generous nature his country becomes en-
deared by her sufferings. But even in earlier days
the bards must have found their best subjects for
song among the picturesque and romantic details of
Irish story. The antiquity to which it mounted ex-
cited imaginative sympathies: the dimness with
which large tracts of it were invested gave a more
striking prominence to what remained of it—those
great, half-isolated Records which loomed through

the mist, like mountain behind mountain retiring into more and more remote distance. Some reference to those records, wild as the wildest 'Irish airs,' may perhaps render more easily intelligible an enterprise of verse which many will deem rash, an attempt to add a Gaelic note to that large concert of English poetry, enriched long since by strains indirectly drawn from almost every age and land.

Long before those three golden centuries succeeding her conversion to Christianity, Ireland possessed culture, laws, and a time-honoured monarchy. It was in part for this reason that she at once became the great missionary land of the north, while foreigners flocked in crowds to her colleges. Her Faith was a tree that rapidly 'covered the lands with its branches,' because it had been planted 'by the water side.' If Ireland had to 'wait long for her martyrs,' it was because the genius of her early institutions was less opposed than that of other Western Nations to Christianity. Most of Europe, including Britain and Gaul, had received the Roman civilisation. With Pagan Rome Ireland had had no dealings, closely as she became linked with Christian Rome. She was an Eastern nation in the West, and a Southern in the North. Her civilisation was patriarchal, not military, in essence; its type was the family, not the army; it had more affinity with the Church, when the Church yet dwelt in tents, than with the complex fabric of the State. It was a civilisation of clans. The clan system would have been fatal to a people whose vocation was to create a great political dominion. To a country whose greatness was destined to be a missionary greatness it proved an auxiliary, at once affording to her the type

of those spiritual clans, her convents, of which those
ruled by the great monastic family of St. Columba
proved the most potent, and also withdrawing her
from the larger worldly ambitions. Had the clan
system met with no external interference, civil society
might possibly in Ireland, as in India, have preserved
its original type substantially unchanged to modern
times, without decay, though also without progress.
But, on the other hand, the missionary progress of
Ireland in three centuries exceeded that made by
half the countries of Europe in twice the time. Clan
fights were her sports; but Religion was her Reality.
To it her genius was attracted. Another Eastern
characteristic, ' Fatalism,' has been attributed to the
Irish race. Her Fatalism meant simply a profound
sense of Religion. The intense Theism which has
ever belonged to the East survived in Ireland as an
instinct no less than as a Faith. The Irish have
commonly found it more easy to recognise the Divine
hand than secondary causes. They have regarded
Religion as the chief possession of man. Such
nations are ever attached to the Past.

That Past was indeed too great a thing to be
forgotten. Even in our own days, remote and prosaic,
by the banks of the Boyne, amid more troubled memorials, we stand and wonder at tumuli the winding
galleries of which are supposed to retain the ashes of
those kings of the Tuatha de Danann, who ruled in
Ireland before the Milesian race. In the isles of
Aran, in Kerry, and in Donegal, we still find the remains of cairn and cromlech and rath, of stone forts,
and of those singular houses called ' cloghauns ' with
their steep beehive roofs. The Royal Irish Academy
shows us its silver shields, golden crowns, cups,

torques, spear-heads of bronze, &c. The illuminated
Missals and Breviaries of the Dublin University
prove to us that no sooner had the land become
Christian than it applied to sacred purposes the
skill it had long before possessed. Centuries earlier,
when the neighbouring countries were barbarous, its
Brehon Laws had constituted a complete code of
civil rule ; while many of its social usages, fosterage,
for instance, and the clan tenure of land, hereditary
offices, eric, &c., were as deeply rooted in the national
heart, as when, 1,500 years later, arbitrary laws
endeavoured in vain to eradicate them. The long
list of 118 kings, previous to the time of St. Patrick,
astonishes us at first ; but, on examining the material
records still existing, we find abundant proofs of the
antiquity of Irish civilisation. The traces of the
husbandman's labour remain on the summit of hills
which have not been cultivated within the records of
tradition, and the implements with which he toiled
have been found in the depth of forest or bog.

If the ancient memorials of Ireland are interesting
to us, much more so must they have proved to the
Irish of an earlier day. A green and woody knoll
beside Lough Derg is all that for us remains of Kincora, the palace of the Munster Kings, and home of
Brian the Great. But to a Gael in the fifteenth
century its ruins must have spoken a language as
intelligible as that in which old castles battered by
Mountjoy address us. To the Irishman, prince or
peasant, Nial of the Nine Hostages was as familiar a
name as Bruce was to the Scottish. Bard and
chronicler told how, before St. Patrick had summoned King Laeghaire to believe, Nial had ruled
over all Ireland; how he had been the ancestor of

the tribe of Hi-Nial, from which were descended the
Princes of Tirconnel and Tyrone, at whose name the
children of Norman nobles in the *Pale*, the four
counties round Dublin, trembled; how he had sent
against Britain and Gaul those naval expeditions,
still for us recorded in Roman verse;[1] how he had
leagued with his countrymen in Scotland, those
Scoti who with the Picts had again and again driven
back the Romans behind their further wall till they
left the land defenceless; and how, at last, he had
fallen at sea, in the port of Boulogne, by the hand
of his rival, Eochy. From priest as well as bard he
would have heard of the Irish Numa, King Cormac;
how he had succeeded to his father, A D. 227; how
he had established three colleges, one for war, one
for history, and one for jurisprudence; how he had
reduced the old Brehon law into a code; how he
had assembled at his palace of Tara his bards and
chroniclers, and commanded them to collect all the
ancient annals of Ireland into a series—the 'Psalter
of Tara;' how he had himself written a book called
'The Institutions of a Prince,' and stored in it the civil
wisdom of his time; how, in obedience to law, he
had resigned his throne on becoming disfigured by a
wound; and how it was piously believed that, before
his death, Christianity had reached him, and he had
become a Believer.

Still more often would he have heard the tale of
King Cormac's Grandfather, Conn of the Hundred
Fights, who succeeded to the crown of all Ireland,
A.D. 123, and who was at last compelled to surrender

[1]   'Totam cum Scotus Iernem
        Movit, et infesto spumavit remige Tethys.'
                                CLAUDIAN.

one half of it to Eoghan More (Eugene the Great),
King of Munster. He would have heard how the
latter, on the war breaking out again, had sought
and found allies in Spain, and with them had perished
in a night surprise; how his rival, Conn of the
Hundred Fights, was slain, in the hundredth year of
his age, by a king of Ulster; and how from a king
who united the blood of Conn and of Eugene were
descended the great houses of Munster, those of the
Dalcassian race, as the OBriens, who held sway in
Thomond or north Munster, and those of the Euge-
nian race, as the MacCarthys, who retained it for so
many centuries in Desmond or south Munster, and
were at last obliged to share it with the Norman
Geraldines.

But the records of which every song-loving Gael
heard went up to periods long before the Christian
Era. He heard how, at a time when the bards had
long enjoyed the dignities in Christian times be-
stowed on the clergy, a storm had arisen against this
song-church, accused of inordinate wealth and abused
power. He heard also how it had been saved by the
interposition of St. Columba, himself a Poet. He
heard how, earlier still, King Eochy had constituted
the five provincial kingdoms, as centuries previously
King Ugony More had divided Ireland into twenty-
five for the benefit of his twenty-five sons, compelling
his people to swear by the 'sun and the moon, the
dew, and all elements visible and invisible,' that their
inheritance should not be taken from them for ever.
He heard how Emania, the palace of the Ulster
kings, had been built, before the time of Ugony, by
Queen Macha, who had compelled rival princes to
toil at the foundations, and marked with the point

of her torque the spot where the work was to begin. The annalist of Clonmacnoise told him how for 850 years the Red-branch Knights, the great order of Pagan Chivalry, had gone in and come out among its halls; how another Queen, Maeve, or Maude, who had herself built the Connaught Palace of Cruachan, invaded Ulster at the head of her army; how her Gamanradians of Iorras had fought with the Red-branch Chivalry; and how, centuries later, the three Collas had burned to the ground that Emania of which the only record remaining was then, as it is now, a lonely rath near Armagh. The chronicler would then have told him that the palace of Tara had been built by King Ollamh Fodhla centuries before even that of Emania had been heard of; that in it, reign after reign, was held the great Triennial Assembly of chiefs, bards, and historians; that each warrior had taken the seat appointed for him beneath his own banner, during deliberations conducted with a solemnity half regal, half sacerdotal; that these assemblies continued to take place till A.D. 554, and that it was deserted for ever in consequence of a malison pronounced against it by St. Rodanus of Lothra. Emania had enjoyed more years of splendour than had elapsed between the first Danish invasion and Queen Elizabeth's wars; yet its greatness was over before Ireland had confessed the Christian Faith. Tara had lasted longer than the whole period of Danish, Norman, and Saxon wars united; yet the weeds had begun to creep over its old rath as many centuries before Henry II. had landed in Ireland as elapsed between his enterprise and what in Ireland was called the 'Anglo-Dutch invasion.'

Glancing thus back with the bards from epoch to

epoch, we reach at last the remote one of the Milesian settlement. The most learned among recent antiquarians assure us that a sceptical spirit respecting that settlement is as unphilosophical as a credulous spirit would have been regarded during the last century. They affirm that the whole social system of Ireland having been based upon genealogical claims, her most important institutions were formed for the purpose of recording facts and dates accurately ; and they state that the early chronicles are remarkably confirmed by Science as regards eclipses, astronomical calculations, &c. It is certain that the Gael ever looked upon this period as the authentic beginning of Irish glories, however problematical her earlier legends might be. Rejecting the claims to a greater antiquity, Charles O'Connor, of Balenagar, assigns to the establishment of the Milesian monarchy in Ireland the date of 760 years before our Era, making it thus nearly contemporaneous with the foundation of Rome. A race called Gadelian, or Gaelic, and at a later period called Scoti (as is supposed from their claims to a *Scythian* descent), migrated to Ireland from Spain under the leadership of the six sons of Milesins, king of that country. Their names were Heber, Heremon, Donn, Colpa, Ir, and Amergin. The brothers founded that Gaelic monarchy which had lasted for nearly 2,000 years when the mighty Norman race extended its conquests from England to Ireland, a land the political and religious institutions of which had never wholly recovered the effects of the Danish inroads.

It is with the Norman conquests in Ireland that the present Poem commences. It is necessary to make a few remarks respecting the chief character-

istics of Irish History from that period to the latter
part of the eighteenth century.

The six centuries of Irish History, illustrated by
'INISFAIL,' divide themselves into three portions.
The first endured for about 350 years. Its pre-
dominant characteristic was Outlawry. The Brehon
Law was set aside by the conquering race, and the
English Law was refused to the conquered, refused
by the settler more than by English kings. The
weak were the prey of the strong. Yet even in
those ages of wrong and rapine all was not suffering.
Flowers spring up by the torrent's bed ; and many a
gay song was sung beneath the invader's fortress.
Moreover, in the midst of the Norman settlements
the Gaelic chief held his own, and around him the
old clan life went on as before. Partly through
intermarriages, the Norman nobles, in the remoter
parts of Ireland, became Irish Chiefs, speaking the
national language, and adopting the national usages.
It is thus that Keating, writing his history amid the
storms of the seventeenth century, speaks of this
race : 'Notwithstanding what has been said of the
cruelties and sacrilegious acts of some of those
foreigners who came into Ireland, many of them were
men of virtue and strict piety, who promoted the
service of God and the cause of religion by erect-
ing churches and monasteries, and bestowing large
revenues upon them for their support ; and God
rewarded their charity and acts of mercy with
particular marks of His favour, and not only blessed
them in their own persons, but in a noble and worthy
posterity.' Their gradual amalgamation with the
nation at large is a pledge that no estrangement of

race or class among Ireland's sons can be permanent.

The second period is characterised by the wars of Religion. They completed the estrangement between England and Ireland. They completed also the union of the Gaelic and Norman races in Ireland. When the last great act of the tragedy had come, at the same side the ancient foes fought and fell. The Cromwellian victories, and the confiscation of more than half Ireland at that time, reduced with comparatively few exceptions the chiefs of both the old races to that condition to which the Geraldines of Desmond had previously been brought by the confiscations of Elizabeth, and the Ulster princes by those of James I. This period ends with the dethronement of James II., when the fall of the old Monarchy consummated that of the old Nobility and the old Faith.

The third period is that of the Penal Laws, and lasted till the days of Grattan. A succession of wars, renewed during centuries with recurrent passion, in defence of ancient laws, national existence, and religious freedom, had remained barren of their intended result. Foreign alliances, even during periods when England was torn by dynastic and religious dissensions, had always proved abortive. The struggle had but rendered Ireland famous among the nations, and scattered among them her warriors, as her missionaries had been scattered in old times. Wrong had run its complete circle. But the People *endured*. The Faith for which it had suffered preserved it as an integral People. The chains which had never been broken fell off. A more glorious triumph than that so often sought had been reserved for Ireland. It was awarded, not to a fortunate moment, but to silent years; not to nobles, but to a people—among whom, however, many tempests had sown wide the seed of nobility; not to spasmodic action, but to inflexible fortitude; not to arms, but to faith. When the cloud had rolled by there emerged a People and a Religion.

Persons of the most different prepossessions have arrived at practically the same estimate of Irish History, and in it have thus found the moral of the tale.

The Catholic sees in Ireland an image of the Church herself—for three early centuries the great missionary of the Faith; for three late ones its martyr; ever in tribulation, but never consumed; at one time exalted as a nation, at another deposed from nationhood but to become more powerful as a race, and effecting more in its captivities and dispersions than it could have done if oppression, and the poverty bequeathed by oppression, had never driven it to the margin of waters broader and more lonely than those of Euphrates or Choaspes. To one of a different creed a conclusion morally the same is differently coloured. Justice, he says, ultimately triumphs over wrong. Liberty cannot be trampled down for ever. A Religion is a Cause: and a Cause and a People in permanent union are indomitable. The philosopher shapes the result thus:—The relation between the three periods of Irish History is logical. The Outlawry of the first period rendered it impossible that in the second a new religion should be introduced into Ireland by means of *Law*. Who were to bow before the new laws at variance with the old traditions? Not kernes, who had never had the benefit of law: not

Barons, whose only law had been their own will.
The struggle but identified for ever the National
sentiment with the Catholic sentiment. Equally
close appears to him the connection between the
second and the third period of Irish History. The
Penal Laws of the latter were blunted by the whole-
sale confiscations of the former. Misery became the
pledge for fidelity. To the Irish people, who had
already lost their lands, there remained nothing but
their Faith. During the long night of persecution
its truths shone out like stars, and wrote themselves
indelibly on the heart of the race. Its priests were
its only friends (a power greater than they sought
being thus, but at a later time, forced upon them) :
the next world was its *nearest* hope : and it was not
likely that either would be forsaken. In the end,
permanent instincts and principles triumphed over
temporary necessities. In the failure of persecuting
laws, and in the restoration of Ireland, one man sees
the victory of Faith, another that of Justice, and a
third that of Reason ; three powers that work, on
the long run, to the same result.

In these days few are probably so biassed by
party bitterness as to grudge an epitaph to Virtue
and Calamity in times gone by. But were the History of Ireland rightly studied by the more intelli-
gent and influential of her sons (by the people it has
never been forgotten) how many obstacles would be
removed to kindly feeling between classes ! how
much would misinterpretation of motives be abated !
how zealous would all honourable men be to per-
petuate the right, to redeem the wrong, and to
abolish whatever in the present gives a bitterness,

not known in other countries, to those heroic recollections of the past from which all nations, except
the meanest, derive so much of their moral life.
Ireland has suffered grievously from ignorance of
Irish History, and we are still reminded by some
persons that even the 'pride of knowledge' hardly
exceeds the occasional pride of ignorance. That ignorance was not dispelled by the researches of Ussher
and Ware, Lanigan and OConnor. Let us hope that
the kindred labours of Dr. Petrie, Dr. Todd, Bishop
Graves, Dr. Reaves, and those great, lamented
scholars, Dr. ODonovan and Professor OCurry, labours as distinguished by impartiality as by depth,
may prove more successful. A just and generous
appreciation of periods less remote is equally needful.
The statesman legislates in vain for a country the
history of which he is ignorant of. The philosopher
inculcates in vain that primary duty, obedience to
Law, if—perhaps while applauding nearly every
revolt in recent times, and among foreign nations—
he mistakes for rebellions those movements, in the
past ages of Ireland, which were obviously, on the
contrary, loyal attempts to vindicate, not only the
very essence of liberty, but, yet more, ancient and
often immemorial authority from lawless aggression.
Thus to speak is, not to serve, but to make a mock of
a sacred thing—Loyalty. A timid caution may shrink
from historical studies (as though in an age of educa-
tion the most interesting portion of human knowledge
could be suppressed), but a manly prudence will
enjoin them. On the long run Truth is a peace-
maker. It is only when the present has received
the great interpretation of the past that the paths of
wisdom and virtue lie plain before us.

To such studies poetry may contribute. Sir
Walter Scott added ballads of his own to the Border
Minstrelsy and the Songs of the Jacobites; and in
those of Lord Macaulay and Professor Aytoun, the
Puritans and Cavaliers sing their hate or love as
vividly, and therefore as instructively, as they could
have done in the days of Cromwell and Rupert. In
proportion as poetry makes us acquainted with the
deeper springs of action, and with those imaginative instincts the might of which, like that of the
imponderable agents in the material world, is at once
secret and of all forces the most vast, history forgets
mere party politics in human interests. It is thus
that poetry exercises her high moral function in
connection with history. She deepens our sympathies with those who contended for the Just; yet
she reminds us also of the allowance to be made for
those who were unhappily ranged on the opposite
side, whether by necessity, by custom, or by that
vain and aggressive patriotism to which must be
assigned a place among the illicit affections. Her
spirit is comprehensive. She takes large views of
things—discerning and confessing upon which side,
on the whole, has been the Right, and on which the
Wrong: for, as regards mere detail, it is obvious
that, so long as retaliation remains an attribute of
human nature, there must, in every prolonged
struggle, be much of incidental wrong at both sides.
But her spirit is also penetrating. She recognises
the force of hostile traditions, detects high impulses
under unworthy disguises, and distinguishes between
the individual and the cause. Thus inspired, history
is enabled at once to discharge its two great cor-
relative duties, that to Justice, which so many evade

in *promiscuous* condemnation, and that to Charity, a substitute for which is so often found in impartial indifference.

That the wrong (though by which side it was initiated, and hardened into a policy, there can be no doubt) was not all at one side is a truth which this poem never conceals. To have concealed it would have been a sorry tribute to departed greatness. That greatness can afford such admissions; but a People which aspires to a future cannot afford an imperfect appreciation of the past. Such concealment would have been inconsistent with the whole meaning and scope of this work. It would also have been unjust. Apart from the fact that the greatest nations have often been the most ruthless in their treatment of conquered races (as, for instance, the Roman Republic), the relations of England and Ireland had rapidly run into a hopeless tangle. In England, the last of the three conquests, the Norman, was early condoned by the Saxon race, because it was early completed, and because a new basis for common rights (without which Time creates no prescription) was thus established. In Scotland the attempt to force Episcopacy upon a Presbyterian country was yet sooner forgiven, because it was quickly defeated. But England had never put forth strength enough to make a complete conquest of Ireland, the English King being recognised only as Suzerain by those Irish Princes who had accepted their position as vassals ; and, on the other hand, Ireland had never put forth sufficient unity of action to throw off that rule which he uneasily held, not as King, but as 'Lord of Ireland,' the only title which he had claimed from the reign of Henry II. to that of Henry VIII.

The conquering power, as it was called, thus ere long found itself caught in a snare of its own making —a position from which it could neither recede without disgrace nor advance without aggravated injustice. In that advance it was ever more and more disconcerted by finding, age after age, that Ireland's weakness was as formidable as her utmost strength could have proved, or rather that she possessed a strength of elasticity in an inverse proportion to her strength of robustness. Hatreds became aggravated : and a fatal absence of sympathy produced acts which perhaps hatred alone would not have produced, as has too often chanced in other countries with small shock even to the benevolent. Out of these manifold confusions Providence has at last evoked an unexpected result. Each of the warring nations has attained a liberty beyond the aspirations of either in the sixteenth century. One of them represents predominantly the Celtic genius, and the ancient faith of Christendom ; the other, the grave energies and free institutes of the Teutonic races, and the civilisation most characteristic of the modern world. Their very diversities, assuming these not to be embittered by the revival, in new forms, of religious intolerance, ought but to render the two countries the more eminently supplemental each to the other—the two central factors of an Empire upon which, more than on any beside, the graver hopes of Humanity rest. Such should be the aspiration, not more of the Englishman than of the Irishman who has insight to discern that the loftiest ideal he can form for his country's future is one that by its greatness excludes all petty mimicries of past struggles, and that despises all petty revenges. Those struggles were just, arduous, full of sad dignity, watched by many nations, worthy of long remembrance. To stand in proportion with them, their final result should be one beneficent to far lands and distant times.

'INISFAIL' may be regarded as a National Chronicle cast in a poetic form. Its aim is to embody the *essence* of a nation's history—a theme, I believe, original in poetry. Contemporary historic poems touch us with a magical hand; but they often pass by the most important events, and linger beside the most trivial. Looking back upon the past, as from a vantage-ground, its general proportions become palpable : and the themes to which poetry then attaches herself are either those critical junctures upon which the fortunes of a nation turn, or such accidents of a lighter sort as illustrate the character of a race. A historic series of poems thus becomes possible, the interest of which is continuous, and the course of which reveals an increasing significance. Such a series, however, as it constitutes a Whole, must be read in its proper order if its meaning is to be understood, and if the Unity of the poem is to be felt. The character of Irish History rendered it natural that its illustration should be chiefly lyrical. In this respect I have imitated the example of Ireland's ancient bards, with whom the Ode or the Dirge was as common as the Ballad was with the minstrels of other nations. Throughout, I have endeavoured to be true to the inner spirit of Irish History, faithful to its meaning, and no less to its changes. This accounts for the difference of treatment and tone observable in the three Parts of the poem, a difference which corresponds with the three periods of the history recorded. In Part I. the tone is chiefly legendary, and the treatment objective, because the period of Irish History illustrated in it is that which bordered most nearly upon the legends of Ireland's heroic yet half barbaric time. In Part II. the tone becomes more dramatic, the tragic struggle having reached its agony. In Part III. the more impassioned part of the conflict being over, the tone subsides into the elegiac until the end is approached, and the morning begins to glimmer through the night. To the reader of Irish History those three diversities of character are as notable in its mournful and manifold sequence, as the three distances in a landscape picture. Fidelity to Irish History rendered no less necessary that recurrence to certain fundamental *ideas* which the reader will observe, as the poem advances, in various degrees of development—such ideas as those of a Providence punishing at once and exalting ; the penance of the Norman ; the penance of the Gael ; the Apostolic mission of Ireland ; her undying hope ; the fidelity of her sons in far lands, &c. The same note is struck again and again in the life of a nation as in that of an individual, but ever in a different octave. Everywhere I have endeavoured to make the human prevail over the merely political interest of the theme, and to illustrate Ireland's Faith apart from polemics, and exclusively as a Power of Consolation and Strength. A national Chronicle in verse would, if faithful, be an echo of that voice which comes from the heart of a People, and is heard alike in festive hall and in the village circle, in the church-porch, and on the battle-field. That voice has many tones besides the sadder and more solemn —it records the brief pathetic joy which vanishes

like a flame, and the hope like the perennial fountain.
The main scope, however, of a poem which illustrates
the interior life of a Nation—the biography of a
People—must be moral. The moral of a brief individual life is often hidden. Nations are patriarchs ;
and their lives last long enough to vindicate the ways
of God.

Poetry has ever made its boast of what is called
Poetic Justice. Nowhere is that justice more mani-
fested than in the history of a race. But such a
history must be contemplated from the right point
of view, which can only be that of Religion. It is a
just perspective that reveals the harmony. Such a
harmony would be presented to us by the history of
the world, if we could grasp it as a whole. It is
presented to us in that of the Chosen People (the
only history recorded faithfully and from the true
point of view) : and to the history of that People,
so long as it remained faithful, there will ever be
found points of resemblance in that of other Nations,
so long as they have been faithful, and so long as
their life has been the life from within, not the mere
outward life of material chance and change. In
them will often be found that result which we note
so pre-eminently in the History of Ireland—the
weapons of oppression converted to the ends of right
—outward affliction ending in moral triumph—
Divine strength perfected in man's weakness.

It has been said that Irish History abounds in
touching and dramatic details, but that it is essen-
tially fragmentary. Religion imparts completeness
to it. When Religion threw off the bonds of centuries, a deliverance precious to all who sincerely
respect freedom of thought and freedom of conscience,

Irish History entered on its consummation, and justice won the most remarkable of her triumphs in modern times. Had it been otherwise, Irish History would have been no theme for song. Most unfit for poetry, however pathetic it may be, is any subject the substance of which is but violence and wrong, and the resultant of which is despondency. Under the tumults with which poetry deals there is ever an inner voice of peace. Memory—mournful and faithful—has been called by some the great Inspirer of Poetry. There is a Hope, the sister of devout Memory, which is its inspirer no less. Such Hope may stand on a tombstone; but her eyes are fixed on heaven; and if her Song begins in dirges it ends in hymns.

A. DE V.

CONTENTS.

ANTAR AND ZARA

OR

'THE ONLY TRUE LOVERS'

AN EASTERN ROMANCE

B

It is not to the credit of our modern civilisation that so little should be heard among us of those Christian communities which have held their own during so many centuries, on the citied slopes of the Lebanon, and on the adjacent plains. Several of them have existed from periods earlier than those in which the foundations of our oldest monarchies were laid. The Maronites derive their name from Maron, a hermit of the fourth century, whose cell, on the banks of the Orontes, gradually attracted a Christian population about it. In the seventh and eighth centuries, when the sword of the False Prophet was carrying all before it, they retreated from the uplands of the Euphrates, and Mesopotamia, to the fastnesses of the Lebanon. The Melchites, a race of unquestionably Arab origin, and whose religious offices are still celebrated in Arabic, emigrated to Syria before the Christian era, and became Christian in the fourth century. Weakened by their hereditary feuds, they retain, notwithstanding, all the pride of their ancient stock, and not less all its heroism, its generosity, its hospitality, its sense of honour, and its passion for poetry and eloquence. The devotion of both these races to their Faith is sufficiently attested by their having retained it during so many centuries of wrong, and in spite of so many persecutions. In the massacres of 1860 alone about 12,000 of them perished.

A philosophic as well as a religious interest
belongs to those races which still keep so much of
what belonged to the feudal and monastic system of
Europe in the middle ages, and combine them with
the patriarchal traditions of the world's morning.
Much that we possess they lack ; but, among them,
some of the affections—patriotism and love, for
instance—retain a meaning which appears to grow
daily more rare amid the boasted civilisation of the
West. That meaning is illustrated alike in their
lives and their poetry. It has been observed that
the religious poetry of the East sometimes resembles
love poetry. The converse remark may no less be
made. Eastern love-poetry is wide in its range, and
has occasionally been almost as epicurean as the basest
of our own : but its more characteristic specimens
resemble the early poetry of religion or patriotic
devotion, so ardently do they breathe the spirit of
self-sacrifice. To many readers the present poem,
perhaps a presumptuous attempt, will be an experi-
ment new, not only as regards its spirit, but its form
also—that of a story narrated in songs. It was
composed, in substance, twelve years ago, when the
author was in the East, and when public attention
had been recently drawn to the Christians of the
Lebanon, though neither permanently nor effectually, by persecutions not less horrible than those
which their fellow-Christians in Turkey have endured
within the last few months.

ANTAR AND ZARA; OR, THE ONLY TRUE LOVERS.

AN EASTERN ROMANCE.

PART I.

HE SANG.[1]

I.

O wind of night! what doth she at this hour
  In those high towers half lost in rock and brake?
Where is she? Sits she lonely in her bower?
  If she sits pensive, is it for my sake?

Perchance she joins the dance with other maids:—
  With whom? By whose are those white fingers
    pressed?
Perhaps for sleep her tresses she unbraids
  While moonbeams fill the chamber of her rest.

---

[1] Throughout this poem the lover's songs are in the longer metre; the lady's in the shorter. In the 1st and 3rd parts the songs are all his; in the 2nd and 4th, all hers; in the 5th and 6th, the two classes are mixed.

Tell her, O wind! that I have laid my head
   Here, on the rough stem of the prostrate pine
Which leans across the dried-up torrent's bed,
   And dream at times her face, and dream it mine.

Once in the palm-grove she looked back on me;
   A wild brier caught her zone: I saw it fall!
Large is the earth, the sun, the stars, the sea—
   For me that rosy girdle clasps them all.

II.

By night I crossed the tremulous poplar bound
   Which cools the south wind with its babbling
      bower;
I heard the river's murmur 'mid that sound,
   And smelt the fragrance of the trampled flower.

Where that pure crystal makes thy morning bath
   A white tent glimmered. Round it, rank on rank,
The crimson oleanders veiled the path,
   And bent or rose, as swelled the breeze or sank.

I entered not.   Beside that river's brim
   I sat.   Thy fawn, with trailing cord, drew near:
When from my knee its head it lifted, dim
   Seemed those dark eyes, by day so large and clear.

Go back, poor fawn, and house thee with thy kind!
   Where, amid rocks and mountains cold with snow,
Through high-arched forests sweep the hart and hind;
   Go back: go up: together let us go.

III.

Tell her that boasts—that slender is and tall—
  I have a cypress in a sunny space :
Tell her that blushes, by my garden wall
  A rose-tree blushes, kindling all the place.

Tell her that sweetly sings and softly moves,
  A white swan winds all night below my trees ;
My nightingale attunes the moon-lit groves—
  Can I not portion out my heart with these ?

If I were dead, my cypress would lament,
  My rose-tree shed its leaves upon my grave,
My nightingale weep long in forest tent—
  She would not mourn me dead that scorns to save.

IV.

Thou cam'st, thou cam'st ! And with thee came
    delight,
  Not mine alone.   The little flowers and leaves
Shook at the first gleam of thy garment white :
  And still yon myrtle thrills, yon almond heaves.

Thou spak'st ! That voice, methinks, is heard on
    high :
  The buds and blooms in every amaranth wreath
By Angels worn expand in ecstasy,
  And in pure light a heavenlier fragrance breathe.

Hail, Land that gav'st her birth ! Hail, precinct old !
  Hail, ancient Race, the Lebanonian crown !
The Turk hath empire, and the Frank hath gold :
  Virtue and Beauty, these are thy renown !

V.

Thou wentest : with thy going came my night :
  As some deep vale when sudden sinks the sun,
Deep, yet suspended on the mountain height
  And girt by snows, am I when thou art gone.

With death those hills, so late all amethyst,
  At once are clad : the streams are filmed with ice :
The golden ether changeth into mist :
  Cold drops run down the beetling precipice :

The instant darkness cometh as a wind,
  Or falleth as the falling of a pall :—
Return, my light of life, my better mind,
  My spirit's day, my hope, my strength, mine all !

VI.

Breathe, healthful zephyrs, airs of Paradise,
  Breathe gently on that alabaster brow ;
Shake the dark lashes of those violet eyes ;
  Flatter those lids that such high grace allow :

Those cheeks, pure lilies, capture with sweet stealth,
  And warm with something of a rose-like glow ;

Those tremulous smiles, costlier than miser's wealth,
  Draw out; detain : those tresses backward blow !

Thus much is yours.   'Tis mine where once she
      strayed
  To gather flowers that ne'er shall meet her sight;
To watch, close shrouded in the tall rock's shade,
  High up one little casement's glimmering light.

VII.

Seest thou, O Maid ! some star by us unseen,
  Buried from us in depths of starless space ?
Know'st thou some joy of lesser joys the queen,
  That lights so sweet a mystery in thy face ?

That face is as the face of them that bask
  In some great Tidings, or the face of one
Who late hath set his hand upon some task
  By God ordained, that shall for God be done.

That light is as the light of them who bent—
  That shepherd choir—above the Babe new born :
Upward from Him thy day is ever sent,
  A lifelong kindling of the Bethlehem morn !

VIII.

Since that strange moment, Love was as a breeze,
  And I a leaf that breeze wafted along :
Onward 'twixt magic heavens and mystic seas
  We passed.   If I was weak, yet Love was strong.

On, ever on, through mountainous defiles,
  By Love sustained, upborne, on piloted,
I wound o'er laughing lakes and happy isles :
  I asked not whither, and I felt no dread.

I breathed, methought, some everlasting spring :
  I passed, in rapturous, endless, aimless quest
(A dew-drop hanging on an eagle's wing)
  Through some rich heaven and ever-deepening
    West.

That dream had end. Once more I saw her face :
  No love it looked : the sweet lips breathed no
    sound :
Then fell I, stone-like, through the fields of space,
  And lay, dead bulk, upon the bleeding ground.

IX.

River that windest in thy jewell'd bed,
  The palms of her soft feet beside thee move :
But gentleness and peace are round thee spread,
  And therefore I am gone from what I love.

Nightly on thee the stars thou lov'st shall gaze:
  Thee from thy heaven no envious cloud can sever:
In vain to her I love mine eyes I raise ;
  And therefore, happy stream, farewell for ever !

Pale passion slays or dies. I would die young,
  Live while I live ; then sink without a sigh,
As some swift wave, from central ocean sprung,
  Subsides into the prone tranquillity.

X.

O heart whereon her Name was graved so long !
  Heart held at last to hers, henceforth be snow !
For love's sake let me do to love no wrong :
  There are who watch her. To the wars I go.

There are who watch her : and in fields far off
  There are who wait my banner, name my name ;
My House was ne'er the upstart Moslem's scoff :
  Its orphaned son will ne'er his fathers shame.

This is the grove where, by yon meeting streams,
  She too her love confessed—how falteringly !
From that glad hour a Church to me it seems :
  I leave it : I must leave it though I die.

Here as I slept, an Angel—not to sense
  Revealed—above me traced the Sacred Sign :
' Here is Love's palace : Duty calls thee hence :
  Alone where Duty stands are Church and Shrine.'

PART II.

SHE SANG.

I.

I HEARD his voice, and I was dumb
  Because to his my spirit cleaved.
He called me from afar : I come.
  Because I loved him, I believed.

He said, ' Though love be secret yet,
  Eternity its truth shall prove.'
It seemed not gift, but ancient debt
  Discharged, to answer love with love.

II.

Love bound a veil above my brow ;
  He wrapt it round me, o'er and o'er ;
He said, ' My little Nun art thou,
  My solitary evermore.

' Where hid'st thou when the falcons fly ;
  The flung jereed in music shrills ?
When sweep the Arab horsemen by
  Through valleys of the terraced hills ?

' Where are thy childhood's blithesome ways ?
  The tales, the dances, and the sports ?
The bards that sang thy beauty's praise
  Amid the hundred-columned courts ? '

Love took from me all gifts save one :
  The veil that shrouds me is his gift :
Love ! say to him I love, ' Alone
  That veil of severance thou canst lift.'

III.

Thy herald near me drew and knelt :
  I knew from whom the missive came
Ere yet I saw, ere yet I felt
  Thy sigil-mark, or kissed thy name.

I read—'twas like a thousand birds,
  Music confused of Paradise :
At last the words became *thy* words ;
  Thy voice was in them, and thine eyes

Above them shone in love and power,
  And flashed the meaning on the whole :
We were not severed, friend, that hour :
  One day shall blend us, soul with soul.

IV.

That face is valorous and grave :
  To it, despite thine unripe spring,
Thy spirit's strength thy future gave :
  It is the countenance of a King.

Look down, strong countenance, strong yet fair,
  Through all this weak, unstable soul !
Like stars sea-mirrored, kindle there
  His virtues—Truth and Self-control !

Not beauty, nor that youthful grace
  Uncareful girlhood's natural dower,
Suffice. A child of royal race,
  A hero's wife should walk in power.

V.

Like some great altar rises vast
  That rock whereon our City stands ;
With grey woods girt ; with shade far cast
  At morn dividing distant lands.

She fears nor war, nor summer drouth,
   By runnels pierced whose sparkling tide
Is drawn from mountains of the South
   O'er myriad arches far descried.

Around her cliff-like, marble zone,
   From tower to tower, from gate to gate,
At eve, when sunset changes stone
   To gold, her Princes walk in state ;

And Priests entoning anthems sweet,
   The People's strength ; and maiden choirs
That, passing, make them reverence meet ;
   And orphaned babes, and sonless sires.

High up, with many a cloistered lawn,
   And chapelled gallery widely spread,
Extends, flower-dressed at eve and dawn,
   The happy ' City of the Dead.'

There sit I, musing day by day ;
   I sing my psalm ; I pray for thee :
' If men could love, not hate,' I say,
   ' How like to heaven this earth would be ! '

VI.

On crimson silk, 'mid leaf and flower
   I traced thy Name in golden thread ;
A harper harped beneath my bower :
   I rose and brought him wine and bread.

He sang ;—methought he sang of thee !
   ' *My* Prince ! ' I cried—' how knew'st him thou ?

His victories in the days to be ?
 His heaven-like eyes, and king-like brow ? '

' O Maid ! I have not seen thy Prince :
 Old wars I sang ; old victories won
In my far-distant land long since ;—
 I sang the birth of moon and sun.'

VII.

My childhood was a cloistered thing :
 No wish for human love was mine :
I heard our hooded Vestals sing
 The praises of their Love Divine.

The village maids with rival glee,
 Flower-filleting their unclipt hair,
Sang thus, ' The meadow flowers are we ! '
 I thought the convent flowers more fair.

Yet false I am not.   Still I climb
 Through love to realms this earth above ;
And those whom most I loved that time
 Only for love's sake fled from love.

VIII.

I often say, now thou art gone,
 ' How hard I seemed when he was here ! '
I feared to seem too quickly won :
 Love also came at first with fear.

I sang me dear old songs which proved
   That many a maid had loved ere I:
No secret knew I till I loved:
   I loved, yet loved reluctantly.

My heart with zeal more generous glowed
   When he I loved was Danger's mate.
Great Love in this his greatness showed—
   He lifted thee to things more great.

IX.

He culled me grapes—the vintager;
   In turn, for song the old man prayed:
I glanced around; but none was near:
   With veil drawn tighter, I obeyed.

' Were I a vine, and he were heaven,
   That vine would spread a vernal leaf
To meet the beams of morn and even,
   And think the April day too brief.

' Were he I love a cloud, not heaven,
   That leaf would spread and drink the rain;
Warm summer shower, and dews of even
   Alike would take, and think them gain.

' It would not shrink from wintry rime
   Or echoes of the thunder-shock,
But watch the advancing vintage-time,
   And meet it, reddening on the rock.'

X.

Dear tasks are mine that make the weeks
    Too swift in passing, not too slow:
I nurse the rose on faded cheeks,
    Bring solace to the homes of woe.

I hear our vesper anthems swell;
    I track the steps of Fast and Feast;
I read old legends treasured well
    Of Maccabean chief or priest.

I hear, on heights of song and psalm,
    The storm of God careering by:
Beside His Deep, for ever calm,
    I kneel in caves of Prophecy.

O Eastern Book! It cannot change!
    Of books beside, the type, the mould—
It stands like yon Carmelian range
    By *our* Elias trod of old!

PART III.

HE SANG.

I.

BESIDE the well she stood, and water drew;
    The bowl, high held in both her hands, I drained;
She smiled, and sparkles showered of gelid dew
    On my hot hair, and brows with travel stained.

'O maiden! by thy lambs, and by thy kids,
   And by that holy, hospitable hand,
Know'st thou her name whom Love to name forbids,
   That fairest Fair One of the far-off land?'

Her eyes grew large; in wonder half, half ruth,
   She spake, like one who sorrowed, yet forgave:
'*Our* land a land of beauty is, O youth!
   Her maids are fair and good; *her* sons are brave.'

'O maiden! by those eyes, and quivering lids,
   Forgive! From thee Love hides not his sweet lore!
Breathe it to none—not even thy lambs and kids '—
   Then whispered I thy Name, but told no more.

II.

How base the soldier's revel o'er his wine!
   The tale around the encampment fire; the song!
Would I might hear, O Maid! no voice but thine,
   Or clash of swords that meet to right the wrong!

Why must his earthlier nature taint, or vex
   Man's race? His heart is brave; his thoughts are
     large;
Benigner Angels guard thy happier sex,
   The Angels that have innocence in charge.

The brightest of that band I saw in dream
   To thee make way: a lily stem she bore;
Then vanished, lost in thee, as gleam in gleam
   Is lost: thou glittered'st brighter than before.

III.

Who shall ascend into thy realm, O Love?
  It is a garden on a mountain steep:
From heaven it hangs, the woods, the clouds above;
  Sees many rivers into ocean creep.

Round it are icy spires; that vale they guard;
  But who can breathe the airs that past them blow?
Within it blooms the rose, and drops the nard;
  But who can clasp the roses of the snow?

The bird there singing sings as sings a bride;
  But who her mystic chant can understand?
O Maid, I saw thee ere we met, and cried,
  ' The land she treads on is a virgin land!'

IV.

Gladdening, as if in founts of Eden dipped,
  Thy beauty cheers and strengthens hearts forlorn,
Not like dark Islam's glances, venom-tipt;—
  Dove's eyes thou hast, the love-lights of the morn.

Thy Father's joy art thou, thy Mother's boast;
  Upon the dusty track by pilgrims trod
Laugheth the cripple; and the warlike host
  Divides before thee, giving thanks to God.

The merchants praise thee, and the wandering guest—
  ' Her veil down streams with such a humble pride,
Fairer that veil alone than all the West
  Irreverent boasts of charms that scorn to hide!'

V.

'Is thy love fairer than each other maiden ? '
   The young maids ask me.   Answer find I none :
I know but this ;—she shines on hearts grief-laden
   Like visitant from star more near the sun.

Above her vesture's hem a lustre hovers :
   Whiter her veil than earliest white of dawn,
Now lifted as on sighs of happy lovers,
   Around her now, like mist o'er Hesper, drawn.

Sweet is her voice, as though with Saint and Angel
   Her converse had been ever, and were still :
She seems to waft with her some high evangel,
   So light her step, so frank with all good-will.

Let her be child, or girl, or maid, or woman—
   I know not what she is.   Alone I know
She moves o'er earth like creature more than human,
   Missioned from God to spread His peace below.

VI.

When, travel-worn, on thee I chance to muse,
   Breeze-like the fragrance comes across my heart
Of spring-flowers breathing sweetness through their
     dews ;
   So blissful and so bountiful thou art.

That hour I sing no song ; but all my soul
  Inly with laughter loud of music rings :
The anthems of a Spirit o'er me roll ;
  Of virtue, loveliness, and love he sings.

All light, the fields of Duty round me spread ;
  Beyond them Honour sits, with thee beside :
A heaven all glory flashes overhead ;
  An earth all rapture trembles like a bride.

VII.

Changed is my love from what it was when first
  Forth from my heart that dream of fair and good,
Like Eve from side of sleeping Adam, burst,
  And by me, when I woke, in glory stood.

That dream wert thou ! A dream, and yet how true !
  Still, still I see thee oft beside that brook,
Standing 'mid lilies in the evening dew,
  Within thy hand a little open book.

Dear are such memories ; dearer far than these
  Art thou—now known ; a lovely human soul
Running on levels of some spirit-breeze
  With wingèd feet to Virtue's glittering goal.

The songs and sufferings of our Native Land,
  The Faith that lifts her high all griefs above,
These, and thy daily tasks of heart and hand,
  Thee too have raised—and with thee raised my love.

VIII.

My hand, made strong by years of manly strife,
   Has taught my heart to love in manly sort ;
I know thee now—a maid—one day a wife ;
   Thy home a war-tent, not the fairy court.

Mine Arab sires their towers cross-crowned had
     raised,
   Like thine, on crag and peak, and dwelt therein,
Hundreds of years ere first in scorn they gazed
   Far down on crescent flags of Saladin.

Seldom for us the unequal strife hath ceased :
   Age after age that martyr-crown we bear,
Here in our old, untamed, inviolate East,
   The Church for three short centuries bore else-
     where.

Wife of our race must share the heroic mould :
   A mother 'mid our mothers with calm eye
Must look on death : like that great heart of old
   Must give her own—if God so wills—to die !

IX.

From things that be around thee stand apart,
   For I thy Lover am, and fight afar :
A sword I send thee, that betwixt thy heart
   And alien things henceforth there may be war.

I send thee not the trophies I have won,
   Tokens of town redeemed, or rescued shrine :

I send a sword ; thy life is now begun :
  Look up ! In heaven, too, hangs the Sword, a Sign !

With this commandment have I bound thine eyes,
  That, fixed and set, henceforth no more they
    swerve.
Mine are they.   She my life who glorifies
  On me must gaze not, but that Cause I serve !

X.

In single fight we met : the Invader fell ;
  Two hosts stood mute, one gloomy, both amazed ;
His eyes, the eyes of one that hears his knell,
  On me, and not my lifted sword, were raised.

Forth from that shivered helm outstreamed afar
  His locks dust-stained. From out those eyes there
    shone,
Baleful in death, Hate's never-setting star :
  He hoped no mercy, and he asked for none.

Then cried my heart, 'A sister's hands have twined,
  How oft! those locks ; a Mother's lips have pressed :
Perhaps this morn the cassia-shaking wind
  Waved them, rich-scented, o'er his true love's
    breast.'

'Foe of my Race,' I said, 'arise; live free;
  But lift no more against the Faith thy sword !'
Was it thy prayer, or but the thought of thee,
  Rescued that sentenced warrior and restored ?

PART IV.

SHE SANG.

I.

It came ! it reached me from afar ;
    I kissed the seal, the cords unwove ;
Came wafted from the fields of war
    On all the odorous airs of love.

Close hid I sang ; close hid I sighed
    In places where no echoes were,
Where dashed the streams through gorges wide,
    And sprays leaned back on moistened air.

I sang a song, half sighs yet proud,
    And smothered by those downward rills,
A music proud, and yet not loud,
    As when her babe a Mother stills.

II.

Behold ! for thee, and for thy love
    I fain would make my spirit fair :
For this I strive ; for this I strove :
    My toil, though late, shall blossom bear.

Before thy face thy plant shall rise ;
    Thy light shall lift it, bloom and flower :
O love me ! Thou art great and wise :—
    Heart-greatness is the woman's dower.

Thou mad'st me as a warrior young
    That yearns to flesh a maiden sword,
That burns for battle with the strong,
    That pants to crush some rebel horde.

Rebels I count all things in me
    That bear no impress of my King!
'Fair is a great king's jealousy;
    His worth he knoweth;' thus I sing.

III.

I stood upon a rock what time
    The moon rushed up above the plain:
The crags were white like frosty rime;
    Her beams upon me beat like rain.

It was her harvest month of might:
    The vales and villages were glad;
I cried—my palms against the light—
    Like one with sudden pinions clad,

'Whom seek'st thou, O thou rising moon
    That broad'nest like a Warrior's shield?
Whom seest thou? Thou shalt see him soon,
    My Warrior 'mid the tented field!

'He reaches now some gorge's mouth;
    Upon his helmet thou shalt shine!—
Seest thou, O moon, from north to south,
    Another Loved One like to mine?'

IV.

No merchant from the isles of spice
  Who stands in hushed hareem or hall,
Who spreads his goods, and names the price,
  Was I, O friend!   I gave thee all.

When I had all things from me cast
  Except thy gifts, that hour I found
A gift I, too, might give at last—
  The being thou had'st made and crowned!

I am not nothing since thy vow
  Enriched my heart.   *That* wealth is mine:
'Nothing' I call myself, that thou
  May'st hear, O love! and call me thine.

V.

High on the hills I sat at dawn
  Where cedar caverns, branching, breathe
Their darkness o'er the deep-dewed lawn,
  While slowly bloomed in heaven a wreath

Of eastern lilies.   Soon the sun
  Ascended o'er the far sea-tide
Smiting to glory billows dun
  And clouds and trees; and loud I cried,

' Thou too shalt rise, *my* sun—thou too—
  O'er darkling hearts in might shalt rise,

And change to kingdoms just and true
   Nocturnal worlds of wrongs and lies.'

And every wind from vale and glen
   Sang loud, ' He, too, shall rise and shine !
A Warrior he, a chief of men,
   A Prince with power ; and he is thine.'

VI.

Men praised my words. Thy spirit dwells
   Within me, strangely linked with mine :
At times my mind's remotest cells
   Brighten with thoughts less mine than thine.

A gleam of thee on me they cast :
   They wear thy look ; they catch thy tone :
A kingdom in my breast thou hast :—
   The words they praised were not mine own.

VII.

A chance was that—our meeting first ?
   At morn I read a quaint old book
That told of maiden palace-nursed
   Who met a Prince beside a brook.

' Beside *our* brook the lilies blow,'
   I thought, ' green-girt, and silver-tipped ; '
And, musing on their bells of snow,
   At eve adown the rocks I tripped.

Sudden I saw thee !—saw thee take
    Toward me thy path !   I turned, and fled :
So swiftly pushed I through the brake
    My girdle dropped :—yet on I sped.

Had I but guessed that past the dates
    That hour the Stranger made his way,
I ne'er had left my maiden mates
    Beside that brook, alone, to stray.

VIII.

Surely my thoughts, ere first we met,
    Were loyal to their future Lord ;
My being, scarce my own as yet,
    Was strung with thine in just accord.

When first I saw, through showers aslant,
    The snowy Lebanonian line,
When first I heard the night-bird's chant,
    Even then my beating heart was thine.

When minstrels sang the sacred strife,
    And thus I wept, ' The Land made free
By patriot's sword is as a wife
    Whose head is on her husband's knee,'

Then, too, I nursed this hope sublime :
    To thine my spirit strove to reach :—
Let no one say there lived a time
    When we were nothing, each to each !

IX.

How oft in dreams that end in tears
 I see that convent near the snow
Wherein I lived those seven sweet years,
 And seven times saw the lilies blow;

There sent to couch on pavements cold,
 Fearless to suffer and to dare,
And reverence learn from nuns dark-stoled
 Who live in penance and in prayer.

There, too, of Love they sang—there, too—
 Yet not this love of maid and youth!
To that first love O keep me true,
 Thou Who art Love at once and Truth!

Have I not heard of hearts that nursed
 This human love, yet wronged their troth?
That first, great love they outraged first:—
 Falsehood to that was death to both!

X.

Now glorious grows my Warrior's name:
 The very babes his praises spread:
But late released, in crowds they came
 Around me, clamouring, 'Give us bread!'

His light was on them! Freed by him,
 A Land redeemed I saw them tread!
I gazed on them with eyes tear-dim:
 I blessed them, and I gave them bread.

'What man is this?' our Ancients sought:
  'This Chief we know not can we trust?'
Thou gav'st them back, unbribed, unbought,
  Their towers far off, their state august.

Thou gav'st to princes proved of yore
  Victory, by carnage undisgraced;
To matrons, hearts unpierced by war;
  To maids, their nuptials high and chaste.

To others, these:—but what to me?
  I speak it not: I know it well:
The fawn whose head is on my knee
  As well as I that gift might tell!

PART V.

THEY SANG.

I.

SUDDEN, in golden arms he came:
  I stood begirt with maiden bands:
Sudden he came, all bright like flame;
  Upon my head he laid his hands.

'This day past victories I disown:
  This day I seek the battle-field
A stranger chief, a knight unknown,
  Without a blazon on my shield.

' Not man, but He the worlds Who made,
   My hope shall frustrate or approve '—
I only bent my knee, and said,
   ' Victor or vanquished, thee I love.'

II.

They set me on a milk-white horse;
   Our household tribe around me trod:
Like rivers down a rocky course
   On rushed the warriors vowed to God.

I rode, the victor's destined prize,
   Last stake when hope was all but gone:
The flashes from a virgin's eyes
   Like music swept those warriors on!

'Twas theirs their Maid Elect to guard,
   The direful battle's tender guest:
'Twas mine to watch, inspire, reward;
   To honour all—to crown the best.

But who that Stranger Chief from far
   That like some brave ship tempest-tossed
Bore on o'er all the waves of war;
   Redeemed a battle all but lost?

I knew.   The victor's crown I dropp'd
   Upon thy brows, my destined Lord:
That eve thou sat'st—O boon unhoped—
   The first time by my Father's board!

III.

The victory ours, the feasting o'er,
　　The Victor rose,—he gazed around ;
' Emir ! I claim the prize of war,
　　Thy daughter's hand.'   My Father frowned.

' Uplift her in thine arms,' he said ;
　　' Then scale yon hillside smooth and dry :
That done, my daughter thou shalt wed :
　　To halt—forget not—is to die.'

I stood : my beating heart cried out,
　　' Thou canst not fail ! '   That cry he heard !
He raised me 'mid the warriors' shout ;
　　Forward he rushed without a word.

His breath came quick : his brows grew dark :
　　' My brother, lover, spouse,' I cried :
He reeled : his eyes were stiff and stark :
　　I wept, ' This day thou winn'st thy Bride ! '

He fell—but on the summit won,
　　Amid the vast and wide acclaim :
He lay, a dead man, in the sun :
　　I kissed his lips, and felt no shame.

Round him the warriors stood amazed ;
　　His love—'twas that brought back his life :
Upon him long my father gazed,
　　Then spake, ' My son, behold thy Wife ! '

IV.

On carpets heaped my Mother sate :
   I sate, I nestled on her knee ;
The gathering murmur neared the gate :
   My mantle, purple as the sea,

I drew about my little feet,
   And nearer sought my Mother's breast :
He came ; she spake, not slow to greet
   With courteous words the victor-guest.

Slowly my veil my Mother's hands
   Lifted, to boast the battle's prize ;—
' Prince ! thou would'st give thy life and lands,
   If I but raised it to her eyes ! '

V.

I knew thee half when first we met ;
   I knew thee well when seldom seen ;
When we had parted, plainlier yet
   I read thy nature—nay, thy mien.

Thine earliest glance my tremors stayed ;
   Then softly, and by slow degrees,
With thee my confidence I made,
   And wondering learned I too could please.

But now that we are drawn so near,
   I lose thee in thine own fair light ;
Vanish the outlines once so clear :—
   I know thee more by faith than sight.

VI.

Upon my shoulder, lightly as a bird,
  Her white hand lit : then back she fled, afraid ;
Beside my seat once more she stood, nor stirred,
  But loosed her hair, and round me dropped its
    shade.

Down to my feet it fell—a sudden night :
  She spake, ' Thy darkness and eclipse am I ;
But thou my sunrise art, and all my light ;—
  Still to weak things Love grants the victory.'

More dulcet than the viol rang her laugh ;
  Low laughed her Mother ; laughed her nurse full
    loud :
' Not *thee* I fear,' she cried, indignant half,
  And kissed—methought—the head o'er which she
    bowed.

VII.

My Lyre reproved my childish mirth :
  My Lute, remembering sad, old years,
Complained, ' Thy feet are yet on earth ;
  Thou caroll'st in the vale of tears.'

I hung my head : ashamed I moved ;
  I answered soft with whispering voice,
' O Love ! 'tis thou that stand'st reproved ;
  The fault is thine, if I rejoice.

' Not less this covenant have I made :
  I will not fold my hands in sleep
Till aid to those who cry for aid
  I stretch—have wept with them that weep.'

VIII.

He sang, ' I dreamed.   Of thee, all night, one thought
   Shone like a white flower on a darkling mere,
Or like one star that flashes, rapture-fraught,
   Through some blue gulf of heaven serene, and clear.'

She sang, ' I dreamed not: happiest sleep is deep :
   I woke as wakes the young bird in the woods :—
Thy spirit must have hung above my sleep,
   A bower balm-breathing from a thousand buds.'

We strove in song ; we sang, my love and I,
   In vales spring-flushed, and where the rock's
      broad breast
Echoed the untaught, ecstatic harmony:
   We warred in happy songs ; but hers was best.

IX.

Thou art not mine as I am thine:
   As great, or greater, is thy love ;
But loftier thoughts above thee shine,
   And lordlier aims before thee move.

The hand now clasping mine—that hand
   Let drop this hand to grasp the sword ;
It hurled in ruin from our Land
   The Impostor Prophet's sons abhorred.

Manhood fell on thee with my tears
   At parting.   With a woman's joy
I loved the warrior 'mid his peers—
   'Twas girlish fancy loved the boy.

X.

Mother of him I loved and love,
  My Mother too, ere long, to be !
With loving words his choice approve,
  And take thy daughter to thy knee :

So shall mine eyes, up-gazing still,
  Thine eyes in filial reverence watch ;
My hand be subject to thy will ;
  My heart from thine its impulse catch.

The young can learn, and I am young
  And labour to be good and true—
Tell her, O thou that know'st ! I long
  To give her age its honours due.

XI.

He sang, ' Upon the myrtle's silver stem
  Thy name I carved. Henceforth that tree is mine ! '
Low-laughing 'neath her vine-wrought anadem
  She sang, ' Thy name I graved upon the pine !

' The feebler hand the stronger bark subdued—
  Say, is it lordlier, bound and tamed to lead
The forest-monarch from his sunburnt wood,
  Or snare some little bird that took no heed ? '

We sang on heights where flowers snow-girdled sprang
  To passionate life : the eagle o'er us sailed :
Down plunged the torrents, and the grey cliffs rang :
  We clashed our songs in war ; but hers prevailed.

XII.

Methought to thine my Angel spake :—
　Near us he seemed, and yet above—
‘ Two children these ; their sport they take ;
　They teach each other how to love.’

Thine Angel answered thus to mine :
　‘ When Virtue, perfected by pain,
Hath changed earth-love to love divine,
　Then, stooping, we will lift the twain

‘ From this dull cave of mortal life
　Low-roofed, and dimly lit with spars,
To realms with Love’s whole glories rife,
　And over-vaulted by the stars,

‘ Where souls that love their God are one ;
　Where He Who made them is their joy :—
Play on—too young for love—play on !
　Your sports are sports of girl and boy ! ’

XIII.

Two hands—they meet ; they part—’tis better so ;
　Parted, they meet to shape one coronal :
Two feet—they meet ; they part, now swift, now
　　slow :
　They pace to music through one palace hall.

Two eyes—they move in concord : wanderers long,
　At last they rest on one unmoving star :
Two mouths, in kisses met, dispart in song—
　Sweet are our meetings ; sweet our partings are.

XIV.

I come, I go; yet neither shall repine:
  Sad is the parting; the return is sweet:
Once more the Battle with a voice divine
  Decrees our severance. Soon once more we meet.

We part not, save in seeming. We are one,
  In spirit one; in spirit we rejoice;
Two voices are we, blent in unison,
  Two echoes of one mountain-thrilling voice.

Nearer we are than words, than thought, can reach;
  Nearer we shall be; nearest, met on high;
Nearest as *not* belonging each to each,
  But both to Him—that Love Who cannot die.

PART VI.

THEY SANG.

I.

THE people met me at the rescued gate,
  On streaming in the immeasurable joy,
Warriors with wounds, grey priests, old men sedate,
  The wife, the child, the maiden, and the boy.

Others slow followed—some as from a tomb,
  Their face a blank, and vacant; blinded some;
Some that had whitened in the dungeon's gloom;
  Some, from long years of lonely silence, dumb.

Anatomies of children with wild glare,
  Like beasts new caught; and man-like spectres
    pale;
And shapes like women, fair, or one time fair,
  (Unhappiest these), that would not lift the veil.

Then saw I what is wrought on man by men:
  Then saw I woman's glory and her shame:
Then learned I that which Freedom is—till then
  The soldier, not of her, but of her name.

The meaning then of Country, Virtue, Faith,
  Flashed on me, lightning-like: I pressed my
    brow
Down on the wayside dust, and vowed till death
  My life to these. *That* was my bridal vow.

II.

A dream was mine that not for long
  Our joy should have its home on earth;
That love, by anguish winged, and wrong,
  Should early seek its place of birth;

That all thy hand hath done and dared
  Should scantlier serve our Country's need
Than some strange suffering 'twixt us shared—
  Her last great harvest's sanguine seed.

I saw false friends their treaties snap
  Like osiers in a giant's hand;
I saw the flames our cities wrap;
  Saw, drowned in blood, our Christian Land.

I saw from far the nations come
    To avenge the lives they scorned to save,
Till, ransomed by our martyrdom,
    A People carolled o'er our grave !

III.

Still to protect the lowly in their place,
    The Power unjust to meet, defiant still,
Is ours; and ours to subjugate the base
    In our own hearts to God's triumphant Will.

We, playmates once amid the flowers and rills,
    Are now two hunters chasing hart and hind,
Two shepherds guarding flocks on holy hills,
    Two eaglets launched along a single wind.

What next ?   Two souls—a husband and a wife—
    Bearing one Cross o'er heights the Saviour trod;—
What last ?   Two Spirits in the life of life
    Singing God's love-song under eyes of God.

IV.

A dream was mine when six years old :—
    Against my Mother's knee one day,
Protected by her mantle's fold,
    All weary, weak, and wan I lay.

Then dreamed I that in caverns drear
   . I roamed forlorn.   The weeks went by

From month to month, from year to year:
   At last I laid me down to die.

An Angel by me stood, and smiled;
   He wrapt me round; aloft he bore;
He swept with me o'er wood and wild;
   He laid me at my Mother's door.

When first we met, with heart that yearned
   How oft I saw that face! Ah! me,
How slowly, seeing, I discerned
   That likeness strange it bears to thee!

v.

If some great Angel thus bespake,
   ' Near, and thy nearest, he shall be,
Yet thou—a dreamer though awake—
   In him but thine own Thought shalt see;'

If some great Angel thus bespake,
   ' Near, and his nearest, thou shalt be,
Yet still his fancy shall mistake
   That beauty he but dreams, for thee;'

If, last, some pitying Angel spake,
   ' Through life unsevered ye shall be,
And fancy's dream suffice to slake
   Your thirst for immortality;'

Then I would cry for Love's great sake,
   ' O Death! since Truth but dwells with thee,
Come quick, and semblance substance make—
   In heaven abides Reality.'

VI.

Upon my gladness fell a gloom :
   Thee saw I—on some far-off day—
My Husband, by thy loved one's tomb :
   I could not help thee where I lay.

Ah, traitress, I, to die the first !
   Ah, hapless thou, to mourn alone !—
Sudden that truth upon me burst,
   Confessed so oft ; till then unknown ;

There *lives* Who loves him !—loves and loved
   Better a million-fold than I !
That Love with countenance unremoved
   Looked on him from eternity.

That Love, all Wisdom and all Power,
   Though I were dust, would guard him still,
And, faithful at the last dread hour,
   Stand near him, whispering, 'Fear no ill ! '

VII.

' Fear not to love; nor deem thy soul too slight
   To walk in Human Love's heroic ways :
Great Love shall teach thee how to love aright,
   Though few the elect of earth who win his praise.

' Fear not, O Maid ! nor doubt lest wedded life
   Thy childhood's heavenward hope should blot or
      blur;
There needs the vestal heart to make the Wife ;
   The best that once it clasped survives in her.

' All love is Sacrifice—a flame that still
  Illumes, and cleanses, though with fire, the breast;
It frees and lifts the clearer heart and will;
  A heap of ashes pale it leaves the rest.'

Thus spake the Hermit from his stony chair;
  Then long time watched her speeding towards her
    home,
As when a dove through sunset's roseate air
  Sails to her nest o'er crag and ocean's foam.

VIII.

' We knew thee from thy childhood, princely Maid ;
  We watched thy growing greatness hour by hour :
Palm-like thy Faith uprose : beneath its shade
  Successive every virtue came to flower.

' Good-will was thine, like fount that overflows
  Its marge, and clothes with green the thirsty sod :
Good thoughts, like Angels, from thy bosom rose,
  And winged through golden airs their way to God.

' To Goodness, Reverence, Honour, from the first
  Thy soul was vowed. It was that spiritual troth
That fitted maid for wife, and in her nursed
  The woman's heart—not years nor outward growth.

' Walk with the Holy Women praised of old
  Who served their God and sons heroic bore : '—
Thus sang the matrons, touching strings of gold
  While maidens wreathed with flowers the bridal
    door.

IX.

' Holy was Love at first, all true, all fair,
    Virtue's bright crown, and Honour's mystic feast,
Purer than snows, more sweet than morning air,
    More rich than roses in the kindling east.

' Then were the hearts of lovers blithe and glad,
    And steeped in freshness like a dew-drenched
      fleece :
Then glittered marriage like a cloud sun-clad
    Or flood that feeds the vales with boon increase.

' Then in its innocence great Love was strong—
    Love that with Innocence renews the earth :
Then Faith was sovran, Right supreme o'er Wrong :
    Then sacred as the altar was the hearth.

' With Hope's clear anthem then the valleys rang ;
    With songs celestial thrilled the household
      bowers : '—
Thus to the newly wed the minstrels sang
    As home they paced; while children scattered
      flowers.

X.

Circling in upper airs we met,
    Singing God's praise, and spring-tide new :—
On two glad Spirits fell one net
    Inwov'n of sunbeams and of dew.

One song we sang ; at first I thought
    Thy voice the echo of mine own :

We looked for naught ; we met unsought :
We met, ascending toward the Throne.

XI.

Life of my better life ! this day with thee
    I stand on earthly life's supremest tower ;
Heavenward across the far infinity
    With thee I gaze in awe, yet gaze in power.

Love first, then Fame, illumed that bygone night :
    How little knew I then of God or man !
Now breaks the morn eternal, broad and bright;
    My spirit, franchised, bursts its narrow span.

Sweet, we must suffer ! Joys, thou said'st, like these
    Make way for holy suffering. Let it come !
Shall that be suffering named which crowns and
    frees ?
    The happiest death man dies is Martyrdom.

Never were bridal rites more deeply dear
    Than when of old to bridegroom and to bride
That Pagan Empire cried, ' False gods revere ! '—
    They turned ; they kissed each other; and they
    died.

XII.

Fair is this Land through which we ride
    To that far keep, our bridal bower :
A sacred Land of strength and pride,
    A Land of beauty and of power.

A mountain Land through virtue bold,
   High built, and bordering on the sun;
A prophet-trodden Land, and old;
   Our own unvanquished Lebanon!

The hermit's grot her gorges guard—
   The Patriarch's tomb.   There snowy dome
And granite ridges sweet with nard
   O'er-gaze and fence the patriot's home.

No realm of river-mouth and pelf;
   No traffic bourne of corn and wine;
God keeps, and lifts her, to Himself:—
   His bride she is, as I am thine.

That Moslem deluge onward rolled:—
   The Faith, enthroned 'mid ruins, sat
Here, in her Lebanonian hold,
   Firm as the ark on Ararat.

War still is hers, though loving peace;
   War—not for empire, but her Lord;—
A lion Land of slow increase;
   For trenchant is the Moslem sword.

XIII.

Alas! that sufferer weak and wan
   Whom, yester-eve, our journey o'er,
Deserted by the caravan,
   We found upon our gallery floor!

How long she gasped upon my breast!
   We bathed her brows in wine and myrrh;—

How death-like sank at last to rest
  While rose the sun! I feared to stir.

All night I heard our bridal bells
  That chimed so late o'er springing corn :
Half changed they seemed to funeral knells—
  She, too, had had her bridal morn!

Revived she woke. The pang was past :
  She woke to live, to smile, to breathe :
Oh! what a look was that she cast,
  Awaking, on my nuptial wreath!

XIV.

High on the hills the marriage feast was spread :
  Descending, choir to choir the maidens sang,
' Safe to her home our beauteous Bride is led,'
  While, each to each, the darkening ledges rang.

From vale and plain came up the revellers' shout :
  Maidens with maidens danced, and men with men ;
Till, one by one, the festal fires burned out
  By lonely waters. There was silence then.

Keen flashed the stars, with breath that came and
    went,
  Through mountain chasms :— around, beneath,
    above,
They whispered. glancing through the bridal tent,
  ' We too are lovers : Heaven is naught but Love ! '

INISFAIL

A LYRICAL CHRONICLE OF IRELAND

In Three Parts

A dirge devoutly breathed o'er sorrows past.

WORDSWORTH

TO

The Memory of

THE FAITHFUL AND THE TRUE;

OF THOSE AMONG THE SONS OF IRELAND

WHO, DURING THE AGES OF HER AFFLICTION,

SUSTAINED A JUST CAUSE

IN THE SPIRIT OF LOYALTY AND LIBERTY,

AND SULLIED THAT CAUSE

BY NO CRIME

INISFAIL

A LYRICAL CHRONICLE OF IRELAND

PART I.

E 2

ADVERTISEMENT.

THE period of Irish history illustrated by the follow-ing poem is that included between the latter part of the twelfth century and the latter part of the eight-eenth. That period presents the singleness of scope which poetry needs. It begins with the evening twilight that succeeded a long and radiant, though often stormy, day; it keeps the watches of a tragic night; and it ends with the happier omens of return-ing dawn. To these six centuries belongs also a re-markable unity of spirit. All the struggles that shook them were characterised by the spirit of Liberty, nor less by that of Loyalty, whether directed to Gaelic princes, to Norman chiefs, who had become Irish, to Charles, or to James. Recent, and ancient, Irish history have, each of them, a spirit of its own. ' Inisfail ' is restricted by its theme to the intermedi-ate period, which begins with Strongbow and ends with Grattan; but in its bard-songs occasional allu-sions are made to Ireland's heroic time, that of her Kings and Saints, who flourished previous to the Danish incursions. In the first Part those allusions relate chiefly to the old Pagan Kings, in the third Part to Christian Saints. The work of the Kings had passed away for ever; that of her Saints had be-queathed to Ireland the imperishable hope. Truth of costume required such bardic allusions, which are also, perhaps, not without their poetic use, supplying, as they do, something analogous to the golden back-ground the old painters were fond of.

PART I.

THE THREE WOES.

THAT Angel whose charge is Eire sang thus, o'er the
  dark isle winging :—
  By a virgin his song was heard at a tempest's
  ruinous close :
'Three golden ages God gave while your tender corn-
  blade was springing :
  Faith's earliest harvest is reap'd.   To-day God
  sends you Three Woes.

'For ages three, without Laws ye shall flee as beasts
  in the forest :
  For an age, and a half age, Faith shall bring not
  peace but a sword :
Then Laws shall rend you, like eagles, sharp-fang'd,
  of your scourges the sorest :
  When these Three Woes are past, look up, for your
  Hope is restored.

'The times of your dole shall be twice the time of
  your foregone glory :
  But fourfold at last shall lie the grain on your
  granary floor—'

The seas in vapour shall fleet, and in ashes the moun-
    tains hoary :
  Let God do that which He wills.   Let His People
    endure and adore !

THE WARNINGS.
A.D. 1170.

I.

In the heaven were Portents dire :
   On the earth were sign and omen :
Bleeding stars and rain of fire
   Dearth and plague foreran the foemen.
Causeless tremors on the crowd
Fell, and strong men wept aloud :
Ere the Northmen cross'd the seas,
Said the bards, were signs like these.

II.

Aodh saw at break of day
   An oak with blood-beads on its lichen :—
All its branches rushed one way,
   Like an army panic-stricken.
Aodh cried, ' I see a host
That flees, as one that flies a ghost.'
Mad he died at noon : ere night
The Stranger's sails were up in sight.

III.

Time was given us to repent :
   Prophets smote them, plain and city :

But we scorn'd each warning sent,
   And outwrestled God's great pity.
'Twixt the blood-stained brother bands
Mitred Laurence raised his hands,
Raised Saint Patrick's cross on high :
We despised him ; and we die.

A BARD SONG.

I.

Our Kings sat of old in Emania and Tara :
   Those new kings whence are they ?   Their names
   are unknown !
Our Saints lie entomb'd in Ardmagh and Killdara ;
   Their relics are healing ; their graves are grass-
   grown.
Our princes of old. when their warfare was over,
   As pilgrims forth wander'd ; as hermits found
   rest :
Shall the hand of the stranger their ashes uncover
   In Benchor the holy, in Aran the blest ?

II.

Not so,[1] by the race our Dalriada planted !
   In Alba were children ; we sent her a man.

---

[1] Innumerable authorities—Irish, English, and Scotch—
record that beginning of Scotch, as distinguished from
Caledonian, history, the establishment of an Irish colony in
Western Scotland, at that time named Alba—a colony from
which that noble country derived its later name, the chief
part of its population, and its Royal House, from which,
through the Stuarts, our present Sovereign is descended.
This settlement is recorded by the Venerable Bede.

Battles won in Argyle in Dunedin they chanted ;
    King Kenneth completed what Fergus began.
Our name is her name : she is Alba no longer :
    Her kings are our blood, and she crowns them at
        Scone ;
Strong-hearted they are, and strong-handed, but
        stronger
When throned on our Lia Fail, Destiny's stone.

THE HOUSE NORMAN.

Among the churches sacked and burnt by Dermod and
his Norman allies, was that of the Monastery of Kells, to
which the headship of the great Order of St. Columba had
been transferred several centuries previously, when Iona
was wasted by the Danes.   The monks are supposed to have
been interrupted, while celebrating the obsequies of their
slaughtered brethren, by the return of the despoilers.

I.

THE walls are black : but the floor is red !
    Blood !—there is blood on the convent floor !
Woe to the mighty : that blood they shed :
    Woe, woe, de Bohun !   Woe, woe, le Poer !
Fitz-Walter, beware ! the years are strong :
De Burgh, de Burgh ! God rights the wrong.
Ye have murder'd priests : the hour draws nigh
When your sons unshriven, without priest, shall die.

II.

Toll for the Mighty Ones : brethren toll !
    They stand astonish'd ! what seek they here ?

Through tower and through turret the winds on
   roll,
But the yellow lights shake not around the bier.
They are here unbidden !—stand back, ye proud !
God shapes the empires as wind the cloud.
The offence must come : but the deed is sin :
Toll the death-bell : the death-psalms begin.

III.

The happy dead with God find rest :
   For them no funeral bell we toll.
Fitz-Hugh ! Death sits upon thy crest !
   De Clare ! Death sits upon thy soul !
Toll, monks, the death-bell ; toll for them
Who masque under helmet and diadem :—
Death's masque is Sin. The living are they
Who live with God in eternal day !

IV.

Fitz-Maurice is sentenced ! Sound, monks, his
   knell !
   As Roderick fell must de Courcy fall.
Toll for Fitz-Gerald the funeral bell :
   The blood of O'Ruark is on Lacy's wall.
The lions are ye of the robber kind !
But when ye lie old in your dens and blind
The wolves and the jackals on you shall prey,
From the same shore sent. Beware that day !

V.

Toll for the Conquerors : theirs the doom !
   For the great House Norman : its bud is nipt !

Ah, princely House, when your hour is come
  Your dirge shall be sung not in church but crypt !
We mourn you in time.   A baser scourge
Than yours that day will forbid the dirge !
Two thousand years to the Gael God gave :—
Four hundred shall open the Norman's grave !

Thus with threne and with stern lament ·
  For their brethren dead the old monks made moan
In the convent of Kells, the first day of Lent,
  One thousand one hundred and seventy-one.

PECCATUM PECCAVIT.

A BARD SONG.

I.

WHERE is thy brother ?   Heremon, speak !
  Heber the son of Milesius, thy sire ?
The orphans' wail and the widow's shriek
  For ever ring on the air of Eire !
And whose, O whose was the sword, Heremon,
  That smote Amergin, thy brother and bard ?—
The Fate of thy house or a mocking Demon
  Upheaved thy hand o'er his forehead scarr'd !

II.

Woe, woe to Eire !   That blood of brothers
  Wells up from her bosom renewed each year ;
'Twas hers the shriek—that desolate Mother's :—
  'Twas Eire that wept o'er that first red bier !

The priest has warn'd, and the bard lamented :
    But warning and wailing her sons despisèd ;
The head was sage, and the heart half-sainted ;
    But the sword-hand was evermore unbaptised ![1]

THE MALISON.

I.

THE Curse of that land which in ban and in blessing
    Hath puissance through prayer and through
      penance, alight
On the False One who whisper'd, the Traitor's hand
    pressing,
    'I ride without guards in the morning—good-
      night !'
O beautiful serpent !   O woman fiend-hearted !
    Wife false to O'Ruark ![2] Queen base to thy trust !
The glory of ages for ever departed
    That hour from the isle of the saintly and just.

[1] Between the brothers who founded the great Milesian
or Gaelic dynasty in Ireland, about B.C. 760, there was strife,
as between the brothers who founded Rome nearly at the
same date. Heremon and Heber divided Ireland between
them. A dispute having arisen between them, a battle was
fought at Geashill, in the present King's County, in which
Heber fell by his brother's hand. This may be called Ireland's 'Original Sin,' the typical fount of many woes. In
the second year of his reign Heremon also slew his brother,
Amergin, in battle.

[2] The story of the Irish Helen is well known. Dervorgil, the wife of O'Ruark, Prince of Breffny, fled with
Dermod Mac Murrough, King of Leinster. The latter,
on his deposition, went to England, where he contracted

II.

The Curse of that land on the princes disloyal,
  Who welcomed the Invader, and knelt at his knee!
False Dermod, false Donald—the chieftains once
    royal
Of the Deasies and Ossory, cursed let them be !
Their name and their shame make eternal. Engrave
    them
  On the cliffs which the great billows buffet and
    stain :
Like billows the nations, when tyrants enslave them,
  Swell up in their vengeance—not always in vain !

III.

But praise in the churches, and worship and honour
  To him who, betray'd and deserted, fought on !
All praise to King Roderick, the chief of Clan-
    Connor,
  The King of all Erin, and Cathall his son !
May the million-voiced chant that in endless expan-
    sion
  Sweeps onward through heaven his praises pro-
    long ;
May the heaven of heavens this night be the mansion
  Of the good king who died in the cloisters of
    Cong !

alliances with Henry II. and Strongbow against Roderick
O'Connor, the last Gaelic king of all Ireland. Dervorgil
ultimately found a refuge at Mellifont, where she lived in
penance and works of charity. Dermod died at Ferns,
under circumstances of strange horror. Exhausted by
domestic discords, as well as the calamities of his country,
Roderick retired to the monastery he had founded at Cong.
He died there at the age of eighty-two, and was interred
at Clonmacnoise, the burial-place of the Irish kings.

THE LEGENDS.

A BARD SONG.

I.

THE woods rose slowly; the clouds sail'd on;
  Man trod not yet the island wide:
A ship drew near from the rising sun;—
  At the helm was the Scythian Parricide.
Battles were lost and battles were won;
  New lakes burst open; old forests died:
For ages once more in the land was none:
  God slew the race of the Parricide.

II.

There is nothing that lasts save the Pine and Bard:
  I, Fintan the bard, was living then!
Tall grows the Pine upon Slieve-Donard:
  It dies: in the loud harp it lives again.
Give praise to the bard and a huge reward!
  Give praise to the bard that gives praise to men:
My curse upon Aodh, the priest of Skard,
  Who jeers at the bard-songs of Ikerren!

HYMN

ON THE FOUNDING OF THE ABBEY OF ST. THOMAS THE
MARTYR (A BECKET), IN DUBLIN, A.D. 1177.

THUS with expiatory rite
  The English priest and Erin's sang,
And loud Fitz-Adelm's towers that night
  With music and with feasting rang.

I.

Rejoice, thou race of man, rejoice!
　To-day the Church renews her boast
Of England's Thomas; and her voice
　Is echoed by the heavenly host.
Rejoice, whoever loves the right;
　Rejoice, ye faithful men and true:
The Prince of Peace o'errules the fight;
　The many fall before the few.

II.

Great is the priestly charge, and great
　The line to which that charge is given!
It comes not, that pontificate,
　Save from the great High Priest in heaven!
A frowning king no equal brook'd:
　His minions cried, 'Obey or die!'
Thomas, like Stephen, heavenward look'd,
　And saw the Son of Man on high.

III.

Thou King of kings, and Lord of lords,
　That world Thy blood redeemed is Thine!
The Cross, not sceptres, and not swords,
　Leads on the march of things divine.
Lo, loss is gain; and gain is loss;
　God lives: His Gospel is not bound:
The Saviour conquered from the Cross;
　His Martyr from the bleeding ground.

IV.

·Thus sang, that hour, with voices blent,
  Vivian and Laurence, side by side;
When Henry, King and Penitent,
  Strewed ashes on his royal pride.
That hour two nations pledged their troth :
  They sware, whate'er the years might bring,
That Martyr's Faith should clasp them both ;
  That Martyr's God should reign, their King.

THE LEGENDS.

A BARD-SONG.

I.

DEAD is the Prince of the Silver Hand,
  And dead Eochy the son of Erc !
Ere lived Milesius they ruled the land
  Thou hast ruled and lost in turn, O'Ruark !
Two thousand years have pass'd since then,
  And clans and kingdoms in blind commotion
Have butted at heaven and sunk again
  As great waves sink in the depths of ocean.

II.

Last King of the Gaels of Eire, be still !
  What God decrees must come to pass :
There is none that soundeth His way or will :
  His hand is iron, and earth is glass.

Where built the Firbolgs shrieks the owl;
  The Tuatha bequeath'd but the name of Eire:
Roderick, our last of kings, thy cowl
  Outweighs the crown of thy kingly sire!

THE FAITHFUL NORMAN.

I.

PRAISE to the valiant and faithful foe!
  Give us noble foes, not the friend who lies!
We dread the drugg'd cup, not the open blow;
  We dread the old hate in the new disguise.
To Ossory's Prince they had pledged their word:
  He stood in their camp, and their pledge they
    broke;
Then Maurice the Norman upraised his sword;
  The cross on its hilt he kiss'd, and spoke:

II.

' So long as this sword or this arm hath might
  I swear by the cross which is lord of all,
By the faith and honour of noble and knight
  Who touches yon Prince by this hand shall fall!'
So side by side through the throng they pass'd;
  And Eire gave praise to the just and true.
Brave foe! the Past truth heals at last:
  There is room in the great heart of Eire for you!

SONG.

I.

WILLOW-LIKE maid with the long loose tresses,
　With locks like Diarba's, and fairy foot,
That gatherest up from the streamlet its cresses,
　Above that caroller bending mute,
Those tresses black in a fillet bind,
Or beware of Manannan the god of the wind!

II.

No fear of the Stranger with feet like those;
　No fear of the robbers that couch in the glen:
But the Wind-god blows on thy cheek a rose,
　Then back returns to kiss it again.
Manannan, they say, is the God in air—
So sang the Tuatha—Bind close thy hair!

III.

The red on her cheek was brightening still;
　A smile ran o'er it and made reply
As she cast from the darkling and sparkling rill
　The flash of a darkling and sparkling eye;
Then over her shoulder her long locks flung
And homeward tripp'd with a mirthful song.

THE LEGENDS.

A BARD SONG.

I.

THEY fought ere sunrise at Tor Conainn ;
   All day they fought on the hoarse sea-shore ;
The sun dropp'd downward ; they fought amain ;
   The tide rose upward ; they fought the more.
The sands were cover'd ; the sea grew red ;
   The warriors fought in the reddening wave ;
That night the sea was the Sea-King's bed ;
   The Land-King drifted by cliff and cave.

II.

Great was the rage in those ancient days
   (We were pagans then) in the land of Eire ;
Like eagles men vanquish'd the noontide blaze ;
   Their bones were granite ; their nerves were wire.
We are hinds to-day ! The Nemedian kings
   Like elk and bison of old stalk'd forth ;
Their name—the 'Sea Kings'—for ever clings
   To the 'Giant Stepping Stones' round the North.

THE BARD ETHELL.

THIRTEENTH CENTURY.

I.

I AM Ethell, the son of Conn ;
   Here I bide at the foot of the hill ;

I am clansman to Brian and servant to none ;
  Whom I hated I hate ; whom I loved love still.
Blind am I.   On milk I live,
   And meat (God sends it) on each Saint's Day,
Though Donald Mac Art—may he never thrive—
  Last Shrovetide drove half my kine away !

II.

At the brown hill's base, by the pale blue lake,
  I dwell, and see the things I saw ;
The heron flap heavily up from the brake,
  The crow fly homeward with twig or straw,
The wild duck, a silver line in wake,
  Cutting the calm mere to far Bunaw.
And the things that I heard though deaf I hear ;
From the tower in the island the feastful cheer :
The horn from the wood ; the plunge of the stag,
With the loud hounds after him, down from the crag.
Sweet is the chase, but the battle is sweeter ;
More healthful, more joyous, for true men meeter !

III.

My hand is weak ; it once was strong :
  My heart burns still with its ancient fire :
If any man smites me he does me wrong,
  For I was the Bard of Brian Mac Guire.
If any man slay me—not unaware,
  By no chance blow, nor in wine and revel,
I have stored beforehand a curse in my prayer
  For his kith and kindred : his deed is evil.

IV.

There never was King, and there never will be,
In battle or banquet like Malachi !

The Seers his reign had predicted long;
He honour'd the Bards, and gave gold for song.
If rebels arose he put out their eyes;
   If robbers plunder'd or burn'd the fanes
He hung them in chaplets, like rosaries,
   That others, beholding, might take more pains:
There was none to women more reverent-minded,
   (For he held his mother, and Mary, dear;)
If any man wrong'd them that man he blinded
   Or straight amerced him of hand or ear.
There was none who founded more convents—none;
   In his palace the old and poor were fed;
The orphan walked, and the widow's son,
   Without groom or page to his throne or bed.
In council he mused, with great brows divine,
And eyes like the eyes of the musing kine,
Upholding a Sceptre o'er which, men said,
Seven Spirits of Wisdom like fire-tongues played.
He drain'd ten lakes and he built ten bridges;
   He bought a gold book for a thousand cows;
He slew ten Princes who brake their pledges;
   With the bribed and the base he scorn'd to carouse.
He was sweet and awful; through all his reign
God gave great harvests to vale and plain;
From his nurse's milk he was kind and brave:
And when he went down to his well-wept grave
Through the triumph of penance his soul uprose
To God and the Saints.   Not so his foes!

v,

The King that came after! ah woe, woe, woe!
He doubted his friend and he trusted his foe.

He bought and he sold : his kingdom old
  He pledged and pawn'd to avenge a spite :
Nó Bard or prophet his birth foretold :
  He was guarded and warded both day and night :
He counsell'd with fools and had boors at his feast ;
He was cruel to Christian and kind to beast :
Men smiled when they talk'd of him far o'er the
    wave :
Paid were the mourners that wept at his grave !
God plagued for his sake his people sore :—
  They sinn'd ; for the people should watch and pray
That their prayers, like angels at window and door,
  May keep from the King the bad thought away !

VI.

The sun has risen : on lip and brow
  He greets me—I feel it—with golden wand.
Ah, bright-faced Norna ! I see thee now ;
  Where first I saw thee I see thee stand !
From the trellis the girl look'd down on me :
  Her maidens stood near : it was late in spring :
The grey priests laugh'd as she cried in glee
  ' Good Bard, a song in my honour sing ! '
I sang her praise in a loud-voiced hymn
To God who had fashion'd her, face and limb,
For the praise of the clan and the land's behoof :
So she flung me a flower from the trellis roof.
Ere long I saw her the hill descending—
  O'er the lake the May morning rose moist and
    slow :
She pray'd me (her smile with the sweet voice blend-
    ing)
  To teach her all that a woman should know.

Panting she stood : she was out of breath :
    The wave of her little breast was shaking :
From eyes still childish and dark as death
    Came womanhood's dawn through a dew-cloud
        breaking.
Norna was never long time the same :
    By a spirit so strong was her slight form moulded
The curves swell'd out from the flower-like frame
    In joy ; in grief to a bud she folded :
As she listen'd her eyes grew bright and large
Like springs rain-fed that dilate their marge.

VII.

So I taught her the hymn of Patrick the Apostle,
    And the marvels of Bridget and Columkille :
Ere long she sang like the lark or the throstle,
    Sang the deeds of the servants of God's high Will :
I told her of Brendan who found afar
Another world 'neath the western star ;
Of our three great bishops in Lindisfarne isle ;
Of St. Fursey the wondrous, Fiacre without guile ;
Of Sedulius, hymn-maker when hymns were rare ;
Of Scotus the subtle who clove a hair
Into sixty parts, and had marge to spare.
To her brother I spake of Oisin and Fionn,
And they wept at the death of great Oisin's son.[1]

---

[1] The publications of the Ossianic Society have made
us familiar with Fionn Mac Cumhal (the Fingal of McPher-
son), chief of the far-famed Irish militia, instituted in the
third century to protect the kingdom from foreign invasion.
Its organisation rendered it an army of extraordinary effi-
ciency ; but, existing as a separate power, it became in time
as formidable to the native sovereigns as to foreigners.
The terrible battle of Gavra was its ruin. In it Oscar, the

I taught the heart of the boy to revel
  In tales of old greatness that never tire,
And the virgin's, up-springing from earth's low level,
  To wed with heaven like the altar fire.
I taught her all that a woman should know :
  And that none might teach her worse lore I gave
    her
A dagger keen, and I taught her the blow
  That subdues the knave to discreet behaviour.
A sand-stone there on my knee she set,
And sharpen'd its point—I can see her yet—
I held back her hair and she sharpen'd the edge
While the wind piped low through the reeds and
  sedge.

VIII.

She died in the convent on Ina's height :—
  I saw her the day that she took the veil :
As slender she stood as the Paschal light,
  As tall and slender and bright and pale !
I saw her ; and dropp'd as dead : bereaven
Is earth when her holy ones leave her for heaven :
Her brother fell in the fight at Beigh :
May they plead for me, both, on my dying day !

IX.

All praise to the man who brought us the Faith !
'Tis a staff by day and our pillow in death !

son of Oisin (or Ossian), and consequently the grandson of
Fionn, fell in single combat with the Irish king Carbry, and
nearly his whole army perished with him, A.D. 284. To
this day Fionn and Oisin are household names in those
parts of western Ireland in which the traditional Gaelic
poetry is recited.

All praise, I say, to that blessed youth
　.Who heard in a dream from Tyrawley's strand
　　That wail, ' Put forth o'er the sea thy hand ;
In the dark we die: give us hope and Truth ! '
But Patrick built not on Iorras' shore
　　That convent where now the Franciscans dwell :
Columba was mighty in prayer and war;
　　But the young monk preaches as loud as his bell
That love must rule all and all wrongs be forgiven,
Or else, he is sure, we shall reach not heaven !
This doctrine I count right cruel and hard :
And when I am laid in the old churchyard
The habit of Francis I will not wear ;
Nor wear I his cord, or his cloth of hair
In secret.　Men dwindle : till psalm and prayer
Had soften'd the land no Dane dwelt there !

X.

I forgive old Cathbar who sank my boat :
　　Must I pardon Feargal who slew my son ;—
Or the pirate, Strongbow, who burn'd Granote,
　　They tell me, and in it nine priests, a nun,
And—worst—Saint Finian's old crosier staff ?
At forgiveness like that I spit and laugh !
My chief, in his wine-cups, forgave twelve men ;
And of these a dozen rebell'd again !
There never was chief more brave than he !
　　The night he was born Loch Gur up-burst :
He was bard-loving, gift-making, loud of glee,
　　The last to fly, to advance the first.
He was like the top spray upon Uladh's oak,
　　He was like the tap-root of Argial's pine :
He was secret and sudden : as lightning his stroke :
　　There was none that could fathom his hid design !

He slept not : if any man scorn'd his alliance
He struck the first blow for a frank defiance
With that look in his face, half night half light,
Like the lake gust-blacken'd yet ridged with white !
There were comely wonders before he died :
The eagle barked, and the Banshee cried ;
The witch-elm wept with a blighted bud :
The spray of the torrent was red with blood :
The chief, return'd from the mountain's bound,
Forgat to ask after Bran, his hound.
We knew he would die : three days were o'er ;—
He died.   We *waked* him for three days more.
One by one, upon brow and breast
The whole clan kiss'd him.   In peace may he rest !

XI.

I sang his dirge.   I could sing that time
Four thousand staves of ancestral rhyme :
To-day I can scarcely sing the half :
Of old I was corn and now I am chaff !
My song to-day is a breeze that shakes
    Feebly the down on the cygnet's breast :
'Twas then a billow the beach that rakes,
    Or a storm that buffets the mountain's crest.
Whatever I bit with a venomed song
    Grew sick, were it beast, or tree, or man :
The wrong'd one sued me to right his wrong
    With the flail of the Satire and fierce Ode's fan.
I sang to the chieftains : each stock I traced
Lest lines should grow tangled through fraud or
    haste.
To princes I sang in a loftier tone,
Of Moran the Just who refused a throne ;

Of Moran whose torque would close, and choke
The wry-neck'd witness that falsely spoke.
I taught them how to win love and hate,
Not love from all ; and to shun debate.
To maids in the bower I sang of love :
And of war at the feastings in bawn or grove.

XII.

Great is our Order ; but greater far
    Were its pomp and power in the days of old,
When the five Chief Bards in peace or war
    Had thirty bards each in his train enroll'd ;
When Ollave Fodhla in Tara's hall
    Fed bards and kings : when the boy, king Nial,
Was train'd by Torna : when Britain and Gaul
    Sent crowns of laurel to Dallan Forgial.
To-day we can launch the clans into fight :
    That day we could freeze them in mid career !
Whatever man knows, was our realm by right :
    The lore without music no Gael would hear.
Old Cormac, the brave blind king, was bard
Ere fame rose yet of O'Daly and Ward.
The son of Milesius was bard—' Go back,
   ' My People,' he sang ; ' ye have done a wrong !
Nine waves go back o'er the green sea track ;
    Let your foes their castles and coasts make strong.
To the island ye came by stealth and at night :
She is ours if we win her in all men's sight ! '
For that first song's sake let our bards hold fast
To Truth and Justice from first to last !
'Tis over ! some think we err'd through pride,
Though Columba the vengeance turned aside.
Too strong we were not : too rich we were :
Give wealth to knaves :—'tis the true man's snare !

XIII.

But now men lie: they are just no more :
  They forsake the old ways : they quest for new :
They pry and they snuff after strange false lore
  As dogs hunt vermin !   It never was true :—
I have scorn'd it for twenty years—this babble
That eastward and southward a Saxon rabble
Have won great battles, and rule large lands,
And plight with daughters of ours their hands !
We know the bold Norman o'erset their throne
Long since ! Our lands ! Let them guard their own !

XIV.

How long He leaves me—the great God—here !
  Have I sinn'd some sin, or has God forgotten ?
This year I think is my hundredth year :
  I am like a bad apple, unripe yet rotten !
They shall lift me ere long, they shall lay me—the
    clan—
By the strength of men on mount Cruachan !
God has much to think of ! How much He hath seen
And how much is gone by that once hath been !
On sandy hills where the rabbits burrow
  Are Raths of Kings men name not now :
On mountain tops I have tracked the furrow
  And found in forests the buried plough.
For one now living the strong land then
Gave kindly food and raiment to ten.
No doubt they wax'd proud and their God defied ;
  So their harvest He blighted or burned their
    hoard ;
  Or He sent them plague, or He sent the sword :

Or He sent them lightning; and so they died
Like Dathi, the king, on the dark Alp's side.

XV.

Ah me that man who is made of dust
 Should have pride toward God! 'Tis a demon's
  spleen!
I have often fear'd lest God, the All-just,
 Should bend from heaven and sweep earth clean,
Should sweep us all into corners and holes,
Like dust of the house-floor, both bodies and souls!
I have often fear'd He would send some wind
In wrath; and the nation wake up stone-blind.
In age or in youth we have all wrought ill:
I say not our great king Nial did well
(Although he was Lord of the Pledges Nine)
 When, beside subduing this land of Eire,
He raised in Armorica banner and sign,
 And wasted the British coast with fire.
Perhaps in his mercy the Lord will say,
'These men! God's help! 'Twas a rough boy
  play!'
He is certain—that young Franciscan Priest—
God sees great sin where men see least:
Yet this were to give unto God the eye
(Unmeet the thought) of the humming fly!
I trust there are small things He scorns to see
In the lowly who cry to Him piteously.
Our hope is Christ. I have wept full oft
 He came not to Eire in Oisin's time;
Though love, and those new monks, would make
  men soft
 If they were not harden'd by war and rhyme.

I have done my part : my end draws nigh :
I shall leave old Eire with a smile and sigh :
She will miss not me as I miss'd my son :
Yet for her, and her praise, were my best deeds done.
Man's deeds ! man's deeds ! they are shades that
    fleet,
Or ripples like those that break at my feet.
The deeds of my chief and the deeds of my King
Grow hazy, far seen, like the hills in spring.
Nothing is great save the death on the Cross !
   But Pilate and Herod I hate, and know
   Had Fionn lived then he had laid them low
Though the world thereby had sustain'd great loss.
My blindness and deafness and aching back
With meekness I bear for that suffering's sake ;
And the Lent-fast for Mary's sake I love,
And the honour of Him, the Man above !
My songs are all over now :—so best !
They are laid in the heavenly Singer's breast
Who never sings but a star is born :
May we hear His song in the endless morn !
I give glory to God for our battles won
   By wood or river, on bay or creek ;
For Norna—who died ; for my father, Conn :
   For feasts, and the chase on the mountains bleak :
I bewail my sins, both unknown and known,
   And of those I have injured forgiveness seek.
The men that were wicked to me and mine ;—
(Not quenching a wrong, nor in war nor wine)
I forgive and absolve them all, save three :—
May Christ in His mercy be kind to me !

KING MALACHI.

A BARD-SONG.

I.

'Twas a holy time when the Kings, long foemen,
　　Fought, side by side, to uplift the serf;
Never triumph'd in old time Greek or Roman
　　As Brian and Malachi at Clontarf.
There was peace in Eire for long years after:
　　Canute in England reign'd and Sweyn;
But Eire found rest, and the freeman's laughter
　　Rang out the knell of the vanquished Dane.

II.

Praise to the King of eighty years
　　Who rode round the battle-field, cross in hand!
But the blessing of Eire and grateful tears
　　To the King who fought under Brian's command!
A crown in heaven for the King who brake,
　　To staunch old discords, his royal wand:
Who spurned his throne for his People's sake,
　　Who served a rival and saved the land!

SAINT PATRICK AND THE KNIGHT;

OR, THE INAUGURATION OF IRISH CHIVALRY.

I.

'Thou shalt not be a Priest,' he said;
　　'Christ hath for thee a lowlier task:

Be thou His soldier !   Wear with dread
   His cross upon thy shield and casque !
Put on God's armour, faithful knight !
   Mercy with justice, love with law ;
Nor e'er except for truth and right
   This sword, cross-hilted, dare to draw.'

II.

He spake, and with his crosier pointed
   Graved on the broad shield's brazen boss
(That hour baptised, confirmed, anointed
   Stood Erin's chivalry) the Cross ;
And there was heard a whisper low—
   Saint Michael, was that whisper thine ?
'Thou Sword, keep pure thy virgin vow,
   And trenchant shalt thou be as mine.'

THE BALLAD OF THE BIER THAT CONQUERED;

OR, O'DONNELL'S ANSWER.

A.D. 1257.

Maurice Fitz Gerald, Lord Justice, marched to the
north-west, and a furious battle was fought between him
and Godfrey O'Donnell, Prince of Tirconnell, at Creadran-
Killa, north of Sligo, A.D. 1257. The two leaders met in
single combat, and severely wounded each other. It was of
the wound he then received that O'Donnell died, after
triumphantly defeating his great rival in Ulster, O'Neill.
The latter, hearing that O'Donnell was dying, demanded
hostages from the Kinel Connell. The messengers who
brought this insolent message fled in terror the moment

they had delivered it ;—and the answer to it was brought
by O'Donnell on his bier. Maurice Fitz Gerald finally retired to the Franciscan monastery which he had founded at
Youghal, and died peacefully in the habit of that Order.

LAND which the Norman would make his own !
(Thus sang the Bard 'mid a host o'erthrown,
While their white cheeks some on the clench'd hand
    propp'd,
And from some the life-blood unheeded dropp'd)
There are men in thee that refuse to die,
Though they scorn to live, while a foe stands nigh !

I.

O'Donnell lay sick with a grievous wound :
   The leech had left him ; the priest had come ;
The clan sat weeping upon the ground,
   Their banners furl'd, and their minstrels dumb.

II.

Then spake O'Donnell, the King : ' Although
My hour draws nigh, and my dolours grow ;
And although my sins I have now confess'd,
And desire in the Land, my charge, to rest,
Yet leave this realm, nor will I nor can,
While a stranger treads on her, child or man.

III.

I will languish no longer a sick King here :
My bed is grievous ; build up my Bier.
The white robe a King wears over me throw ;
Bear me forth to the field where he camps—your
   foe,
With the yellow torches and dirges low.

The heralds have brought his challenge and fled ;
The answer they bore not I bear instead.
My People shall fight, my pain in sight,
And I shall sleep well when their wrong stands
    right.'

IV.

Then the clan rose up from the ground, and gave ear,
And they fell'd great oak-trees and built a Bier ;
Its plumes from the eagle's wing were shed,
And the wine-black samite above it spread
Inwov'n with sad emblems and texts divine,
And the braided bud of Tirconnell's pine,
And all that is meet for the great and brave
When past are the measured years God gave,
And a voice cries ' Come ' from the waiting grave.

V.

When the Bier was ready they laid him thereon ;
And the army forth bare him with wail and moan :
With wail by the sea-lakes and rock-abysses ;
With moan through the vapour-trail'd wildernesses ;
And men sore wounded themselves drew nigh
And said, ' We will go with our King and die ; '
And women wept as the pomp pass'd by.
The yellow torches far off were seen ;
No war-note peal'd through the gorges green ;
But the black pines echo'd the mourners' keen.

VI.

What said the Invader, that pomp in sight ?
  ' They sue for the pity they shall not win.'

But the sick King sat on his Bier upright,
And said, ' So well!   I shall sleep to-night:—
Rest here my couch, and my peace begin.'

VII.

Then the war-cry sounded—' Lamb-dearg Aboo ! '
And the whole clan rush'd to the battle plain:
They were thrice driven back, but they closed anew
That an end might come to their King's great
pain.
'Twas a nation, not army, that onward rush'd,
'Twas a nation's blood from their wounds that
gush'd:
Bare-bosom'd they fought, and with joy were slain;
Till evening their blood fell fast like rain;
But a shout swell'd up o'er the setting sun,
And O'Donnell died, for the field was won.

So they buried their King upon Aileach's shore;
And in peace he slept;—O'Donnell More.

THE DIRGE OF ATHUNREE.

A.D. 1316.

This great battle marked an epoch in Irish history.   In
it the Norman power at last triumphed over that of the
Gael, which had long been enfeebled by the divisions in
the royal house of O'Connor.   From this period also the
Norman barons more rapidly than before became Irish
chiefs.   As such they were accepted by Ireland.   The power
of the English crown, on the other hand, gradually de-
clined till it became unknown beyond the narrow limits of
a part of the Pale.   It rose again after the accession of
Henry VII.

I.

ATHUNREE! Athunree!
Erin's crown, it fell on thee!
Ne'er till then in all its woe
Did her heart its hope forego.
Save a little child—but one—
The latest regal race is gone.
Roderick died again on thee,
     Athunree!

II.

Athunree! Athunree!
A hundred years and forty-three
Winter-wing'd and black as night
O'er the land had track'd their flight:
In Clonmacnoise from earthy bed
Roderick raised once more his head :—
Fedlim floodlike rushed to thee,
     Athunree!

III.

Athunree! Athunree!
The light that struggled sank on thee!
Ne'er since Cathall the red-handed
Such a host till then was banded.
Long-haired Kerne and Galloglass
Met the Norman face to face;
The saffron standard floated far
O'er the on-rolling wave of war;
Bards the onset sang on thee,
     Athunree!

IV.

Athunree !   Athunree !
The poison tree took root in thee !
What might naked breasts avail
'Gainst sharp spear and steel-ribbed mail ?
Of our Princes twenty-nine
Bulwarks fair of Connor's line,
Of our clansmen thousands ten
Slept on thy red ridges.   Then—
Then the night came down on thee,
    Athunree !

V.

Athunree !   Athunree !
Strangely shone that moon on thee !
Like the lamp of them that tread
Staggering o'er the heaps of dead,
Seeking that they fear to see.
O that widows' wailing sore !
On it rang to Oranmore ;
Died, they say, among the piles
That make holy Aran's isles ;—
It was Erin wept on thee,
    Athunree !

VI.

Athunree !   Athunree !
The sword of Erin brake on thee !
Thrice a hundred wounded men,
Slowly nursed in wood or glen,
When the tidings came of thee
Rushed in madness to the sea ;

Hurled their swords into the waves,
Raving died in ocean caves:—
Would that they had died on thee,
    Athunree!

VII.

Athunree! Athunree!
The heart of Erin burst on thee!
Since that hour some unseen hand
On her forehead stamps the brand:
Her children ate that hour the fruit
That slays manhood at the root;
Our warriors are not what they were;
Our maids no more are blithe and fair;
Truth and Honour died with thee,
    Athunree!

VIII.

Athunree! Athunree!
Never harvest wave o'er thee!
Never sweetly-breathing kine
Pant o'er golden meads of thine!
Barren be thou as the tomb;
May the night-bird haunt thy gloom,
And the wailer from the sea,
    Athunree!

IX.

Athunree! Athunree!
All my heart is sore for thee,
It was Erin died on thee,
    Athunree!

THE DIRGE OF EDWARD BRUCE.

A.D. 1318.

I.

He is dead, dead, dead!—
   The man to Erin dear!
The King who gave our Isle a head—
   His kingdom is his bier.
He rode into our war;
   And we crown'd him chief and prince,
For his race to Alba's shore
   Sailed from Erin, ages since.
Woe, woe, woe!
   Edward Bruce is cold to-day;
He that slew him lies as low,
   Sword to sword and clay to clay.

II.

King Robert came too late!—
   Long, long may Erin mourn!
Famine's rage and dreadful Fate
   Forbade her Bannockburn!
As the galley touch'd the strand
   Came the messenger of woe;
The King put back the herald's hand—
   'Peace,' he said, 'thy tale I know!
His face was in the cloud;
   And his wraith was on the surge.'—
Maids of Alba, weave his shroud!
   Maids of Erin, sing his dirge!

THE TRUE KING.

A BARD-SONG.

A.D. 1399.

I.

HE came in the night on a false pretence;
　As a friend he came; as a lord remains:
His coming we noted not—when—or whence;
　We slept: we woke in chains.
Ere a year they had chased us to dens and caves;
　Our streets and our churches lay drown'd in
　　blood;
The race that had sold us their sons as slaves
　In our Land as conquerors stood!

II.

Who were they, those princes that gave away
　What was theirs to keep, not theirs to give?
A king holds sway for a passing day;
　The kingdoms for ever live!
The tanist succeeds when the king is dust:
　The king rules all; yet the king hath nought:
They were traitors not kings who sold their trust;
　They were traitors not kings who bought!

III.

Brave Art Mac Murrough!—Arise, 'tis morn!
　For a true king the nation waited long,
He is strong as the horn of the unicorn,
　This true king who rights our wrong!

He rules in the fight by an inward right;
  From the heart of the nation her king is grown;
He rules by right; he is might of her might;
  Her flesh, and bone of her bone!

THE BALLAD OF QUEEN MARGARET'S FEASTING.

A.D. 1451.

A singularly picturesque narrative of this event is given
in an old Irish Chronicle, translated by Duald Mac Ferbis,
one of Ireland's 'chief bards,' for Sir James Ware, in the
year 1666, and republished in the 'Miscellany of the Irish
Archæological Society,' vol. i. 1846. The chronicler thus
concludes: 'God's blessing, the blessing of all the Saints,
and of every one, blessing from Jerusalem to Inis Glaaire, be
on her going to heaven; and blessed be he who will reade
and heare this for blessing her Soul; and cursed be that sore
in her breast that killed Margaret.'

I.

Fair she stood—God's queenly creature!
  Wondrous joy was in her face;
Of her ladies none in stature
  Like to her, and none in grace.
On the church-roof stood they round her,
  Cloth of gold was her attire;
They in jewell'd circle wound her;—
  Beside her Ely's King, her sire.

II.

Far and near the green fields glitter'd
  Like to flowery meads in Spring,

Gay with companies loose-scatter'd
  Seated each in seemly ring,
Under banners red or yellow:
  There all day the feast they kept
From chill dawn and noontide mellow
  Till the hill-shades eastward crept.

III.

On a white steed at the gateway
  Margaret's husband, Calwagh, sate:
Guest on guest, approaching, straightway
  Welcomed he with love and state.
Each pass'd on with largess laden,
  Chosen gifts of thought and work,
Now the red cloak of the maiden,
  Now the minstrel's golden torque.

IV.

On the wind the tapestries shifted;
  From the blue hills rang the horn;
Slowly toward the sunset drifted
  Choral song and shout breeze-borne.
Like a sea the crowds unresting
  Murmur'd round the grey church-tower;
Many a prayer amid the feasting,
  For Margaret's mother rose that hour!

V.

On the church-roof kerne and noble
  At her bright face look'd, half dazed;
Nought was hers of shame or trouble;—
  On the crowds far off she gazed:

Once, on heaven her dark eyes bending,
  Her hands in prayer she flung apart:
Unconsciously her arms extending
  She bless'd her People in her heart.

VI.

Thus a Gaelic queen and nation
  At Imayn till set of sun
Kept with feast the Annunciation,
  Fourteen hundred fifty-one.
Time it was of solace tender ;—
  'Twas a brave time, strong yet fair !
Blessing, O ye Angels, send her
  From Salem's towers and Inisglaaire !

THE WEDDING OF THE CLANS.

A GIRL'S BABBLE.

I go to knit two clans together;
  Our clan and this clan unseen of yore :—
Our clan fears nought ! but I go, O whither ?
  This day I go from my Mother's door.

Thou redbreast sing'st the old song over,
  Though many a time thou hast sung it before ;
They never sent thee to some strange new lover :—
  I sing a new song by my Mother's door.

I stepp'd from my little room down by the ladder,
  The ladder that never so shook before ;
I was sad last night : to-day I am sadder,
  Because I go from my Mother's door.

The last snow melts upon bush and bramble;
  The gold bars shine on the forest's floor;
Shake not, thou leaf! it is I must tremble,
  Because I go from my Mother's door.

From a Spanish sailor a dagger I bought me;
  I trail'd a rose-tree our grey bawn o'er;
The creed and my letters our old bard taught me;
  My days were sweet by my Mother's door.

My little white goat that with raised feet huggest
  The oak stock, thy horns in the ivies frore,
Could I wrestle like thee—how the wreaths thou
    tuggest!—
  I never would move from my Mother's door.

O weep no longer, my nurse and Mother!
  My foster-sister, weep not so sore!
You cannot come with me, Ir, my brother—
  Alone I go from my Mother's door.

Farewell, my wolf-hound, that slew Mac Owing
  As he caught me and far through the thickets
    bore:
My heifer, Alb, in the green vale lowing,
  My cygnet's nest upon Lorna's shore!

He has killed ten chiefs, this chief that plights me
  His hand is like that of the giant Balor:
But I fear his kiss; and his beard affrights me,
  And the great stone dragon above his door.

Had I daughters nine with me they should tarry;
  They should sing old songs; they should dance at
    my door;

They should grind at the quern;—no need to
  marry !
O when will this marriage-day be o'er ?

THE IRISH NORMAN;

OR, LAMENT FOR THE BARON OF LOUGHMOE.

I.

WHO shall sing the Baron's dirge ?
  Not the corded brethren hooded
    With the earth-hued cloak and cowl :—
  'Mid the black church mourner-crowded,
    While the night winds round it howl,
Let them, in the chancel kneeling,
Lift the hymns to God appealing :
Let them scare the Powers of Evil,
Striking dumb the accusing devil :
Let them angel-fence the Soul
That flies forward to its goal :
Prayer can quicken : fire can purge :
Yet they shall not sing his dirge !

II.

Who shall sing the Baron's dirge ?
  Not the ceremonial weepers
    Blackening o'er the place of tombs :
  Though their cry might wake the sleepers
    In the dark that wait their dooms ;
Though their dreadful ululation
Sounds the death-note of a nation ;

Though the far-off listeners shiver
  (Wave-tossed seamen, weary reapers)
    Shiver like to funeral plumes,
While the long wail like a river
Rolls beyond the horizon's verge ;
Yet they shall not sing his dirge !

III.

Who shall sing the Baron's dirge ?
  Not the minstrels of his presence,
    Harpers of his halls and towers :
  Let them, 'mid the bowery pleasance,
    Sing that flower among the flowers,
Female beauty :—swift its race is
As the smiles on infant faces !
O, ye conquering years and hours !
Children that together played
Love and wed, and then are laid
  Grey-haired beneath the yew-tree bowers,
Passing gleams in glooms that merge—
Yet they shall not sing his dirge !

IV.

Who shall sing the Baron's dirge ?
  Sing it castles that he wasted
  Like to old oaks thunder-blasted,
Wasted with the sword or fire !
Sternness God with sweetness mateth ;
Next to him that well createth
Is the just and brave Destroyer !
The man that sinned, the same must fall,
Though Peter by him stood and Paul !
They his clansmen, they his gleemen,
They that wear the garb of freemen

Wore the sackcloth, wore the serge:—
Let them sing the Baron's dirge.

V.

Who shall sing the Baron's dirge?
  Whoso fain would sing it faileth,
  Triumph so o'er grief prevaileth!
Double-fountained was his blood,
A Gaelic spring, a Norman flood!
To his bosom truth he folded
  With a youthful lover's zeal:
God's great Justice seemed he, moulded
  In a statued shape of steel!
Men were liars; kerne and noble;
He consumed them like to stubble!
The orphan's shield, the traitor's scourge—
Sing, fierce winds, the Baron's dirge!

VI.

Who shall sing the Baron's dirge?
  O thou dread Almighty Will!
    Man exulteth; woman plaineth;
    But the Will Supreme ordaineth,
  And the years its fate fulfil.
All our reason is unreason;
  All our glory ends in woe:
Thou didst raise him for a season,
  Thou once more hast laid him low!
But his strong life sought Thee ever;
Sought Thee like a mountain river
Lost at last in the sea surge—
No! we will not sing his dirge!

VII.

Who shall sing the Baron's dirge ?
  'Twas no time of sobs or sighing :
  Grave, yet glad, he lay a dying.
Heralds through the vales were sent
  Bidding all men pray for grace
That he rightly might repent
  Sins of his and all his race :
Well he worked : three days his spirit
Throve in prayer and waxed in merit.
The blessed lights aloft were raised :
On the Cross his dim eyes gazed
To the last breath's ebb and gurge—
No ! for him we chant no dirge !

THE STATUTE OF KILKENNY.

The celebrated Statute of Kilkenny, passed A.D. 1362, is
thus described by an English historian, Mr. Plowden :—'It
was enacted that intermarriages with the natives, or any
connection with them *as fosterers, or in the way of gossipred,*
should be punished as high treason ; that the use of their
name, language, apparel, or customs should be punished
with the forfeiture of lands and tenements ; that to submit
to be governed by the Brehon Laws was treason ; that the
English should not make war upon the natives without the
permission and authority of Government ; that the English
should not permit the Irish to graze upon their lands ; that
they should not admit them to any benefice or religious
privilege, or even entertain their bards.'

Of old ye warr'd on men : to-day
  On women and on babes ye war ;

The noble's child his head must lay
 Beneath the peasant's roof no more!

I saw in sleep the infant's hand
 His foster-brother's fiercely grasp;
His warm arm, lithe as willow wand,
 Twines me each day with closer clasp!

O infant smiler! grief-beguiler!
 Between the oppressor and the oppress'd
O soft, unconscious reconciler,
 Smile on! through thee the Land is bless'd.

Through thee the puissant love the poor;
 His conqueror's hope the vanquish'd shares:
For thy sake by a lowly door
 The clan made vassal stops and stares.

Our vales are healthy. On thy cheek
 There dawns each day a livelier red:
Smile on! Before another week
 Thy feet our earthen floor will tread!

Thy foster-brothers twain for thee
 Would face the wolves on snowy fell:
Smile on! the 'Irish enemy'
 Will fence their Norman nursling well.

The nursling as the child is dear;—
 Thy Mother loves not like thy nurse!
That babbling Mandate steps not near
 Thy cot but o'er her bleeding corse!

THE DAYS OF OUTLAWRY.

I.

A CRY comes up from wood and wold,
   A wail from fen and marish,
'Grant us your Laws, and take our gold;
   Like beasts dog-chased we perish.'—
The hunters of their kind reply,
   'Our sports we scorn to barter;
We rule! the Irish enemy
   Partakes not England's charter.'

II.

A cry comes up for ever new,
   A wail of hopeless anguish,
'Your Laws, your Laws!—our Laws ye slew;
   In living death we languish.'—
'Not so! We keep our hunting-ground;
   We chase the flying quarry.
Hark, hark, that sound—the horn and hound!
   Away! we may not tarry!'

III.

Sad Isle, thy laws are Norman lords [1]
   That, dower'd by Henry's bounty,

---

[1] In the reign of Edward I. those Irish who lay contiguous to the county lands, finding themselves in a position of utter outlawry, the ancient Brehon Law of Ireland not being recognised by England, and English law not being extended to them, applied to the king for the protection of the latter. The incident is thus narrated by Plowden in his 'History of Ireland:'—'They consequently offered, through Ufford, the chief governor, 8,000 marks to the king, pro-

On cities sup 'mid famish'd hordes,
  And dine on half a county !
A laughing giant, Outlawry,
  Strides drunk o'er hill and heather ;
Justice to him is as a fly
  'Twixt mail'd hands clash'd together.

IV.

O memory, memory, leave the graves
  Knee-deep in grass and darnel !
Wash from a kingdom, winds and waves,
  The odour of the charnel !
Be dumb, red graves in valleys deep,
  Black towers on plains blood-sloken :—
Dark fields, your thrilling secrets keep,
  Nor speak till God hath spoken !

THE THREE CHOIRS;

OR, THE CONSECRATION OF ST. PATRICK.

WHILE holy hands on Patrick laid
  The great Priest consecrated,

vided he would grant the free enjoyment of the laws of England to the whole body of Irish natives indiscriminately.' Edward was disposed to accept the offer, but in the words of Plowden :—'These politic and benevolent intentions of Edward were thwarted by his servants, who, to forward their own rapacious views of extortion and oppression, prevented a convention of the king's barons and other subjects in Ireland. . . . The cry of oppression was not silenced; the application of the Irish was renewed, and the king repeatedly solicited to accept them as free and faithful subjects.'

Three mystic choirs—so sang the bards—
    Their anthems matched and mated;

The first, that Roman choir which chants
    O'er tombs of Paul and Peter;
The next a Seraph band, with note
    By distance rendered sweeter.

The third rang out from Fochlut's wood
    Where once their ululation
Lost Erin's babes to Patrick raised—
    ' Redeem a wildered nation ! '

Ring out once more, from Erin's shore !
    From Rome, from Heaven, for ever
Roll on thou triple Psalm, that God
    May answer and deliver !

THE BALLAD OF TURGESIUS THE DANE;

OR, THE GIRL DELIVERER.

THE people sat amid the dust and wept:
    ' In darker days than these God burst the chain,'
(Thus sang the harper as the chords he swept),
    ' Hear of the Girl Deliverer and the Dane.'

PART I.

Twin ivy wreaths her forehead wound,
    A green wreath and a yellow :
Her hair a gleaming dusk in ground
    Wi'h ends of sunshine mellow.

H 2

Fair rose her head the tall neck o'er;
   Her neck in snows was bedded :
Some crown, they swore, unseen she bore—
   That queenly head it steadied.

Her sable vest in front was laced
   With laces red as coral ;
Her golden zone in gems was traced
   With leafy type and moral.

As treading hearts her small feet went
   In love-suspended fleetness :
And hearts thus trodden forth had sent
   An organ-sob of sweetness.

Upon the dais when she stept
   Meath's peopled hall rang loudly :
Their hundred harps the minstrels swept :
   Her sire looked round him proudly.

The Dane beside him, darkening, sate,
   At once his guest and victor ;
Green Erin's scourge—the true King's fate—
   The sceptred serf's protector.

' Sir King ! our worship grows but small !
   Here Gaels alone find honour :
A white girl cannot cross your hall
   But all men gaze upon her !

' My speech is short : yon stands my fort !
   Ere three nights thither send her
With twenty maidens of her court,
   Your fairest, to attend her.'

PART II.

The Dane strides o'er his stony floor,
　A strong, fierce man, yet hoary :
The low sun fires the purple moor
　With mingled gloom and glory.

The tyrant stops; he stares thereon :
　Sun-touched, his armour flashes :
His rough grey hair a glow hath won
　Like embers seen through ashes.

His mail'd hand grasps his tangled beard :
　He laughs that red sun watching,
Till the roofs laugh back like a forest weird
　The laughter of Wood-gods catching.

'My Sea-Kings! mark yon furnace-sheen !
　The Fire-god is not thrifty !
No flame like that these eyes have seen
　For winters five-and-fifty !

'My sire lay dead : the ship sailed north,
　The pyre and the corse on bearing :
Six miles it sailed; the flame sprang forth
　Like sea-vext Hecla glaring !

'We'll pledge him to-night in the blood-red wine :
　'Tis wrought, the task he set me !
From coast to coast this Isle is mine :
　Not soon will her sons forget me !

'I have burned their shrines and their cities sacked ;
　Their Fair Ones our castles cumber ;
We were shamed to-night if the bevy lacked
　The fairest from their number.

' Young wives for us all ; too many by half !
   Strange mates—the hind with the dragon ! '
He laughed as when the reveller's laugh
   Rings back from the half-drained flagon.

PART III.

The girl hath prayed at her Mother's grave,
   And kissed that grave, and risen :
She hath swathed a knife in a silken glaive :
   She is calm, but her great eyes glisten.

Between silk vest and spotless breast
   A dagger she hath hidden ;
With lips compressed gone forth, a guest
   Unhonoured—not unbidden.

Through moonshine wan on moves she, on :
   But who are those, the others ?
They are garbed like maids, but maids are none :
   They are lovers of maids, and brothers.

The gates lie wide : they enter in :
   Loud roars the riot and wassail :
They hear at times 'mid the conquerors' din
   The harp of the Gaelic vassal.

The Dane has laid on her head his hand,
   The love in his eye is cruel :
Out leap the swords of that well-masked band :
   Two nations have met in duel !

'Twas God their sentence on high that wrote !
   'Tis a righteous doom—that slaughter !
His Sea-Kings lie drowned in the castle moat,
   And the Tyrant in Annin water.

From mountain to mountain the tidings flashed :
  It pealed from turret to turret :
Like a sunlit storm o'er the plains it dashed :
  It hung o'er the vales like a spirit.

'Twas a maiden's honour that crowned the right :
  'Twas a vestal claim, scarce noted
By the power which trampled it out of sight,
  That rose on the wrong, and smote it !

The harper ceased : aloud the young men cried,
  ' That maid is Erin ! Live, O maid, for ever ! '
' Not Erin but her Faith,' the old priests replied :
  ' Her Faith—that only—shall the Land deliver ! '

EPILOGUE.

At my casement I sat by night, while the wind
  remote in dark valleys
  Voluminous gather'd and grew, and waxing swell'd
    to a gale :
Now mourning like seas heart-grieved, now sobbing
  in petulant sallies :
  Far off, 'twas a People's moan ; hard by, but a
    widow's wail.

To God there is fragment none : nothing single ; no
  isolation :
  The ages to Him are one : round Him the Woe,
    and the Wrong
Roll like a spiritual star, and the cry of the desolate
  Nation :—
  The Souls that are under the Altar respond in
    music ' How long ? '

By the casement I sat alone till sign after sign had
    descended:
  The Hyads rejoin'd their sea, and the Pleiads by
    fate were down borne:
And then with that distant dirge a tenderer anthem
    was blended,
  And, glad to behold her young, the bird gave
    thanks to the morn.

INISFAIL

A LYRICAL CHRONICLE OF IRELAND

PART II.

THE WARS OF RELIGION

PART II.

Prologue.

'CAN THESE BONES LIVE?'

A VOICE from the midnoon call'd, 'Arise, be alone,
  and remove thee;
  Descend into valleys of bale, and look on the visions
  of night;
From the stranger flee, and be strange to the men
  and the women that love thee,
  That thy wine may be tears, and that ashes may
  mix with the meats of delight.

'To few is the Vision shown, and to none for his
  weal or from merit:
  As lepers they live who see it; as those that men
  pity or hate:
And to few is the Voice reveal'd; yet to them who
  hear and can bear it
  Though bitterness cometh at first, yet sweetness
  cometh more late.'

Then in vision I saw a Corse—death-cold; but the
  Angels had draped it
  In light; and that light divine round the unseal'd
  death-cave was strewn;

And an anthem rush'd o'er the worlds; but the
    tongue that moulded and shaped it
Was a great storm through ruins borne; and the
    lips that spake it were stone.

PLORANS PLORAVIT.

A.D. 1583.

SHE sits alone on the cold grave-stone
    And only the dead are nigh her;
In the tongue of the Gael she makes her wail:
    The night wind rushes by her.

'Few, O few are the leal and true,
    And fewer shall be, and fewer;
The land is a corse; no life, no force:
    O wind with sere leaves strew her!

'Men ask what scope is left for hope
    To one who has known her story:—
I trust her dead!   Their graves are red;
    But their Souls are with God in glory.'

ROISIN DUBH;[1]

OR, THE BLEEDING HEART.

I.

O WHO art thou with that queenly brow
    And uncrown'd head?

[1] Roisin Dubh signifies the 'Black little Rose,' and was
one of the mystical names under which the bards celebrated
Ireland.

And why is the vest that binds thy breast,
  O'er the heart, blood-red ?
Like a rose-bud in June was that spot at noon,
  A rose-bud weak;
But it deepens and grows like a July rose :
  Death-pale thy cheek !

II.

' The babes I fed at my foot lay dead;
  I saw them die :
In Ramah a blast went wailing past ;
  It was Rachel's cry.
But I stand sublime on the shores of Time,
  And I pour mine ode,
As Miriam sang to the cymbals' clang,
  On the wind to God.

III.

' Once more at my feasts my Bards and Priests
  Shall sit and eat :
And the Shepherd whose sheep are on every steep
  Shall bless my meat !
Oh, sweet, men say, is the song by day,
  And the feast by night ;
But on poisons I thrive, and in death survive
  Through ghostly might.'

THE DIRGE OF DESMOND.

Rush, dark Dirge, o'er hills of Erin ! Woe for Desmond's name and race!
Loving Conqueror whom the Conquered caught so
  soon to her embrace :

There's a veil on Erin's forehead : cold at last is
    Desmond's hand :—
Halls that roofed her outlawed Prelates blacken like
    a blackening brand.

Strongbow's sons forsook their Strong One, served
    so long with loving awe ;
Roche the Norman, Norman Barry, and the Baron
    of Lixnaw :
Gaelic lords—that once were Princes—holp not—
    Thomond or Clancar :
Ormond, ill-crowned Tudor's kinsman, ranged her
    hosts, and led her war.

One by one his brothers perished : Fate down drew
    them to their grave :
Smerwick's cliffs beheld his Spaniards wrestling
    with the yeasty wave.
Swiftly sweep the eagles westward, gathering where
    the carcase lies :
There's a blacker cloud behind them : vultures next
    will rend their prize.

'Twas not War that wrought the ruin !   Sister
    portents, yoked for hire,
Side by side dragged on the harrow—Famine's
    plague, and plague of Fire :
Slain the herds, and burned the harvests, vale and
    plain with corpses strown,
'Mid the waste they spread their feast; within the
    charnel reigned—alone.

In the death-hunt she was nigh him; she that
    scorned to leave his side :
By her Lord she stood and spake not, neck-deep in
    the freezing tide :

Round them waved the osiers; o'er them drooped
    the willows, rank on rank :
Troopers spurred; and bayed the bloodhounds, up
    and down the bleeding bank.

From the East sea to the West sea rings the death-
    keen long and sore :
Erin's Curse be his that led them, found the hovel,
    burst the door !
O'er the embers dead an old man silent bent with
    head to knee:
Slowly rose he: backward fell they :—' Seek ye
    Desmond ? I am he.'

London Bridge ! thy central archway props that grey
    head year by year:
But to God that head is holy; and to Erin it is
    dear :
When that bridge is dust, that river in the last fire-
    judgment dried,
The man shall live who fought for God; the man
    who for his country died.

WAR-SONG OF MAC CARTHY.

I.

Two lives of an eagle, the old song saith,
    Make the life of a black yew-tree;
For two lives of a yew-tree the furrow's path
    Endures on the grassy lea :
Two furrows shall last till the time is past
    God willeth the world to be ;

For a furrow's time has Mac Carthy stood fast,
  Mac Carthy in Carbery.

II.

Up with the banner whose green shall live
  While lives the green on the oak !
And down with the axes that grind and rive
  Keen-edged as the thunder-stroke !
And on with the battle-cry known of old,
  And the clan-rush like wind and wave ;
On, on ! the Invader is bought and sold ;
  His own hand hath dug his grave !

FLORENCE MAC CARTHY'S FAREWELL TO HIS ENGLISH LOVE.

I.

ENGLAND's fair child, Evangeline !
In that far-distant land of mine
  There stands a Yew-tree among tombs !
For ages there that tree hath stood,
A black pall dash'd with drops of blood ;
  O'er all my world it breathes its glooms.

II.

Evangeline ! Evangeline !
Because my Yew-tree is not thine,
  Because thy Gods on mine wage war,
Farewell !   Back fall the gates of brass ;
The exile to his own must pass :
  I seek the land of tombs once more.

TO THE SAME.

W<small>E</small> *seem* to tread the self-same street,
  To pace the self-same courts or grass;
Parting, our hands appear to meet:
  O vanitatum vanitas!

Distant as earth from heaven—or hell—
  From thee the things to me most dear:
Ghost-throng'd Cocytus and thy will
  Between us rush.   We might be near.

Thy world is fair: my thoughts refuse
  To dance its dance or drink its wine;
Nor canst thou hear the reeds and yews
  That sigh to me from lands not thine.

THE DIRGE OF KILDARE.

A.D. 1595.

T<small>HE</small> North wind clanged on the sharp hill-side:
The mountain muttered: the cloud replied;
'There is one rides up through thy woods, Tyrone!
That shall ride on a bier of the pine branch down.'

The flood roars over Danara's bed:
'Twas green at morning: to-night 'tis red:
What whispers the raven to oak and cave?
'Make ready the bier and make ready the grave.'

Kildare, Kildare!   Thou hast left the bound
Of hawk and heron, of hart and hound;

With the hunter's art come to the Lion's lair :
He is mighty of limb and old.   Beware !

Beware, for on thee that eye is set
Which glared upon Norreys at Clontibret :
And that hand is lifted, from horse to heath
Which hurled the giant they mourn in Meath !

Kildare, Kildare !   There are twain this hour
With brows turned north from Maynooth's grey
    tower :
The Mother sees nought : the bride shall see
The Herald and Death-flag far off—not thee.

WAR-SONG OF TIRCONNELL'S BARD AT THE BATTLE OF BLACKWATER.

AUGUST 14, A.D. 1598.

At this battle the Irish of Ulster were commanded by
' Red Hugh ' O'Neill, Prince of Tyrone, and by Hugh O'Donnell (called also 'Red Hugh '), Prince of Tirconnell.   Queen
Elizabeth's army was led by Marshal Bagnal, who fell in the
rout with 2,500 of his force.   Twelve thousand gold pieces,
thirty-four standards, and all the artillery of the vanquished
army were taken.

I.

GLORY to God, and to the Powers that fight
    For Freedom and the Right !
We have them then, the Invaders !   There they stand
    At last on Oriel's land !
And there the far-famed Marshal holds command,

Bagnal, their bravest! at his right
That recreant, neither chief nor knight,
' The Queen's O'Reilly,' he that sold
His country, clan, and church for gold.
They have pass'd the gorge stream-cloven,
   And the mountain's purple bound ;
Now the toils are round them woven,
   Now the nets are spread around !
Give them time : their steeds are blown ;—
   Let them stand and round them stare,
   Breathing blasts of Irish air :
Our eagles know their own !

II.

Twin Stars !   Twin regents of our righteous war !
This day remember whose, and who ye are—
Thou that o'er green Tir-owen's Tribes hast sway !
Thou whom Tirconnell's vales obey !
   The line of Nial, the line of Conn
   So oft at strife, to-day are one !
   To Erin both are dear ; to me
   Dearest he is, and needs must be
   My Prince, my chief, my child, on whom
   So early fell the dungeon's doom.
   O'Donnell ! hear this day thy Bard !
   By those young feet so maim'd and scarr'd,
   Bit by the winter's fangs when lost
   Thou wandered'st on through snows and frost,
Remember thou those years in chains thou worest,
   Snatch'd in false peace from unsuspecting halls,
And that one thought, of all thy pangs the sorest,
   Thy subjects groan'd the upstart Stranger's thralls !
     That thought on waft thee through the fight :
     On, on, for Erin's right !

III.

Seest thou yon stream whose tawny waters glide
Through weeds and yellow marsh lingeringly and
      slowly?
    Blest is that spot and holy!
There, ages past, Saint Bercan stood and cried,
' This spot shall quell one day the Invaders' pride ! '
    He saw in mystic trance
      The blood-stain flush yon rill :
    On, hosts of God, advance ;
      Your country's fates fulfil !
    Be Truth this day your might !
    Truth lords it in the fight !

IV.

    O'Neill !   That day be with thee now
When, throned on Ulster's regal seat of stone,
    Thou sat'st and thou alone ;
While flocked from far the Tribes, and to thy hand
    Was given the snow-white wand,
Erin's authentic sceptre of command !
Kingless a People stood around thee !   Thou
Didst dash the alien bauble from thy brow,
    And for a coronet laid down
That People's love became once more their Mon-
    arch's crown !
    True King alone is he
In whom made one his People share the throne :
Fair from the soil he rises like a tree :
    Rock-like the Tyrant presses on it, prone !
      Strike for that People's cause !
      For Gaelic rights ; for Brehon laws :
The sage traditions of civility ;
Pure hearths, and Faith set free !

V.

Hark ! the thunder of their meeting !
Hand meets hand, and rough the greeting !
Hark ! the crash of shield and brand ;
They mix, they mingle, band with band,
Like two horn-commingling stags
Wrestling on the mountain crags,
Intertwisted, intertangled,
Mangled forehead meeting mangled !
Lo ! the wavering darkness through
I see the banner of Red Hugh ;
Close beside is thine, O'Neill !
Now they stoop and now they reel,
Rise once more and onward sail,
Like two falcons on one gale !
O ye clansmen past me rushing,
Like mountain torrents seaward gushing,
Tell the chiefs that from this height
Their chief of Bards beholds the fight ;
That on theirs he pours his spirit ;
Marks their deeds and chants their merit ;
While the Priesthood evermore,
Like him that ruled God's host of yore,
With arms outstretch'd that God implore !

VI.

Mightiest of the line of Conn,
On to victory ! On, on, on !
It is Erin that in thee
Lives and works right wondrously !
Eva from the heavenly bourne
Upon thee her eyes doth turn,

She whose marriage couch was spread
'Twixt the dying and the dead !
Parcell'd kingdoms one by one
For a prey to traitors thrown ;
Pledges forfeit, broken vows,
Roofless fane and blazing house ;
All the dreadful deeds of old
Rise resurgent from the mould,
For their judgment peal is toll'd !
All our Future takes her stand
Hawk-like on thy lifted hand.
States that live not, vigil keeping
In the limbo of long weeping ;
Palace-courts and minster-towers
That shall make this isle of ours
Fairer than the star of morn,
Wait thy mandate to be born !
Chief elect 'mid desolation
Wield thou well the inspiration
Thou drawest from a new-born nation !

VII.

Sleep no longer Bards that hold
Ranged beneath me harps of gold !
Smite them with a heavier hand
Than vengeance lays on axe or brand !
Pour upon the blast a song
Linking litanies of wrong,
Till, like poison-dews, the strain
Eat into the Invader's brain.
On the retributive harp
Catch that death-shriek shrill and sharp,
Hers, though choked in blood, whose lord
Perish'd, Essex, at thy board !

Peerless chieftain! peerless wife!
From his throat, and hers, the knife
Drain'd the mingled tide of life!
Sing the base assassin's steel
By Sussex hired to slay O'Neill!
Sing, fierce Bards, the plains sword-wasted,
Sing the cornfields burnt and blasted,
That when raged the war no longer
Kernes dog-chased might pine with hunger!
Pour around their ears the groans
Of half-human skeletons
From wet cave or forest-cover
Foodless deserts peering over,
Or upon the roadside lying
Infant dead and mother dying,
On their mouth the grassy stain
Of the wild weed gnaw'd in vain;—
Look upon them hoary Head
Of the last of Desmonds dead;
Head that evermore dost frown
From the Bridge of London down!
She that slew him from her barge
Makes that Head this hour the targe
Of her insults cold and keen,
England's Caliph, not her Queen!
—Portent terrible and dire
Whom thy country and thy sire
Branded with a bastard's name,
Thy birth was but thy lightest shame!
To honour recreant and thine oath;
 Trampling that Faith whose borrow'd garb
 First gave thee sceptre crown and orb,
Thy flatterers scorn, thy lovers loathe
That idol with the blood-stained feet
Ill-throned on murder'd Mary's seat!

VIII.

Glory be to Him alone who holds the nations in His
hand !

The plain lies bare ; the smoke drifts by ; they fly—
the invaders—band o'er band !

Sing, ye priests, your deep Te Deums ; bards, make
answer loud and long,

In your rapture flinging heavenward censers of
triumphant song.

Isle for centuries blind in bondage lift once more
thine ancient boast,

From the cliffs of Inishowen southward on to
Carbery's coast !

We have seen the Right made perfect, seen the Hand
that rules the spheres

Glance like lightning through the clouds, and backward roll the wrongful years.

Glory fadeth, but this triumph is no fleeting barren
glory ;

Rays of healing it shall scatter on the eyes that read
our story :

Upon nations bound and torpid as they waken it shall
shine

As on Peter in his chains the Angel shone with light
divine.

From the unheeding, from the unholy it may hide,
like Truth, its ray ;

But when Truth and Justice conquer on their crowns
its beam shall play :

O'er the ken of troubled despots it shall trail a meteor's
glare ;

For the blameless it shall glitter as the star of
morning fair :

Whensoever Erin triumphs then its dawn it shall
    renew ;
Then O'Neill shall be remember'd, and Tirconnell's
    chief, Red Hugh !

THE TRUE VICTORY.

A WARRIOR by his stone-dead lord
    Fast bleeding sat, and heard on high
Three Angels making of a sword,
    Who sang right merrily :

' We shape the Sword of conquering days :—
    What jewels shall that sword emboss ?
Not deeds, but sufferings ; shame, not praise,
    The victories of the Cross.'

THE SUGANE EARL.

A.D. 1601.

I.

'TWAS the White Knight that sold him—his flesh
    and his blood !
    A Fitz-Gerald betray'd the Fitz-Gerald :
Death-pale the false friend in the 'mid forest stood ;
    Close by stood the conqueror's herald !

At the cave-mouth he lean'd on his sword, pale and
    dumb,
  But the eye that was on him o'erbore him :
' Come forth,' cried the White Knight ; — one
    answer'd, 'I come !'
  And the Chief of his house stood before him !

II.

' Cut him down,' said the Outlaw with cold smile and
    stern,
   ' 'Twas a bold stake ; but Satan hath won it !'—
In the days of thy father, Earl Desmond, no kerne
  Had heard that command, and not done it !
The name of the White Knight shall cease, and his
    race !
  His castle down fall, roof and rafter !
This day is a day of rebuke ; but the base
  Shall meet what he merits hereafter !

THE LAMENT OF THE FOE TURNED
FRIEND.

I.

THERE clung a mist about mine eye,
  Or else round him a mist there clung :
From war to war the years went by,
  And still that cloud between us hung :
That, that he was I saw him not,
  Old friend, old comrade, fellow-man :
I saw but that which chance had wrought ;
  A rival house, a hostile clan.

II.

In vain one Race, one Faith were ours :
    A common Land, a common Foe :
Vainly we chased through Lorha's bowers,
    In boyhood paired, the flying roe :
Sea-caves of Irr ! in vain by you
    Our horses stemmed the heaving floods,
While freshening gales of morning blew
    The sunrise o'er the mountain woods !

III.

Ah spells of Fate ! Ah Wrath and Wrong !
    Ah Friend that once my dearest wert !
Where lay thine image hid so long
    But in the centre of my heart ?
Thou fell'st ! a flash from out the past
    One moment showed thee as of yore :
Death followed fast—a midnight blast;
    And that fair crest was seen no more.

IV.

Ah, great right hand, so brave yet kind !
    Ah, sovereign eyes ! ah, lordly mirth !
Thy realm to-day—like me—sits blind :
    And endless winter chills thy hearth.
This day I see thee in thy spring,
    Though seventy winters make me grey :
This night my bards thy praise shall sing :
    This night for thee my priests shall pray.[1]

---

[1] In Ireland there were occasions when the chief who
had pursued an ancient enemy to the death became his
sincerest mourner. A chronicler of the 17th century affirms

THE PHANTOM FUNERAL;

OR, THE DIRGE OF THE LAST DESMOND.

A.D. 1601.

James Fitz-Garret, son of the 'Great Earl of Desmond,' had been sent to England when a child as a hostage, and was for seventeen years kept a prisoner in the Tower, and educated in the Queen's religion. James Fitz-Thomas, the 'Sugane Earl,' having meantime assumed the title and prerogatives of Earl of Desmond, the Queen sent her captive to Ireland, attended by persons devoted to her, and provided with a *conditional* patent for his restoration. When he reached Kilmallock, on his way to Kerry, wheat and salt were there showered on him by the people, in testimony of loyalty.

---

that an instance of such a change was found in the Earl of Ormond of Elizabeth's time, called ' Black Thomas.' ' Now, good reader, let there be a truce to words, and listen to the whistling of the lash.—. . . There was then in Ireland Thomas Butler, Earl of Ormond, who changed his religion in the court of Elizabeth. Brooding over the scandal he had given by his apostacy, he resolved to be reconciled to the Church in his last days. He therefore made his peace with God, edified all by his piety, and soon after, losing the ineffable blessing of sight, was gathered to his fathers. Now, ere he died, he was heard to lament two actions of his life—first, that he had ever renounced that holy religion in his youth which in his old age he was not able to succour ; and, secondly, that he had taken up arms against the Geraldines of Desmond, who were ever the strenuous champions of the Faith, and the bulwarks of their country's liberty. Oh, good God ! why did Ormond conspire to ruin them ? '

('The Rise, Increase, and Exit of the Family of the Geraldines, Earls of Desmond, and Palatines of Kerry.' Written in Latin by Brother Dominicus de Rosario O'Daly, in the seventeenth century, and translated by the Rev. C. P. Meahan.)

The next day was Sunday. When the young Earl left his house, it was with difficulty that a guard of English soldiers could keep a path open for him. From street and window and housetop every voice urged him to fidelity to his ancestral faith. The youth, who did not even understand the language in which he was adjured, having reached a spot where two roads separated, took that one which led to 'the Queen's church,' as it was called; and with loud cries his clan rushed forth from Kilmallock, and abandoned his standard for ever. Shortly afterwards he returned to England, where he fell sick; and in a few months the news of his death reached his ancient palatinate of Kerry.—See the *Pucata Hibernia.*

STREW the bed and strew the bier,
　(Who rests upon it was never man)
With all that a little child holds dear,
　With violets blue and violets wan.

Strew the bed and strew the bier
　With the berries that redden thy shores, Corann
Lay not upon it helmet or spear :—
　He knew them never. He ne'er was man.

Far off he sleeps ; yet we mourn him here ;
　Their tale is falsehood ! he ne'er was man !
'Tis a phantom funeral ! Strew the bier
　With white lilies brushed by the floating swan.

They lie who say that the false Queen caught him
　A child asleep on the mountains wide ;
A captive reared him ; a strange faith taught him ;—
　'Twas for no strange faith that his father died !

They lie who say that the child return'd
　A man unmanned to his towers of pride ;
That his people with curses the false Earl spurn'd ;
　Woe, woe, Kilmallock ! they lie, and lied !

The clan was wroth at an ill report,
　But now the thunder-cloud melts in tears:
The child that was motherless play'd. 'Twas sport!
　A child must sport in his childish years!

Ululah! Ululah! Low, sing low!　　　　　·
　The women of Desmond loved well that child!
Our lamb was lost in the winter snow:
　Long years we sought him in wood and wild.

How many a babe of Fitz-Gerald's blood
　In hut was foster'd though born in hall!
The old stock burgeon'd the fair new bud,
　The old land welcomed them, each and all!

Glynn weeps to-day by the Shannon's tide,
　And Shanid and she that frowns o'er Deal;
There is woe by the Laune and the Carra's side,
　And where the Knight dwells by the woody Feale.

In Dingle and Beara they chant his dirge;
　Far off he faded—our child—sing low!
We have made him a bed by the ocean's surge;
　We have made him a bier on the mountain's brow.

The clan was bereft! the old walls they left;
　With cries they rushed to the mountains drear!
But now great sorrow their heart hath cleft;
　See! one by one they are drawing near!

Ululah! Ululah! Low, sing low!
　The flakes fall fast on the little bier:
The yew-branch and eagle-plume over them throw!
　The last of the Desmond Chiefs lies here.

THE MARCH TO KINSALE.

DECEMBER, A.D. 1601.

1.

O'ER many a river bridged with ice,
  Through many a vale with snow-drifts dumb,
Past quaking fen and precipice
  The Princes of the North are come !
Lo, these are they that, year by year,
  Roll'd back the tide of England's war ;—
Rejoice, Kinsale ! thy help is near !
  That wondrous winter march is o'er.
    And thus they sang, ' To-morrow morn
      Our eyes shall rest upon the foe :
    Roll on, swift night, in silence borne,
      And blow, thou breeze of sunrise, blow ! '

II.

Blithe as a boy on march'd the host
  With droning pipe and clear-voiced harp ;
At last above that southern coast
  Rang out their war-steed's whinny sharp :
And up the sea-salt slopes they wound,
  And airs once more of ocean quaff'd ;
Those frosty woods, the blue wave's bound,
  As though May touched them waved and laugh'd.
    And thus they sang, ' To-morrow morn
      Our eyes shall rest upon our foe :
    Roll on, swift night, in silence borne,
      And blow, thou breeze of sunrise, blow ! '

III.

Beside their watchfires couch'd all night
  Some slept, some danced, at cards some play'd,
While, chanting on a central height
  Of moonlit crag, the priesthood pray'd:
And some to sweetheart, some to wife
  Sent message kind ; while others told
Triumphant tales of recent fight,
  Or legends of their sires of old.
    And thus they sang, ' To-morrow morn
      Our eyes at last shall see the foe :
    Roll on, swift night, in silence borne,
      And blow, thou breeze of sunrise, blow ! '

KINSALE.

JANUARY 3, A.D. 1602.

WHAT man can stand amid a place of tombs,
  Nor yearn to that poor vanquished dust beneath ?
Above a Nation's grave no violet blooms ;
  A vanquished Nation lies in endless death.

'Tis past : the dark is dense with ghost and vision !
  All lost ! the air is throng'd with moan and wail :
But one day more and hope had been fruition :
  O Athunree, thy fate o'erhung Kinsale ! [1]

[1] The inexplicable disaster at Kinsale, when, after their marvellous winter march, the two great northern chiefs of Tirconnell and Tyrone had succeeded in relieving their Spanish allies there, was one of those events upon which the history of a nation turns. We know little more than

What name is that which lays on every head
  A hand like fire, striking the strong locks grey ?
What name is named not save with shame and
  dread ?
Once let us breathe it,—then no more for aye !

Kinsale ! accursed be he, the first who bragg'd
  ' A city stands where roam'd but late the flock ; '
Accursed the day, when, from the mountain dragg'd,
  Thy corner-stone forsook the mother-rock !

DIRGE.

I.

I am black but fair, and the robe I wear
  Is dark as death ;
My cheek is pale, and I bind my veil
  With a cypress wreath.

that it was a night-attack, the secret of which had been
divulged by a deserter. O'Donnell took shipping for
Spain, where he died before the promised aid was furnished,
in the twenty-ninth year of his age, September 10, 1602.
King Philip caused him to be buried in the Cathedral of
Valladolid, and raised there a monument in his honour.
O'Neill fought his way back to Ulster. Lord Mountjoy had
repeatedly wasted the country, so that a terrible famine
reigned. Every day O'Neill was more strictly hemmed in ;
while his allies deserted him and his retainers were starved.
When the news arrived of the death of Red Hugh O'Donnell,
all hope was over. He agreed to the terms proposed to him
by Mountjoy, surrendering his claims as a native prince,
and engaging to resume his title as Earl of Tyrone. Several
days previously the Queen had died ; but Mountjoy had
concealed this event. A few days later the ships of O'Neill's
Spanish allies arrived. He sent them back.

Where the nightshades flower I build the bower
    Of my secret rest:
O kind is sleep to the eyes that weep
    And the bleeding breast.

II.

My palace floor I tread no more;
    No throne is mine;
No sceptre I hold, nor drink from gold
    Of victory's wine:
Yet I rule a Queen in the worlds unseen
    By Sassanach eye;
A realm I have in the hearts of the brave
    And an empery.

III.

In crypt, not aisle, of the ruin'd pile
    All day I lurk,
And in western caves when the ocean raves,
    Through the midnight murk.
But far o'er the sea there is one loves me
    'Neath the southern star:
The Fisherman's ring my help shall bring,
    And heal my scar.

TO NUALA IN ROME.

Nuala was the sister of Red Hugh, and of Roderick
O'Donnell. The latter died an exile in Rome, A.D. 1608.
Nuala left her husband, on his proving a traitor to his
country, and clave to her brother. It was on finding her
weeping at that brother's grave in S. Pietro Montorio, that
O'Donnell's bard addressed to her the tragic ode well-known
through Clarence Mangan's translation: ' O Woman of the
Piercing Wail ! '

THY shining eyes are vague with tears,
 Though seldom and unseen they flow ;
The playmate of thy childish years—
 My friend—at last lies low.

If I—thus late—thy love might win,
 Withheld for his sake—brief the gain ;
I live in battle's ceaseless din:
 Thou liv'st in silent pain.

Nuala ! exile, and the bread
 By strangers doled thy cheek make pale ;
On blue Lough Eirne that cheek was red,
 In western Ruaidh's gale !

The high-neck'd stag looks down no more
 From sunset cliffs upon thy path
In Doire. Not now thou tread'st the shore
 By Aileach's royal Rath.

No more thou hear'st the sea-wind sing
 O'er cairns where Ulster monarchs sleep ;
The linnets of the Latian spring
 They only make thee weep.

To thee no joy from domes enskied,
　　Or ruins of Imperial Rome;
Thou look'st beyond them, hungry-eyed,
　　T'ward thy far Irish home.

On green Tirconnell, now a waste,
　　The sighs of outcasts feed thine own;
Nuala! soon my clarion's blast
　　Shall drown that mingled moan.

In Spain they call us King and Prince,
　　And plight alliance, and betray;
In Rome through clouds of frankincense
　　Slow dawns our better day.

To King or Kaiser, Prince or Pope,
　　I sue not, nor to magic spell;—
Nuala! on this sword my Hope
　　Stands like a God.　Farewell!

────────

THE ARRAIGNMENT;

OR, FIRST AND LAST.

THUS sang thy missioned Bard, O'Neill,
　　At James's Court a threatening guest,
When Ulster died.　Round ranks of steel
　　Ran the sharp whisper ill suppressed.

Ho! space for Judgment! squire and groom!
　　Ho! place for Judgment—and a bier!
We bear a dead man to his tomb:
　　We ask for Judgment, not a tear.

Back, beaming eyes, and cloth of gold,
  Back, plumes, and stars, and herald's gear,
Injustice crowned, and falsehood stoled!
  There lies a lordlier pageant here!

Draw near, Sir King, and lay thy hand
  Upon this dead man's breast! Draw near!
The accusing blood, at God's command,
  Wells forth! The count is summed. Give ear!

Who, partner with a knave abhorred,[1]
  Farmed as his own that Traitor's feud?
Vicarious fought? By others' sword
  Mangled a kingdom unsubdued?

Who reigned in great Religion's name,
  Liegeman and Creedsman of the Pope?
Who vindicates his cleric claim
  By schism and rapine, axe and rope?

Who reads by light of blazing roofs
  His gospel new to Prince and Kerne?
Who tramples under horses' hoofs
  A race expatriate, slow to learn?

From holy Ulster, last discrowned—
  'Twas falsehood did the work, not war—
Who drives her sons by scourge and hound
  To famished Connacht's utmost shore?

Beware false splendours brave to-day!
  Unkingly King, and recreant peers!
Ye hold your prey; but not for aye:
  The hour is yours: but ours the years!

[1] Dermod, King of Leinster, A.D. 1170.

THE SUPPRESSION OF THE FAITH IN ULSTER.

A BARDIC ODE.

A.D. 1623.

Throughout Ulster, and in most parts of Ireland, it had been found impossible to carry the Penal Laws against the Catholic faith fully into effect until the reign of James I. The accession of that prince was hailed as the beginning of an era of liberty and peace. James had ever boasted himself a descendant of the ancient Milesian princes, had had frequent dealings with the Irish chiefs in their wars against Elizabeth, and was believed by them to be, at least in heart, devoted to the religion of his Mother. In the earlier part of his reign, though he refused to grant a legal toleration, he engaged that the Penal Laws should not be executed. In the year 1605 a proclamation was issued, commanding all Catholic priests to quit Ireland under the penalty of death. Next came the compulsory flight of Tirconnell and Tyrone, the Plantation of Ulster, and the swamping of the Irish Parliament by the creation of fictitious boroughs. In 1622 Archbishop Ussher preached before the new Deputy, Lord Faulkland, his celebrated sermon on the text, 'He beareth not the sword in vain.' The next year a new proclamation was published, commanding the departure of all the Catholic clergy, regular and secular, within forty days.

I.

Now we know that they are dead!
They, the Chiefs that kept from scaith
The northern land—the sentenced Faith—
Now we know that they are dead!

II.

Wrong, with Rapine in her leash,
Walk'd her ancient rounds afresh!

Law—late come—with leaden mace
Smites Religion in the face ;—
But the spoiler first had place !

III.

Axes and hammers, hot work and hard !
　From niche and from turret the Saints they cast ;
The church stands naked as the churchyard ;
　The craftsman-army toils fiercely and fast :
They pluck from the altars the precious stones
　As vultures pluck at a dead man's eyes ;
Like wolves down-dragging the flesh from the bones
　They strip the gold from the canopies.
They rifle the tombs ; they melt the bells :
The foundry furnace bubbles and swells !—
Spoiler, for once thou hast err'd ; what ho !
Thou hast loos'd this shaft from an ill-strung bow !
In that Faith thou wouldst strangle, thy Mother died !
Who slew her ? The Usurper our chiefs defied !
Thy heart was with Rome in the days of old ;
Thy counsel was ours ; thy counsel and gold !

IV.

A ban went forth from the regal chambers,
　From the Prince that courted us once with lies,
From the secular synods where he who clambers,
　Not he that walks upright, receives the prize :
' Go back to thy Judah, sad Prophet, go ;
There wail thy wrong, and denounce thy woe ;
But no longer in Bethel thy prophecy sing,
'Tis the chapel and court of Samaria's King ! '
—Let England renounce her church at will,
The children of Erin are faithful still.

For a thousand years has that church been theirs :—
They are God's, not Cæsar's, the creeds and prayers!

V.

Thou that art haughty and full of bread,
The crown falls soon from the unwise head!
Who rear strange altars shall find anon
The lion thereby and sea-sand thereon!
In the deserts of penance they peak and pine
Till fulfilled are the days of the wrath divine.
Thy covenant make with the cave and brier
For shelter by day and by night for fire ;
When the bolt is launch'd at the craggy crest,
And the cedars flame round the eagle's nest !

VI.

A voice from the ocean waves,
   And a voice from the forest glooms,
And a voice from old temples and kingly graves,
   And a voice from the catacombs !
It cries, the King that warreth
   On religion and freedom entwined in one
Down drags in his blindness the fane, nor spareth
   The noble's hall, nor the throne !
I saw in my visions the walls give way
   Of the mystic Babylon ;
I saw the gold Idol whose feet are clay
   On his forehead lying prone ;
I saw a sea-eagle defaced with gore
   Flag wearily over the main ;
But her nest on the cliff she reached no more,
   For the shaft was in her brain.

As when some strong man a stone uplifteth
  And flingeth into floods far down,
So God, when the balance of Justice shifteth,
  Down dasheth the despot's crown,
Down dasheth the realm that abused its trust,
  And the nation that knew not pity,
And maketh the image of power unjust
  To vanish from out the city !

VII.

Wait, my country, and be wise ;—
Thou art gall'd in head and breast,
Rest thou needest, sleep and rest ;
Rest and sleep, and thou shalt rise
And tread down thine enemies.
That which God ordains is best ;
That which God permits is good,
Though by man least understood.
Now His sword He gives to those
Who have wisdom won from woes ;
In them fighting ends the strife :
At other times the impious priest
Slipping on his victim's blood
Falls in death on his own knife !
God is hard to 'scape !   His ire
Strikes the son if not the sire ! [1]
In a time, to God not long,
Thou shalt reckon with this wrong !

---

[1] King James I.'s ' Plantation of Ulster ' was the loss of Ireland to his son, and again to his grandson, and consequently the permanent loss of England.

KING CHARLES'S ' GRACES.'

A.D. 1626.

I.

THUS babble the strong ones, ' The chain is slacken'd!
  Ye can turn half round on your side to sleep!
With the thunder-cloud still your isle is blacken'd;
  But it hurls no bolt upon tower or steep.
Ye are slaves in name: old laws proscribe you;
  But the King is kindly, the Queen is fair;
They are knaves or fools who would goad or bribe
    you
  A legal freedom to claim! Beware!'

II.

We answer thus: our country's honour
  To us is dear as our country's life!
That stigma the foul law casts upon her
  Is the brand on the fame of a blameless wife!
Once more we answer: from honour never
  Can safety long time be found apart:
The bondsman that vows not his bond to sever,
  Is a slave by right and a slave in heart!

SIBYLLA IERNENSIS.

I.

I DREAM'D. Great bells around me peal'd;
  The world in that sad chime was drown'd;
Sharp cries as from a battle-field
  Were strangled in that wondrous sound:

Had all the Kings of earth lain dead,
Had nations borne them lapp'd in lead
To torch-lit vaults with plume and pall,
Such bells had served for funeral.

II.

'Twas work of phantasy! I slept
  Where black Baltard o'erlooks the deep;
Plunging all night the billows kept
  Their ghostly vigil round my sleep.
But I had fed on tragic lore
That day—your annals, ' Masters Four ! '
And every moan of wind and sea
Was as a funeral chime to me.

III.

I woke. In vain the skylark sang
  Above the breezy cliff ; in vain
The golden iris flashed and swang
  In hollows of the sea-pink plain.
As ocean shakes—no longer near—
The listening heart, and haunts the ear,
The Sibyl and that volume's spells
Pursued me with those funeral bells !

IV.

The Irish Sibyl whispers slow
  To one who pass'd her tardy Lent
In purple and fine linen, ' Lo !
  Thou would'st amend—but not repent !
Beware ! Long prospers fearless crime ;
Half courses bring the perilous time !
His way who changes, not his will,
Is strong no more, but guilty still.'

THE BALLAD OF 'BONNY PORTMORE;'

OR, THE WICKED REVENGE.

A.D. 1641.

I.

SHALL I breathe it?   Hush! 'twas dark:—
   Silence!—few could understand:—
   Needful deeds are done—not told.
In your ear a whisper!   Hark!
   'Twas a sworn, unwavering band
      Marching through the midnight cold;
Rang the frost plain, stiff and stark:
      By us, blind, the river rolled.

II.

Silence! we were silent then :-
   Shall we boast and brag to-day?
      Just deeds, blabbed, have found their price!
Snow made dumb the trusty glen;
   Now and then a starry ray
      Showed the floating rafts of ice:
Worked our oath in heart and brain:
      Twice we halted:—only twice.

III.

When we reached the city wall
   On their posts the warders slept:
      By the moat the rushes plained:
Hush! I tell you part, not all!
   Through the water-weeds we crept;
      Soon the sleepers' tower was gained.
My sister's son a tear let fall—
   Righteous deeds by tears are stained.

IV.

Round us lay a sleeping city :—
  Had they wakened we had died :
    Innocence sleeps well, they say.
Pirates, traitors, base banditti,
  Blood upon their hands undried,
    'Mid their spoils asleep they lay !
Murderers ! Justice murders pity !
    Night had brought their Judgment Day !

V.

In the castle, here and there,
  'Twixt us and the dawning East
    Flashed a light, or sank by fits :
' Patience, brothers ! sin it were
  Lords to startle at their feast,
    Sin to scare the dancers' wits ! '
Patient long in forest lair
  The listening, fire-eyed tiger sits !

VI.

O the loud flames upward springing !
  O that first fierce yell within,
    And, without, that stormy laughter !
Like rooks across a sunset winging
  Dark they dashed through glare and din
    Under rain of beam and rafter !
O that death-shriek heavenward ringing ;
    O that wondrous silence after !

The fire-glare showed, 'mid glaze and blister,
  A boy's cheek wet with tears. 'Twas base !

That boy was firstborn of my sister ;
  Yet I smote him on the face !

Ah ! but when the poplars quiver
  In the hot noon, cold o'erhead,
Sometimes with a spasm I shiver ;
  Sometimes round me gaze with dread.

Ah ! and when the silver willow
  Whitens in the moonlight gale,
From my hectic, grassy pillow
  I hear, sometimes, that infant's wail !

THE INTERCESSION.[1]

ULSTER.

A.D. 1641.

IRIEL the Priest arose and said :
  ' The just cause never shall prosper by wrong !
The ill cause battens on blood ill shed ;
  'Tis Virtue only makes Justice strong.

[1] Dr. Leland and other historians relate that the Catholic clergy frequently interfered for the protection of the victims of that massacre, which took place at an early period of the Ulster rising of 1641. They hid them beneath their altars. From the landing of Owen Roe O'Neill all such crimes ceased. They disgraced a just cause, and, doubtless, drew down a Divine punishment. A lamentable list of the massacres committed in the same year, at *the other side*— massacres less generally known—will be found in Bishop Moran's ' Persecutions suffered by the Catholics under Cromwell and the Puritans,' p. 168. It is compiled from a contemporary record.

' I have hidden the Sassanach's wife and child
   Beneath the altar ; behind the porch ;
O'er them that believe not these hands have piled
   The copes and the vestments of holy Church !

' I have hid three men in a hollow oak ;
   I have hid three maids in an ocean cave : '
As though he were lord of the thunder-stroke,
   The old Priest lifted his hand—to save.

But the people loved not the words he spake ;
   And their face was changed, for their heart was
     sore :
They spake no word ; but their brows grew black,
   And the hoarse halls roar'd like a torrent's roar.

  Has the Stranger robb'd you of house and land ?
   In battle meet him and smite him down !
Has he sharpen'd the dagger ? Lift ye the brand !
   Has he bound your Princes ? Set free the clown !

' Has the Stranger his country and knighthood
   shamed ?
   Though he 'scape God's vengeance so shall not ye !
His own God chastens ! Be never named
   With the Mullaghmast slaughter ! Be just and
     free ! '

But the people received not the words he spake,
   For the wrong on their heart had made it sore ;
And their brows grew black like the stormy rack,
   And the hoarse halls roar'd like the wave-wash'd
     shore.

Then Iriel the Priest put forth a curse !
   And horror crept o'er them from vein to vein ;—

A curse upon man and a curse upon horse,
    As forth they rode to the battle-plain.

And there never came to them luck or grace,
    No Saint in the battle-field help'd them more,
Till O'Neill who hated the warfare base
    Had landed at Doe on Tirconnell's shore.

DIRGE OF RORY O'MORE.

A.D. 1642.

Up the sea-sadden'd valley at evening's decline
A heifer walks lowing; 'the Silk of the Kine;'[1]
From the deep to the mountain she roams, and again
From the mountains' green urn to the purple-rimm'd
    main.

Whom seek'st thou, sad Mother? Thine own is not
    thine!
He dropp'd from the headland; he sank in the brine!
'Twas a dream! but in dream at thy foot did he
    follow
Through the meadow-sweet on by the marish and
    mallow!

Was he thine? Have they slain him? Thou seek'st
    him, not knowing
Thyself too art theirs, thy sweet breath and sad low-
    ing!

[1] One of the mystical names for Ireland used by the
bards.

Thy gold horn is theirs; thy dark eye, and thy silk!
And that which torments thee, thy milk, is their milk!

'Twas no dream, Mother Land! 'Twas no dream,
    Inisfail!
Hope dreams, but grief dreams not—the grief of the
    Gael!
From Leix and Ikerren to Donegal's shore
Rolls the dirge of thy last and thy bravest—O'More!

THE BATTLE OF BENBURB.

A BARDIC ODE.

This battle was won by Owen Roe O'Neill over the
Parliamentarian forces, A.D. 1646. The rebels left 3,423 of
their dead on the field.

I.

At even I mused on the wrong of the Gael;—
A storm rushed by me with war-blast not wail,
And the leaves of the forest, plague-spotted and dead,
Like a multitude broken before it fled;
Then I saw in my visions a host back driven
(Ye clansmen be true) by a Chief from heaven!

II.

At midnight I gazed on the moonless skies;—
There glisten'd, 'mid other star-blazonries,
A Sword all stars; then heaven, I knew,
Hath holy work for a sword to do:
Be true, ye clansmen of Nial! Be true!

III.

At morning I look'd as the sun uprose
On hills of Antrim late white with snows;
Was it morning only that dyed them red?
Martyr'd hosts, methought, had bled
On their sanguine ridges for years not few!
Ye clansmen of Conn, this day be true!

IV.

There is felt once more on the earth
   The step of a kingly man:
Like a dead man hidden he lay from his birth,
   Exiled from his country and clan:
This day his standard he flingeth forth;
   He tramples the bond and ban:
Let them look in his face that usurp'd his hearth!
   Let them vanquish him, they who can!
     Owen Roe, our own O'Neill!
      He treads once more our land!
     The sword in his hand is of Spanish steel,
      But the hand is an Irish hand!

V.

I saw in old time with these eyes that fail [1]
   The ship drop down Lough Swilly;

[1] In 1607 a conspiracy, never proved, and probably never undertaken, was suddenly charged against Tyrone and Tirconnell. To avoid arrest the two earls, whose previous submission had rendered them helpless, embarked on board a ship that chanced to have anchored in Lough Swilly. They found refuge in Rome, where their tombs are shown to the traveller in the church of San Pietro, on the Janiculan Hill.

The Four Masters thus record the tragedy:—'They em-

Lessening 'mid billows the snowy sail
  Bent down like a storm-rock'd lily ;
Far, far it bore them, those Sceptres old
That ruled o'er Ulster for ages untold,
The sceptre of Nial and the sceptre of Conn,
Thy Princes, Tirconnell and green Tyrone !
No freight like that since the mountain-pine
Left first the hills for the salt sea-brine !
Down sank on the ocean a blood-red sun
As westward they drifted, when hope was none,
With their priests and their children o'er ocean's
  foam
And every archive of house and home :
Amid the sea-surges their bards sang dirges :
God rest their bones in their graves at Rome !
    Owen Roe, our own O'Neill !
    He treads once more our land !
    The sword in his hand is of Spanish steel,
    But the hand is an Irish hand !

VI.

I saw in old time through the drifts of the snow
A shepherdless People dash'd to and fro,
With hands toss'd up in the wintry air,
With the laughter of madness or shriek of despair.

barked on the festival of Holy Cross, in autumn. This was
a princely company : and it is certain that the sea has not
borne and the wind has not wafted in modern times a
number of persons in one ship more eminent, illustrious, or
noble in race, heroic deeds, valour, feats of arms, and brave
achievements than they. Would that God had but permitted
them to remain in their patrimonial inheritance until the
children had arrived at the age of manhood ! Woe to the
heart that meditated, woe to the counsel that recommended
the project of this expedition ! '

L 2

Dispersed is the flock when the shepherd lies low :
The sword was of parchment : a lie was the blow :
What is Time ?   I can see the rain beat the white
    hair,
And the sleet that defaces the face that was fair,
As onward they stagger o'er mountain and moor
From the Ardes and Rathlin to Corrib's bleak shore :
I can hear the babe weep in the pause of the wind—
' To Connaught ! '   The bloodhounds are baying be-
    hind !—
     Owen Roe, our own O'Neill !
     He treads once more our land !
    The sword in his hand is of Spanish steel,
     But the hand is an Irish hand !

VII.

Visions no more of the dreadful past !
The things that I long'd for are mine at last !
I see them and hold them with heart and eyes ;
On Irish ground, under Irish skies,
An Irish army, clan by clan,
The standard of Ulster on leading the van !
Each chief with his clansmen, tried men like steel ;
Unvanquish'd Maolmora, Cormac the leal !
And the host that meets them right well I know,
The psalm-singing boors of that Scot, Munro !
—We hated you, Barons of the Pale !
But now sworn friends are Norman and Gael ;
For both the old foes are of lineage old,
And both the old Faith and old manners hold.
Montgomery, Conway ! base-born crew !
This day ye shall learn an old lesson anew !
Thou art red with sunset this hour, Blackwater
But twice ere now thou wert red with slaughter !

Another O'Neill by the ford they met ;
And ' the bloody loaming ' men name it yet !
   Owen Roe, our own O'Neill !
     He treads once more our land !
   The sword in his hand is of Spanish steel !
     But the hand is an Irish hand !

VIII.

The storm of the battle rings out !   On ! on !
Shine well in their faces, thou setting sun !
The smoke grows crimson : from left to right
Swift flashes the spleenful and racing light :
The horses stretch forward with belly to ground :
On ! on ! like a lake which has burst its bound !
Through the clangour of brands rolls the laughter of
    cannon :
Wind-borne it shall reach thine old walls, Dun-
    gannon !
Armagh's grey Minster shall chant again
To-morrow at vespers an ancient strain !
On, on !   This night on thy banks, Loch Neagh,
Men born in bondage shall couch them free !
On, warriors launch'd by a warrior's hand !
Four years ye were leash'd in a brazen band ;
He counted your bones, and he meted your might,
This hour he dashes you into the fight !
Strong sun of the battle, great Chief whose eye
Wherever it gazes makes victory,
This hour thou shalt see them do or die !
—They form : there stand they one moment, still !
   Now, now, they charge under banner and sign :
They breast unbroken the slope of the hill,
   It breaks before them, the Invader's line !

Their horse and their foot are crush'd together
Like harbour-locked ships in the winter weather,
Each dash'd upon each, the churn'd wave strewing
With wreck upon wreck, and ruin on ruin.
The spine of their battle gives way with a yell:
Down drop their standards : that cry was their knell !
Some on the bank and some in the river
Struggling they lie that shall rally never.
'Twas God fought for us ! with hands of might
From on high He kneaded and shaped the fight !
To Him be the praise !   What He wills must be :
With Him is the future : for blind are we !
Let Ormond at will make terms or refuse them !
Let Charles the Confederates win or lose them ;
Unbind the old Faith and annul the old strife,
Or cheat us, and forfeit his kingdom and life !
Come hereafter what must cr may
Ulster, thy cause is avenged to-day :
What fraud took from us and force, the sword
That strikes in daylight makes ours, restored !
　　　Owen Roe, our own O'Neill !
　　　　He treads once more our land !
　　　The sword in his hand is of Spanish steel,
　　　　But the hand is an Irish hand !

TRADITOR ISTE.

A WAIL.

I.

Can it be, can it be ?   Can our Great One be
　　Traitor ?
Can the child of her greatest be faithless to Eire ?

The clown and the stranger have wronged—let them
  hate her!
  Old Thomond well knows them; they hate her
  for hire!
Can a brave man be leagued with the rebels and
  ranters
  'Gainst his faith, and his country, his king, and
  his race,
Can he bear the low moanings, the curses, the
  banters?—
  There's a scourge worse than these—the applause
  of the base!

II.

Was the hand that set fire to the Churches descended
  From his hand who upreared them—the strong
  hand, the true?
When the blood of the People and Priesthood ran
  blended
  Who was it looked on, and cried, ' Spare them
  not'? Who?
Some Fury o'erruled thee! Some root thou hadst
  eaten!
  'Twas a Demon that stalked in thy shape. 'Twas
  not thou!
Not tears of the Angels that blood-stain can
  sweeten;
  That Cain-mark not death can erase from thy
  brow!

DIRGE OF OWEN ROE O'NEILL.

A.D. 1649.

So, 'tis over !   Lift the dead !
   Bear him to his place of rest,
Broken heart, and blighted head :
   Lay the Cross upon his breast.

There be many die too late ;
   Here is one that died too soon : [1]
'Twas not Fortune—it was Fate
   After him that cast her shoon.

Toll the church bells slowly : toll !
   God this day is wroth with Eire :
Seal the book, and fold the scroll ;
   Crush the harp, and break the wire.

Lords and priests, ye talked and talked
   In Kilkenny's Council Hall ;
But this man whose game ye baulked
   Was the one man 'mong you all.

'Twas not in the field he fell !
   Sing his requiem, dark-stoled choir !
Let a nation sound his knell :
   God this day is wroth with Eire !

---

[1] The conqueror of Benburb died (by poison as was believed at the time) just after he and Ormond had concluded terms for joint action against Cromwell. Had he not been summoned to Kilkenny when on the point of following up the victory of Benburb, the Puritan army must, within a few days, have been driven out of Ulster.

THE BISHOP OF ROSS.

A.D. 1650.

THEY led him to the peopled wall :
  'Thy sons !' they said, 'are those within !
If at thy word their standards fall,
  Thy life and freedom thou shalt win !'

Then spake that warrior Bishop old,
  'Remove these chains that I may bear
My crosier staff and cope of gold :
  My judgment then will I declare.'

They robed him in his robes of state :
  They set his mitre on his head :
On tower and gate was silence great :
  The hearts that loved him froze with dread.

He spake : 'Right holy is your strife !
  Fight for your Country, King, and Faith·
I taught you to be true in life :
  I teach you to be true in death.

'A priest apart by God is set
  To offer prayer and sacrifice :
And he is sacrificial yet
  The pontiff for his flock who dies.'

Ere yet he fell, his hand on high
  He raised, and benediction gave ;
Then sank in death, content to die :—
  Thy great heart, Erin, was his grave.

DIRGE.

A.D. 1652.

I.

WHOSE were they those voices?   What footsteps
    came near me ?
    Can the dead to the living draw nigh and be
      heard ?
I wept in my sleep; but ere morning to cheer me
    Came a breeze from the woodland, a song from the
      bird.
O sons of my heart! the long-hair'd, the strong-
    handed !
    Your phantoms rush by me with war-cry and
      wail :—
Ye too for your Faith and your Country late banded,
My sons by adoption, mail'd knights of the Pale !

II.

Is there sorrow, O ye that pass by, like my sorrow ?
    Of the Kings I brought forth there remaineth not
      one !
Each day is dishonour'd; disastrous each morrow :—
    In the yew-wood I couch till the daylight is done.
At midnight I lean from the cliff o'er the waters,
    And hear, as the thunder comes up from the sea,
Your moanings, my sons, and your wailings, my
    daughters :
    With the sea-dirge they mix not : they clamour to
      me !

THE WHEEL OF AFFLICTION.

BRIGHT is the Dream-land of them that weep ;
  Of the outcast head on the mountains bare :
Thy Saints, O Eire, I have seen in sleep ;
  Thy Queens on the battle-plain, fierce yet fair.

Three times I dreamed on Tyrawley's shore :
  Through ranks of the Vanished I paced a mile :
On the right stood Kings, and their crowns they
    wore :
On the left stood Priests without gold or guile.

But the vision I saw when the deep I crossed,
  When I crossed from Iorras to Donegal,
By night, on the vigil of Pentecost,
  Was the saddest vision, yet best of all.

From the sea to the sky a Wheel rolled round :
  It breathed a blast on the steadfast stars ;
'Twas huge as that circle with marvels wound—
  The marvels that reign o'er the Calendars.

Then an Angel spake—' That Wheel is Earth ;
  It grinds the wheat of the bread of God : '
And the Angel of Eire, with an Angel's mirth,
  ' The mill-stream from Heaven is the Martyrs'
    blood.'

EPILOGUE.

Like dew from above it fell—from beyond the limits
    of ether;
    From above the courses of stars, and the thrones of
      angelical choirs;
'If God afflicts the Land, then God of a surety is
    with her;
    Her heart-drops counts, like beads, and walks with
    her through the fires.

'Time, and a Time, and Times! Earth's noblest
    birth was the latest:
    That latest birth was Man; his flesh her Redeemer
    wears:
Time, and a Time, and Times! one day the least
    shall be greatest:
    In glory God reaps, but sows below in the valley
    of tears.'

It was no Seraph's song, nor the spheral chime of
    creation,
    That Voice! To earth it stooped as a cloud to the
    ocean flood:
It had ascended in sighs from the anguished heart of
    a nation;—
    The musical echo came back from the boundless
    bosom of God.

INISFAIL

A LYRICAL CHRONICLE OF IRELAND

PART III.

PART III.

PARVULI EJUS.

In the night, in the night, O my Country, the stream
    calls out from afar :
  So swells thy voice through the ages, sonorous
    and vast :
In the night, in the night, O my Country, clear flashes
    the star :
  So flashes on me thy face through the gloom of the
    past.

I sleep not ; I watch : in blows the wind ice-wing'd,
    and ice-finger'd :
  My forehead it cools and slakes the fire in my
    breast ;
Though it sighs o'er the plains where oft thine exiles
    look'd back, and long linger'd,
  And the graves where thy famish'd lie dumb and
    thine outcasts find rest.

For up from those vales wherein thy brave and thy
    beautiful moulder,
  And on through the homesteads waste and the
    temples defiled,

A voice goes forth on that wind, as old as the Islands
and older,
'God reigns: at His feet earth's Destiny sleeps
like a child.'

IN RUIN RECONCILED.

A.D. 1660.

I HEARD a woman's voice that wailed
  Between the sandhills and the sea :
The famished sea-bird past me sailed
  Into the dim infinity.

I saw on boundless rainy moors,
  Far off I saw a great Rock loom ;
The grey dawn smote its iron doors ;
  And then I knew it for a Tomb.

Two queenly shapes before the grate
  Watched, couchant on the barren ground ;
Two regal shades in ruined state,
  One Gael; one Norman ; both discrowned.

THE CHANGED MUSIC.

I.

THE shock of meeting clans is o'er :
  The knightly or the native shout
Pursues no more, by field or shore,
  From rath to cairne, the ruined rout.

O'er dusty stalls old banners trail
  In mouldering fanes : while far beneath
At last the Norman and the Gael
  Lie wedded in the caves of death.

II.

No more the Bard-song ! dead the strains
  That mixed defiance, grief, and laugh :
Old legends haunt no more the plains,
  Half saintly and barbaric half.
Changed is the music.   Sad and slow
  Beyond the horizon's tearful verge
The elegiac wailings flow,
  The fragments of the broken dirge.

THE MINSTREL OF THE LATER DAY.

I.

WHAT art thou, O thou Loved and Lost,
  That, fading from me, leav'st me bare ?
The last trump of a vanquished host
  Far off expiring on the air
So cheats in death the listener's ear
  As thou dost cheat this aching heart :—
To me thy Past looked strangely near ;
  Distant and dim seems that thou art.

II.

O Eire ! the things I loved in thee
  Were dead long years ere I was born :

Yet still their shadows lived for me,
  An evening twilight like the morn :
But daily now with vulgarer hand
  The Present sweeps those phantoms by :—
Like annals of an alien land
  Thy history's self appears to die.

ODE.

THE 'CURSE OF CROMWELL;'

OR, THE DESOLATION OF THE WEST.

  trance I roamed that Land forlorn,
By battle first, then famine worn ;
  I walked in gloom and dread.
The Land remained : the hills were there :
The vales—but few remained to share
  That realm untenanted.

Far-circling wastes, far-bending skies ;
Clouds as at Nature's obsequies
  Slow trailing scarf and pall :—
In whistling winds on creaked the crane :
Grey lakes upstared from moor and plain
  Like eyes on God that call.

Turn where I might, no blade of green
Diversified the tawny scene :
  Bushless the waste, and bare :
A dusky red the hills, as though
Some deluge ebbing years ago
  Had left but seaweed there.

Dark red the vales : that single hue
O'er rotting swamps an aspect threw
   Monotonous yet grand :
Long feared—for centuries in decay—
Like a maimed lion there it lay,
   What once had been a Land.

Yet, day by day, as dropt the sun,
A furnace glare through vapours dun
   Illumed each mountain's head :
Old tower and keep their crowns of flame
That hour assumed ; old years of shame
   Like fiends exorcised, fled.

That hour, from sorrow's trance awaking,
My soul, like day from darkness breaking,
   With might prophetic fired,
To those red hills and setting suns
Returned antiphonal response,
   As gleam by gleam expired.

And in my spirit grew and gathered
Knowledge that Ireland's worst was weathered,
   Her last dread penance paid ;
Conviction that for earthly scath
In world-wide victories of her Faith
   Atonement should be made.

That hour, as one who walks in vision,
Of God's ' New Heavens ' I had fruition,
   And saw, and inly burned :
And I beheld the multitude
Of those whose robes were washed in blood,
   Saw chains to sceptres turned !

And I saw Thrones, and Seers thereon
Judging, and Tribes like snow that shone,
    And diamond towers high-piled,
Towers of that City theirs at last
Through tribulations who have passed,
    And theirs, the undefiled.

A Land become a Monument!
Man works; but God's concealed intent
    Converts his worst to best:
The first of Altars was a Tomb—
Ireland! thy grave-stone shall become
    God's Altar in the West!

PEACE.

SERAPH that from the blue abyss
    O'erlook'st the storms round earth that roll,
While we, by fragments wildered, miss
    The dread perfection of the whole,

Draw near at last!   A moment lean
    Upon that earth's tumultuous breast
Thy hand heart-healing, and serene,
    And grant the anguished planet rest!

THE BALLAD OF THE LADY TURNED BEGGAR.

The Irish who fought for Charles I., and whose estates
were confiscated on that account, looked in vain, with a
few exceptions, for their restoration on the accession of

Charles II. The widow of one of these Royalists, Lord
Roche, in her old age used to be seen begging in the streets
of Cork.

I.

'DROP an alms on shrunken fingers,' faintly with a
 smile she said ;
But the smile was not of pleasure, and unroselike was
 the red :
'Fasts wear thin the pride fantastic ;—one I left at
 home lacks bread.'

II.

Lady ! hard is the beginning — so they say — of
 shameless sinning :
Ay but (loss disguised in winning) easier grows it
 day by day :
May thy shamefaced, sinless pleading to the unhearing
 or unheeding
Lacerate less an inly bleeding bosom ere those locks
 grow grey ;
Locks whose midnight once was lighted with the
 diamond's changeful ray !

III.

Silks worn bare with work's abusing ; cheek made
 wan with hailstorm's bruising ;
Eye its splendour slowly losing ; state less stately in
 decay ;—
Chanting ballad or old ditty year by year she roam'd
 the city :
Love at first is kin to pity ; pity to contempt, men
 say ;
Wonder lessen'd, reverence slacken'd, as the raven
 locks grew grey.

IV.

What is that makes sadness sadder ?   What is that
   makes madness madder ?
Shame, a sharper-venomed adder, gnaws when looks
   once kind betray !
' She is poor: the poor are common !   'Twas a
   countess : 'tis a woman ;
Looks she has at times scarce human : England !
   there should be her stay :
'Twas for Charles the old lord battled—Charles and
   England—so men say.'

V.

Charles ! Whitehall ! the wine, the revel ! No, she
   sinks not to *that* level !
Mime or pander; king or devil; she will die on
   Ireland's shore !
Ne'er, till Portsmouth's brazen forehead grows with
   virtuous blushes florid,
Will she pass that gate abhorrèd, climb that stair-
   case, tread that floor :
Let *that* forehead wear the diamond which Lord
   Roche's widow wore !

VI.

Critic guest through Ireland wending, careless praise
   with cavil blending,
Wonder not, in old man bending, or in beggar boys
   at play,
Wonder not at aspect regal, princely front or eye of
   eagle :

Common these where baying beagle, or the wire-
    hair'd wolf-hound grey
Chased old nobles once through woodlands which the
    ignoble made their prey.
Centuries three that sport renewed they—thrice a
    century—so men say.

THE IRISH SLAVE IN BARBADOES.

BESIDE our shieling spread an oak :
    Close by, a beech, its brother :
Between them rose the pale blue smoke ;
    They mingled each with other.

The gold mead stretched before our door
    Beyond the church-tower taper ;
The river wound into the moor
    In distance lost and vapour.

Amid green hazels, cradle-swung,
    Our babe, with rapture dancing,
Watched furry shapes the roots among,
    With beaded eyes forth glancing.

Ah, years of blessing ! Rich no more,
    Yet grateful and contented,
The lands that Strafford from us tore
    No longer we lamented.

So fared it till that night of woe
    When, from the mountains blaring,
The deep horns rang, ' The foe, the foe ! '
    And fires were round us glaring.

He went: next day our hearth was cold,
  Then came that week of slaughter :—
I woke within the ship's black hold,
  And heard the rushing water.

Ah ! those that seemed our life can die,
  Yet we live on and wither !
Fling out thy fires, thou Indian sky :
  Toss all thy torches hither !

Send, salt morass and swamps of cane,
  Send forth your ambushed fever !
O death, unstrain at last my chain,
  And bid me rest for ever !

ARCHBISHOP PLUNKET.

(THE LAST VICTIM OF THE 'POPISH PLOT.')

JULY 11, A.D. 1681.

'The Earl of Essex went to the king (Charles II.) to
apply for a pardon, and told his Majesty "the witnesses
must needs be perjured, as what they swore could not possibly be true." But his Majesty answered in a passion,
"Why did you not declare this, then, at the trial? I dare
pardon nobody—his blood be upon your head, and not
mine !'—Haverty's *History of Ireland.* See also Bishop
Moran's admirable *Life of Archbishop Plunket.*

WHY crowd ye windows thus, and doors ?
  Why climb ye tower and steeple ?
What lures you forth, O senators ?
  What brings you here, O people ?

Here there is nothing worth your note—
  'Tis but an old man dying:

The noblest stag this season caught,
   And in the old nets lying !

Sirs, there are marvels, but not here :
   Here's but the threadbare fable
Whose sense nor sage discerns, nor seer ;
   Unwilling is unable !

That prince who lurk'd in bush and brake
   While bloodhounds bay'd behind him,
Now, to his father's throne brought back,
   In pleasure's wreaths doth wind him.

The primate of that race, whose sword
   Stream'd last to save that father,
To-day is reaping such reward
   As Irish virtues gather.

His Faith King Charles partakes—and hides !
   Ah, caitiff crowned, and craven !
Not his to breast the rough sea tides ;
   He rocks in peaceful haven.

Great heart !   Pray well in heaven this night,
   From dungeon loosed, and hovel,
For souls that blacken in God's light,
   That know the truth, yet grovel.

THE LAST STRUGGLE.

A.D. 1690.

A CROWNLESS King stands up,
   That King the knaves traduce :
His lineage springs from Irish Kings
   Through Kenneth and through Bruce.

Our strength, our hope, are past;
   Our faith, our truth remain;
With James is right; for James we'll fight,
   'Gainst Dutchman and 'gainst Dane.

They hate him well, those Dutch,
   For on their necks he trod!
He fired their tallest ships, and dyed
   The green sea with their blood.
'Twas treason laid him low—
   Children his bread who brake—
The Saxon spurns that English king
   The Gael will not forsake.

Who calls him Tyrant?   They,
   Those traitors foiled long since,
That strove to snatch his future crown
   From England's patriot Prince!
What plea was theirs that day?
   What crime was his? His Faith!
Despite their laws we'll fight his cause,
   And fight it to the death.

His grandsire filched our lands :
   His father pawned his pledge :
His brother doled us doubtful words
   That wore a double edge :
In James we found at need
   Small love, and succour none :
Not less we propped the father's right;
   We'll not desert the son.

A BALLAD OF SARSFIELD;

OR, THE BURSTING OF THE GUNS.

A.D. 1690.

SARSFIELD rode out the Dutch to rout,
　And to take and break their cannon;
To mass went he at half-past three,
　And at four he cross'd the Shannon.

Tirconnel slept.　In dream his thoughts
　Old fields of victory ran on;
And the chieftains of Thomond in Limerick's towers
　Slept well by the banks of Shannon.

He rode ten miles and he cross'd the ford,
　And couch'd in the wood and waited;
Till, left and right, on march'd in sight
　That host which the true men hated.

' Charge ! ' Sarsfield cried; and the green hill-side
　As they charged replied in thunder;
They rode o'er the plain and they rode o'er the slain,
　And the rebel rout lay under !

He burn'd the gear the knaves held dear,—
　For his King he fought, not plunder;
With powder he cramm'd the guns, and ramm'd
　Their mouths the red soil under.

The spark flash'd out—like a nation's shout
　The sound into heaven ascended;
The hosts of the sky made to earth reply,
　And the thunders twain were blended !

Sarsfield rode out the Dutch to rout,
    And to take and break their cannon ;—
A century after, Sarsfield's laughter
    Was echoed from Dungannon.

A BALLAD OF ATHLONE;

OR, HOW THEY BROKE DOWN THE BRIDGE.

Does any man dream that a Gael can fear ?—
    Of a thousand deeds let him learn but one !
The Shannon swept onward, broad and clear,
    Between the leaguers and worn Athlone.

' Break down the bridge ! '—Six warriors rushed
    Through the storm of shot and the storm of shell :
With late, but certain, victory flushed
    The grim Dutch gunners eyed them well.

They wrenched at the planks 'mid a hail of fire :
    They fell in death, their work half done :
The bridge stood fast ; and nigh and nigher
    The foe swarmed darkly, densely on.

' O who for Erin will strike a stroke ?
    Who hurl yon planks where the waters roar ? '
Six warriors forth from their comrades broke,
    And flung them upon that bridge once more.

Again at the rocking planks they dashed ;
    And four dropped dead ; and two remained :
The huge beams groaned, and the arch down-
    crashed ;—
    Two stalwart swimmers the margin gained.

St. Ruth in his stirrups stood up, and cried,
  ' I have seen no deed like that in France !'
With a toss of his head Sarsfield replied,
  ' They had luck, the dogs ! 'Twas a merry chance !'

O many a year upon Shannon's side
  They sang upon moor and they sang upon heath
Of the twain that breasted that raging tide,
  And the ten that shook bloody hands with Death !

THE REQUITAL.

I.

WE too had our day—it was brief : it is ended—
  When a King dwelt among us ; no strange King
    but ours !
When the shout of a People delivered ascended
  And shook the broad banner that hung on his
    towers.
We saw it like trees in a summer breeze shiver ;
  We read the gold legend that blazoned it o'er :
' To-day !—now or never ! To-day and for ever ! '
  O God, have we seen it to see it no more ?

II.

How fared it that season, our lords and our masters,
  In that spring of our freedom how fared it with
    you ?
Did we trample your Faith ? Did we mock your
    disasters ?
  We restored but his own to the leal and the true.

Ye had fallen !   'Twas a season of tempest and
     troubles :
  But against you we drew not that knife ye had
     drawn ;
In the war-field we met ; but your prelates and
     nobles
  Stood up 'mid the senate in ermine and lawn !

THE LAST MAC CARTHYMORE.

On thy woody heaths, Muskerry—Carbery, on thy
     famish'd shore,
Hands hurl'd upwards, wordless wailings, clamour
     for Mac Carthymore !
He is gone ; and never, never shall return to wild or
     wood
Till the sun burns out in blackness and the moon
     descends in blood.

He, of lineage older, nobler, at the latest Stuart's
     side
Drew once more his father's sword for Charles in
     blood of traitors dyed :—
Once again the stranger fattens where Mac Carthys
     ruled of old,
For a later Cromwell triumphs in the Dutchman's
     muddier mould.

Broken boat and barge around him, sea-gulls piping
     loud and shrill,
Sits the chief where bursts the breaker, and laments
     the sea-wind chill ;

In a barren northern island dinn'd by ocean's endless
  roar,
Where the Elbe with all his waters streams between
  the willows hoar.

Earth is wide in hill and valley;—palace courts and
  convent piles
Centuries since received thine outcasts, Ireland, oft
  with tears and smiles :
Wherefore builds this grey-hair'd Exile on a rock-
  isle's weedy neck ?—
Ocean unto ocean calleth ; inly yearneth wreck to
  wreck !

He and his, his Church and Country, King and kinsmen, house and home,
Wrecks they are like broken galleys strangled by the
  yeasty foam :
Nations past and nations present are or shall be soon
  as these—
Words of peace to him come only from the breast of
  raging seas.

Clouds and sea-birds inland drifting o'er the sea-bar
  and sand-plain ;
Belts of mists for weeks unshifting ; plunge of de-
  vastating rain ;
Icebergs as they pass uplifting aguish gleams
  through vapours frore,
These, long years, were thy companions, O thou last
  Mac Carthymore !

When a rising tide at midnight rush'd against the
  downward stream,
Rush'd not then the clans embattled meeting in the
  Chieftain's dream ?

When once more that tide exhausted died in mur-
    murs toward the main
Died not then once more his slogan, ebbing far o'er
    hosts of slain ?

Pious river! let us rather hope the low monotonies
Of thy broad stream seaward toiling and the willow-
    bending breeze
Charm'd at times a midday slumber, tranquillised
    tempestuous breath,
Music last when harp was broken, requiem sad and
    sole in death.

RELIGIO NOVISSIMA.

THERE is an Order by a northern sea,
    Far in the West, of rule and life more strict
Than that which Basil reared in Galilee,
    In Egypt Paul, in Umbria Benedict.

Discalced it walks ; a stony land of tombs,
    A strange Petræa of late days, it treads !
Within its court no high-tossed censer fumes ;
    The night-rain beats its cells, the wind its beds.

Before its eyes no brass-bound, blazon'd tome
    Reflects the splendour of a lamp high-hung :
Knowledge is banish'd from her earliest home,
    Like wealth : it whispers psalms that once it sung.

It is not bound by the vow celibate,
    Lest, through its ceasing, anguish too might cease ;

In sorrow it brings forth ; and Death and Fate
    Watch at Life's gate, and tithe the unripe in-
      crease.

It wears not the Franciscan's cord or gown ;
    The cord that binds it is the Stranger's chain :
Scarce seen for scorn, in fields of old renown,
    It breaks the clod ; another reaps the grain.

Year after year it fasts ; each third or fourth
    So fasts that fasts of men to it are feast ;
Then of its brethren many in the earth
    Are laid unrequiem'd like the mountain beast.

Where are its cloisters ?   Where the felon sleeps !
    Where its novitiate ?   Where the last wolf died !
From sea to sea its vigil long it keeps—
    Stern Foundress ! is its Rule not mortified ?

Thou that hast laid so many an Order waste,
    A Nation is thine Order !   It was thine
Wide as a realm that Order's seed to cast,
    And undispensed sustain its discipline.

QUOMODO SEDET SOLA.

How sits the City lonely and uncrowned ;
    (Thus the old Priests renewed that Hebrew song)
She sits a widowed queen in weepings drowned ;
    Her friends revile her, who should mourn her wrong.

Behold, her streets are silent and her gate ;
    And as the sea her sorrows are increased—

The Daughter of my People, desolate ;
  And no man mounteth to her solemn feast.

To them that brought her comfort she hath said,
  ' My children strove, and each by each is slain :
I turned from Him to Whom my youth was wed :
  Therefore the heathen hosts my courts profane.

' The bruised reed He brake not; neither cried,
  Nor strove, nor smote : He set the prisoners free :
But sons of mine oppressed His poor, and lied,
  Nor walked in judgment and in equity.'

Thus sang the Priests, and ended, ' Christ was led
  Lamb-like to death.   His mouth He opened not :
He gave His life to raise from death the dead :
  That God Who sends our penance shared our lot.

SPES UNICA.

I.

BETWEEN two mountains' granite walls one star
  Shines in this sea-lake quiet as the grave ;
The ocean moans against its rocky bar ;
  That star no reflex finds in foam or wave.

II.

Saints of our country : if—no more a Nation—
  Vain are henceforth her struggles, from on high
Fix in the bosom of her desolation
  So much the more that Hope which cannot die !

SEDERUNT IN TERRA.

' The Lord hath spread His net about her feet,
   And down hath hurled her wall in heaps around ; '
Thus sang her elders, as their breasts they beat,
   Her virgins with their garlands on the ground.

' The head of Sion to the dust is brought :
   Her Kings are slain or scattered by the sword :
Her ancient Law is made a thing of nought :
   Her Prophets find not vision from the Lord.

' Because they showed thee not thy sin of old,
   Servants this day have lordship o'er thy race :
From thine own wells thou draw'st thy drink for
   gold ;
   And Gentile standards mock thy Holy Place.

' Thy little children made an idle quest—
   " Where—where is bread ? " As wounded men
   they lay
In every street. Upon their mothers' breast
   At last they breathed their souls in death away.'

The Priests made answer, ' Christ on Olivet
   Prayed to His Father. Pray thou well this day.
His chalice passed Him not. Therefore thy debt
   Is cancelled. Watch with Him one hour, and pray.'

DEEP CRIETH UNTO DEEP.

I.

BESIDE that Eastern sea—there first exalted—
  Thus sang, not Bard, but Priest, 'The Cross lies
    low!'
Sad St. Sophia, 'neath thy roofs gold-vaulted
  Who kneels this hour? the blind and turban'd
    Foe!

II.

O Eire! a sister hast thou in thy sorrow!
  If thine the earlier, hers the bitterer moan:
She weeps to-day; great Rome may weep to-
    morrow!
  Claim not that o'er-proud boast—to weep alone.

ADHÆSIT LINGUA LACTANTIS.

'THY woes have made thy heart as iron hard:
  Lo! the sea-monsters yield their young the breast;
But thou the gates of thine increase hast barred;
  And scorn'st to grant thine offspring bread or rest.

'Thy lordly ones within thy womb conceived
  And nursed in scarlet, wither in thy drouth;
The tongue of him, thy suckling babe, hath cleaved
  To that dry skin which roofed his milkless mouth.

'Put down thy lips into the road-side dust;
  And whisper softly through that dust, and say,
"Although He slay me, yet in God I trust;
  He made, and can re-make me. Let Him slay!"'

' Behold ! to tarry for the Lord is good ;
  His faithfulness for ever shall remain ;
His mercies as the mornings are renewed :
  The man that waits Him shall not wait in vain.

' Within thy bones He made His fire to burn
  That thou might'st hate the paths thy feet have
    trod :
Jerusalem, Jerusalem, return ; '
  Thus sang the Priests—' thy refuge is thy God.'

THE PROMISE.

I.

As the church-bells rolled forth their sonorous Evan-
  gel,
  Their last ere the Stranger usurped the old pile,
I heard, 'mid their clangour, the voice of an Angel
  Give words to that music which rushed o'er the
    Isle :
' In thousand-fold echoes, thy God, unforsaking,
  That peal shall send back from the heavenly
    bourne :
O hearts that are broken, O hearts that are break-
  ing,
  Be strong, for the glories gone by shall return.'

II.

Thenceforth in the wood, and the tempests that din
  it,
  In the thunder of mountains, the moan of the
    shore,

That chime I can hear, and the clear song within it,
  The voice of that Angel who sings evermore,
'The Faith shall grow vast though the Faithful grow
    fewer;
  By sorrow uplifted ascendeth *their* Throne
Who resist the ill deed, but not hate the ill-doer,
  Who forgive, unpartaking, all sins but their own.'

Only a reed that sighed :—
  And the Poplar grove hard by
From a million of babbling mouths replied,
  'Who cares, who cares?   Not I!'

Only a dove's low moan :—
  And the new-gorged raven near
Let fall from the red beak the last white bone,
  And answered, half croak, half sneer.

Only the Silk of the Kine,
  Far driven on the foot that bled:
And only old Argial's bleeding pine;
  And the Black Rose that once was red.

ODE.

THE CYCLIC RENOVATION.

I.

THE unvanquish'd Land puts forth each year
  New growth of man and forest;

Her children vanish ; but on her,
   Stranger, in vain thou warrest !
She wrestles, strong through hope sublime,
   (Thick darkness round her pressing)
Wrestles with God's great Angel, Time—
   And wins, though maim'd, the blessing.

II.

As night draws in what day sent forth,
   As Spring is born of Winter,
As flowers that hide in parent earth
   Re-issue from the centre,
Our Land takes back her wasted brood,
   Our Land in respiration,
Breathes from her deep heart unsubdued
   A renovated nation !

III.

A Nation dies : a People lives :—
   Through signs celestial ranging
A Race's Destiny survives
   Unchanged, yet ever changing :
The many-centuried Wrath goes by ;
   But while earth's tumult rages
' In cœlo quies.'   Burst and die
   Thou storm of temporal ages !

IV.

Burst, and thine utmost fury wreak
   On things that are but seeming !
First kill ; then die ; that God may speak,
   And man surcease from dreaming !

That Love and Justice strong as love
  May be the poles unshaken
Round which a world new-born may move
  And Truth that slept may waken !

THE SPIRITUAL RENOVATION.

I.

The Watchman stood on the turret :
  He looked to the south and the east :
But the Kings of the south were sleeping,
  And the eastern Kings at feast.
  Not yet is thy help : not yet
  Hast thou paid the uttermost debt :
Not reached is the worst, thou Weeper :—
  Though thy feet—God meteth their tread—
  Have dinted the green sea's bed,
There are depths in the mid sea deeper !
Not *all* God's waves and His billows
  As yet have gone over thy head,
That Penance and Faith should be lords o'er
    Death,
  And that Hell should be vanquishèd.

II.

I heard thine Angel that sighed
  Three times, ' Descend to the deep.'
I heard at his side the Archangel that cried,
  ' To the depth that is under the deep.'
Who made thee and shaped thee of old,
  It is He in the darkness that lays thee,
With the cerements around thee ninefold ;

That Earth, when the waking is thine,
May look on His Hand divine,
And answer, ' None other might raise thee ! '

III.

Noble, and Chieftain and Prince,
   They were thine in thy day, and died :
The head and the members were scattered long
    since ;—
   Shall a sinew, or nerve abide ?
So long as of that dead clay
   Two atoms together cleave,
God's trumpet that calls thee thou canst not obey,
   His promise receive and believe.
So long as the seed, the husk,
   The body of death, and the prison,
Holds out, undissolved, in the dusk,
   So long in his pains and his chains
The unglorified Spirit remains ;
   The New Body unrisen.

A SONG OF THE BRIGADE.

    The Irish Brigade, consisting originally of soldiers of
James II., took service with more than one continental
sovereign. In many a land it made the name of Ireland
famous. The Brigade was recruited from Ireland till the
latter part of the eighteenth century, and it is said that,
from first to last, nearly 500,000 men belonged to it.

   I SNATCHED a stone from the bloodied brook
     And hurled it at my household door !
   No farewell of my love I took :
     I shall see my friend no more.

I dashed across the churchyard bound :
  I knelt not by my parents' graves :
There rang from my heart a clarion's sound
  That summoned me o'er the waves.

No land to me can native be
  That strangers trample and tyrants stain :
When the valleys I loved are cleansed and free
  They are mine, they are mine again !

Till then, in sunshine or sunless weather,
  By Seine and Loire, and the broad Garonne,
My war-horse and I roam on together
  Wherever God wills.   On ! on !

A SONG OF THE BRIGADE.

RIVER that through this purple plain
Toilest—once redder—to the main,
Go, kiss for me the banks of Seine ;

Tell him I loved, and love for aye,
That his I am though far away—
More his than on the marriage-day.

Tell him thy flowers for him I twine
When first the slow sad mornings shine
In thy dim glass ; for he is mine.

Tell him when evening's tearful light
Bathes those dark towers on Aughrim's height,
There where he fought, in heart I fight.

A freeman's banner o'er him waves !
So be it ! I but tend the graves
Where freemen sleep whose sons are slaves.

Tell him I nurse his noble race,
Nor weep save o'er one sleeping face
Wherein those looks of his I trace.

For him my beads I count when falls
Moonbeam or shower at intervals
Upon our burn'd and blacken'd walls:

And bless him! bless the bold Brigade—
May God go with them, horse and blade,
For Faith's defence, and Ireland's aid!

SONG.

I.

NOT always the winter! not always the wail!
  The heart heals perforce where the spirit is pure!
The apple-tree blooms in the glens of Imayle;
  The blackbird sings loud by the Slane and the
    Suir!
There are princes no more in Kincora and Tara,
But the gold-flower laughs out from the Mague at
  Athdara;
And the Spring-tide that wakens the leaf in the
  bud,
(Sad Mother, forgive us) shoots joy through our
  blood!

II.

Not always the winter! not always the moan!
  Our fathers, they tell us, in old time were free:
Free to-day is the stag in the woods of Idrone,
  And the eagle that fleets from Loch Lene o'er the
    Lee!

The blue-bells rise up where the young May hath
    trod ;
The souls of our martyrs are reigning with God !
Sad Mother, forgive us ! yon skylark no choice
Permits us.   From heaven he is crying 'Rejoice ! '

A SONG OF THE BRIGADE.

A.D. 1706.

I.

WHAT sound goes up among the Alps !
    The shouts of Irish battle !
The echoes reach their snowy scalps ;
    From cliff to cliff they rattle !
In vain he strove—the Duke—Eugene :—
    That flying host to rally :
The squadrons green, they swept it clean
    Beyond Marsiglia's valley.

II.

Who fixed their standards on thy wall,
    Long-leaguered Barcelona !
Unfallen, who saw the bravest fall ?
    Reply, betrayed Cremona !
O graves of Sarsfield and of Clare !
    O Ramillies and Landen,[1]
Their brand we bear : their faith we share,
    Their cause we'll ne'er abandon !

[1] O'Brien, Lord Clare, fell at the battle of Ramillies,
A.D. 1706 ; Sarsfield, Earl of Lucan, on the field of Landen,
A.D. 1693.   Catching in his hand the blood that trickled
from his death-wound, he exclaimed, ' O that this had been
for Ireland ! '

III.

Years passed : again went by the Bard,
    The law that banned him braving :
Where blood of old had stained the sward
    Summer corn was waving :
The tempest of a sudden joy
    Uplifting stave and stanza,
The valleys echoed ' Fontenoy,'
    The wild sea-shore ' Almanza ! '

THE SEA-WATCHER.

I.

THE crags lay dark in strange eclipse :
    From waves late flushed the glow was gone :
The topsails of the far-off ships
    Alone in lessening radiance shone :
Against a stranded boat a maid
    Stood leaning, gunnel to her breast,
As though its pain that pressure stayed :
    Her large eyes rested on the west.

II.

' Beyond the sea ! beyond the sea !
    The weeks, the months, the years go by !
Ah ! when will some one say of me,
    ' Beyond the sky ! beyond the sky ! '
And yet I would not have thee here
    To look upon thy country's shame :
For me the tear : for me the bier :
    For thee fair field, and honest fame.'

THE FRIENDLY BLIGHT.

I.

A MARCH-WIND sang in a frosty wood,
  'Twas in Oriel's land on a mountain.brown,
While the woodman stared at the hard black bud,
  And the sun through mist went down:
' Not always,' it sang, ' shall triumph the wrong,
  For God is stronger than man, they say : '
(Let no man tell of the March-wind's song,
  Till comes the appointed day.)

II.

' Sheaf after sheaf upon Moira's plain,
  And snow upon snow on the hills of Mourne !
Full many a harvest-moon must wane,
  Full many a Spring return !
The Right shall triumph at last o'er wrong :
  Yet none knows how, and none the day : '—
The March-wind sang; and bit 'mid the song
  The little black bud away !

III.

' Blow south-wind on, through my vineyard blow ! '
  So pray'd that land of the palm and vine ;
O Eire, 'tis the north wind and wintry snow
  That strengthen thine oak and pine !
The storm breaks oft upon Uladh's hills ;
  Oft bursts the wave on the stones by Saul ;
In God's time cometh the thing God wills,
  For God is the Lord of all !

THE NEW RACE.

I.

O YE who have vanquish'd the Land and retain it,
  .How little ye know what ye miss of delight !
There are worlds in her heart—could ye seek it or
    gain it—
  That would clothe a true Noble with glory and
    might.
What is she, this Isle which ye trample and ravage,
  Which ye plough with oppression and reap with
    the sword,
But a harp, never strung, in the hall of a savage,
  Or a fair wife embraced by a husband abhorr'd ?

II.

The chiefs of the Gael were the People embodied ;
  The chiefs were the blossom, the People the root !
Their conquerors, the Normans, high-soul'd, and
    high-blooded,
  Grew Irish at last from the scalp to the foot.
But ye !—ye are hirelings and satraps, not Nobles !
  Your slaves, they detest you ; your masters, they
    scorn !
The river lives on ; but its sun-painted bubbles
  Pass quick, to the rapids insensibly borne.

THE BALLAD OF KING CORMAC'S CHOICE.

According to the Irish chronicles, Cormac, King of all
Ireland, renounced the worship of idols about two centuries
before the arrival of St. Patrick, having received in a vision
the promise of the true Faith.

BESIDE the banks of Boyne, where late
    The dire Dutch trumpets blared and rang,
'Mid wounded kernes the harper sate,
    And thus the river's legend sang :

Who shall forbid a King to lie
    Where lie he will, when life is o'er ?
King Cormac laid him down to die;
    But first he raised his hand, and swore :

' At Brugh ye shall not lay my bones :
    Those pagan Kings I scorn to join
Beside the trembling Druid stones,
    And on the northern bank of Boyne.

' A grassy grave of poor degree
    Upon its southern marge be mine
At Rossnaree, where of things to be
    I saw in vision the pledge and sign.

' Thou happier Faith, that from the east
    Slow travellest, set my People free !
I sleep, thy prophet and thy priest,
    By southern Boyne, at Rossnaree.'

He died : anon from hill and wood
    Down flocked the black-robed Druid race,
And round the darkened palace stood,
    And cursed the dead King to his face.

Uptowering round his bed, with lips
   Denouncing doom, and cheeks death-pale,
As when at noontide strange eclipse
   Invests grey cliff and shadowed vale ;

And proved with cymbal'd anthems dread
   The Gods he spurned had bade him die :—
Then spake the pagan chiefs, and said,
   ' Where lie our Kings, this King must lie.'

In royal robes the corse they dressed ;
   They spread the bier with boughs of yew ;
And chose twelve men, their first and best,
   To bear him through the Boyne to Brugh.

But on his bier the great dead King
   Forgat not so his kingly oath ;
And from sea-marge to mountain spring,
   Boyne heard their coming, and was wroth.

He frowned far off, 'mid gorse and fern,
   As those ill-omened steps made way ;
He muttered 'neath the flying hern ;
   He foamed by cairn and cromlech grey ;

And rose, and drowned with one black wave
   Those Twelve on-wading ; and with glee
Bore down King Cormac to his grave
   By southern Boyne, at Rossnaree !

Close by that grave, three centuries past,
   Columba reared his saintly cell ;
And Boyne's rough voice was changed at last
   To music by the Christian bell.

So Christ's true Faith made Erin free,
   And blessed her women and her men ;

And that which was again shall be,
　And that which died shall rise again.

He ceased : the wondering listeners roared
　Accordance to the quivering strings,
And praised King Cormac, Erin's Lord,
　And prophet of the King of kings.

THE IRISH EXILE AT FIESOLE.

I.

HERE to thine exile rest is sweet :
　Here, Mother-land, thy breath is near him !
Thy pontiff, Donat, raised his seat
　On these fair hills that still revere him ;
Like him that thrill'd the Helvetian vale,
　St. Gall's, with rock-resounded anthem : —
For their sakes honour'd is the Gael :
　The peace they gave to men God grant them !

II.

Far down in pomp the Arno winds
　By domes the boast of old Religion ;
The eternal azure shining blinds
　Serene Ausonia's queenliest region.
Assunta be her name ! for bright
　She sits, assumed 'mid heavenly glories ;
But ah ! more dear—though dark like night—
　To me, my loved and lost Dolores !

III.

The mild Franciscans say—and sigh—
  ' Weep not except for Christ's dear Passion ! '
They never saw their Florence lie,
  Like her I mourn, in desolation !
On this high crest they brood in rest,
  The pines their Saint and them embowering,
While centuries blossom round their nest
  Like those slow aloes seldom flowering.

IV.

' Salvete, flores martyrum ! '
  Such was the Roman Philip's greeting,
In banner'd streets with myrtles dumb
  The grave-eyed English college meeting.
There lived an older martyr-land !
  All realms revered her—none would aid her ;
Or reaching forth a tardy hand
  Enfeebled first, at last betrayed her !

V.

Men named that land a ' younger Rome ! '
  She lit the north with radiance golden ;
Alone survives the catacomb
  Of all that Roman greatness olden !
Her Cathall at Taranto sate :
  Virgilius ! Saltzburgh was thy mission !
Who sow'd the Faith fast long, feast late ;
  Who reap'd retain unvex'd fruition.

VI.

Peace settles on the whitening hair;
  The heart that burned grows cold and colder ;

My resurrection spot is there
  Where those Etrurian ruins moulder.
Foot-sore, by yonder pillar's base
  My rest I make, unknown and lowly :
And teach the legend-loving race
  To weep a Troy than theirs more holy.

WINTER SONG.

THE high-piled cloud drifts on as in scorn,
  Like a ghost, half pining, half stately,
Or a white ice-island in silence borne
  O'er seas congeal'd but lately.

With nose to the ground, like a wilder'd hound,
  O'er wood-leaves yellow and sodden
On races the wind, but cannot find
  One sweet track where Spring hath trodden.

The moor is black ; with frosty rime
  The wither'd brier is beaded ;
The sluggard Spring hath o'erslept her time,
  The Spring that was never more needed.

What says the oak-leaf in the night-cold noon,
  And the beech-stock scoffing and surly ?
' Who comes too soon is a witless loon,
  Like the clown that is up too early.'

But the moss grows fair when the trees are bare,
The torpid year finds a pillow there ;
And beside it the fern with its green crown saith
' Best bloometh the Hope that is rooted in death.'

GAIETY IN PENAL DAYS.

BEATI IMMACULATI.

' THE storm has roar'd by ; and the flowers reappear:
Like a babe on the battle-field born, the new year
Through wrecks of the forest looks up on the skies
With a smile like the windflower's, and violet eyes.

' There's warmth in the sunshine ; there's song in
    the wood :
There's faith in the spirit, and life in the blood ;
We'll dance though the Stranger inherits the soil :
We'll sow though we reap not ! For God be the
    toil ! '

O Earth that renewest thy beautiful youth !
The meek shall possess thee ! Unchangeable Truth !
A childhood thou giv'st us 'mid grey hairs reborn
As the gates we approach of perpetual morn !

In the halls of their fathers an alien held feast ;
Their church was a cave and an outlaw their priest ;
The birds have their nests and the foxes have holes—
What had these ? Like a sunrise God shone in their
    souls !

SONG.

I.

YE trumpets of long-buried hosts
    Peal, peal no longer in mine ears !
No more afflict me, wailing ghosts

Of princedoms quell'd and vanished years !
    Freeze on my face, forbidden tears :
And thou, O heart, whose hopes are dead,
Sleep well, like hearts that sleep in lead,
    Embalmed 'mid royal sepulchres.

II.

The stream that one time rolled in blood
    A stainless crystal winds to-day :
Fresh scions of the branded wood
    Detain the flying feet of May :
    The linnet chants 'mid ruins grey :
The young lambs bound the graves among : —
O Mother-land ! he does thee wrong
    That with thy playmates scorns to play.

UNA.

To the knee she stood 'mid rushes,
    And the broad, dark stream swept by her :
Smiles went o'er her, smiles and blushes,
    As the stranger's bark drew nigh her :
Near to Clonmacnoise she stood :
Shannon past her wound in flood.

By her side a wolf-hound wrestled
    With a bright boy bold as Mars ;
On her breast an infant nestled,
    Like to her, but none of hers ;
A golden iris graced her hand—
All her gold was in that wand.

O'er the misty, moorish margin
    Frown'd a ruin'd tower afar ;
Some one said, 'This peasant virgin
    Comes from chieftains great in war !
Princes once had bow'd before her :
Now the reeds alone adore her ! '

Refluent dropt (that bark on gliding)
    The wave it heaved along the bank :
Like worldings still with fortune siding,
    The reed-beds with it backward sank.
Farewell to her !　The rushing river
Must have its way.　Farewell for ever !

DOUBLE-LIVED;

OR, RACES CROWNED.

I.

BEFORE the award, in those bright Halls
    That rest upon the rolling spheres,
Like kingly patriarchs God instals
    Long-suffering Races proved by years ;
They stand, the counterparts sublime
    Of shapes that walk this world of woe,
Triumphant there in endless prime
    While militant on earth below.

II.

As earth-mists build the snowy cloud
    So Spirits risen, that conquered Fate,
Age after age up-borne in crowd,
    That counterpart Assumed create :

Some form the statue's hand or head :
   Some add the sceptre or the crown :
Till the great Image, perfected,
   Smiles on its mortal semblance down.

III.

There stand the Nations just in act,
   Or cleansed by suffering, cleansed not changed :
They stand of martyr souls compact,
   Round heaven's crystalline bastions ranged.
Among those Gods Elect art thou,
   My Country—loftier hour by hour !
The earthly Erin bleeds below :
   The heavenly reigns and rules in power.

ADDUXIT IN TENEBRIS.

THEY wish thee strong : they wish thee great !
   Thy royalty is in thy heart !
Thy children mourn thy widow'd state
   In funeral groves.   Be what thou art !

Across the world's vainglorious waste,
   As o'er Egyptian sands, in thee
God's hieroglyph, *His* shade is cast—
   A bar of black from Calvary.

Around thee many a land and race
   Have wealth or sway or name in story ;
But on that brow discrown'd we trace
   The crown expiatory.

SONG.

I.

O woods that o'er the waters breathe
  A sigh that grows from morn till night;
O waters with your voice like death,
  And yet consoling in your might ;
Ye draw, ye drag me with a charm,
  As when a river draws a leaf,
From silken court and citied swarm
  To your cold homes of peace in grief.

II.

In boyhood's pride I trod the shore
  While slowly sank a crimson sun
Revealed at moments, hid once more
  By rolling mountains, gold or dun :
But now I haunt its marge when day
  Hath laid his fulgent sceptre by,
And tremble over waters grey
  Long windows of a hueless sky.

THE BATTLE OF CLONTARF;

OR, THE KING'S SACRIFICE.

The battle of Clontarf, fought A.D. 1014, annulled for
ever the Danish power in Ireland. During two centuries and
more the sons of the North had landed on the Irish coasts,
sacked the monasteries, burned the cities and churches, and
in many places well-nigh destroyed the Christian civilisa-

tion of earlier times, although they were never able to establish a monarchy in Ireland.   The native dynasties for the
most part remained; and Brian the Great, then King of all
Ireland, though aged and blind, led forth the native hosts
against the invaders for one supreme effort.   He placed his
son Murrough in command; but he offered up, notwithstanding, his life for his country, and wrought her deliverance.   His sons and his grandson partook his glory and his
fate.   His death was a favourite theme with the chroniclers
and bards of ancient Erin.

By green Clontarf they thronged the unhappy shore
   Whence James had fleeted like a transient guest:—
' We had Kings of late; we had Kings of yore,'
   Thus sang the Bard; ' but the first were best! '

And the shouts of the anguished around him rang,
   From streaming eyes forth flashed the fire,
As thus King Brian's death he sang,
   The blind old King who died for Eire.

I.

   ' Answer, thou that from the height
   Look'st to left, and look'st to right,
   Answer thou, how goes the fight? '

II.

Thus spake King Brian, by his tent
Kneeling, with sceptred hands that leant
Upon that altar which, where'er
He marched, kept pure his path with prayer.
For after all his triumphs past
   That made him wondrous 'mid his peers,.
On the blind King God's will had cast
   The burden of his fourscore years:

And therefore when that morn, at nine,
　He rode along the battle's van,
No sword he lifted, but the Sign
　Of Him Who died for man.
King Brian's fleshly strength decayed,
　Three times in puissance waxed his spirit,
　And tall like oak-trees towered his merit,
And like a praying host he prayed :—
From nine to twelve, with crown on head,
Full fifty prayers the King had said;
And unto each such power was given,
It shook the unopening gates of heaven.

III.

' O King, the battle goes this hour
　As when two seas are met in might,
When billow billow doth devour,
　And tide with tide doth fight:

' I watch the waves of war ; but none
　Can see what banners rise or fall;
Sea-clouds on rush, sea-crests on run,
　And blood is over all.'

IV.

Then prayed the King once more, head-bare,
And made himself a cross in prayer,
With outstretched arms, and forehead prone,
Staid on that topmost altar-stone
Gem-charged, and cleansed from mortal taint,
And strong with bones of many a Saint.
In youth his heart for God had yearned,
And Eire: now thrice his youth returned:

A child full oft, ere woke the bird,
The convent's nocturns he had heard,
In old Kincora, or that isle
Which guards, thus late, its wasted pile,
While winds of night the tall towers shook;
And he would peer into that Book
Which lay, lamp-lit, on eagle's wings, ·
   Wherein God's Saints in gold and blue
Stood up, and Prophets stood, and Kings;
   And he the Martyrs knew,
And maids, and confessors each one,
   And—tabernacled there in light—
   That blissful Virgin enough bright
To light a burnt-out sun.
The blazoned Letters well he kenned
   That stood like gateways keeping ward,
   Before the Feast-Days set, to guard
Long ways of wisdom without end:
He knew the music notes black-barred,
   And music notes, like planted spears,
Whereon who bends a fixed regard
   The gathering anthem hears,
Like wakening storms 'mid pines that lean
Ere sunrise o'er some dusk ravine.—
The thoughts that nursed his youth, that hour
Were with his age, and armed with power.

v.

So fifty Psalms he sang, and then
Rolled round his sightless eyes again,
And spake—'Thou watcher on the height,
Make answer quick, how goes the fight?'

VI.

' O King, the battle goes as when
  The mill-wheel circles round and round :
The battle reels ; and bones of men
  Beneath its wheel are ground :

' The war-field lies like Tomar's wood
  By axes marred, or charred with fire,
When, black o'er wood-ways ruin-strewed,
  Rises the last oak spire.'

VII.

Then to his altar by the tent
Once more King Brian turned, and bent
Unsceptred hands and head discrowned
Down from that altar to the ground,
In such sort that the cold March air
With fir-cones swept his snow-white hair ;
And prayed, ' O Thou that from the skies
  Dost see what is, and what must be,
Make mine and me Thy Sacrifice,
  But set this People free ! '

VIII.

That hour, he knew, in many a fane
Late ravaged by the Pagan Dane,
God's priests were offering, far and wide,
The Mass of the Presanctified :
For lo ! it was Good Friday morn,
And Christ once more was crowned with thorn :
God's Church, he knew, from niche and shrine
  Had swept those gauds that time consumes,

Whate'er sea-cave, or wood, or mine
   Yield from their sunless wombs :
Veiled were the sacred images,
He knew, like vapour-shrouded trees,
Vanished gold lamp, and chalice rare;
The astonished altars stripped and bare,
Because upon the cross, stone-dead,
Christ lay that hour disraimented.

IX.

He prayed—then spake—' How goes the fight ? '
Then answer reached him from the height :—

X.

' O King, the battle goes as though
   God weighed two nations in His scale ;
And now the fates of Eire sink low,
   Now theirs that wear the mail :

' O King, thy sons, through God's decree,
   Are dead—save one, the best of all,
Murrough—and now, ah woe is me !
   I see his standard fall ! '

XI.

It fell : but as it fell, above
Through lightning-lighted skies on drove
A thousand heavenly standards, dyed
In martyrdom's ensanguined tide ;
And every tower, and town, and fane
   That blazed of old round Erin's shore,
Down crashed, it seemed, in heaven again ;—
   So dire that thunder's roar !

The wrath had come : the Danes gave way ;
For Brian's prayer had power that day ;
Seaward they rushed, the race abhorred—
The sword of prayer had quelled their sword.
So fled they to the ship-thronged coast ;
    But, random-borne through Tolga's glade,
A remnant from that routed host
    Rushed by where Brian prayed ;
And, swinging forth his brand, down leap'd
    Black Brodar, he that foremost rode,
And from the kingly shoulders swept
    The old head, praising God ;
And cried aloud, ' Let all men tell
That Brodar, he that leagues with Hell,
That Brodar of the magic mail
Slew Brian of the Gael.'

XII.

Him God destroyed ! The Accursed One lay
    Like beast, unburied where he fell :
But Brian and his sons this day
    In Armagh Church sleep well.
And Brian's grandson strong and fair,
Clutching a Sea-King by the hair,
Went with him far through Tolga's wave—
Went with him to the same sea-grave.
So Eire gave thanks to God, though sad,
    And took the blessing and the bale,
And sang, in funeral garments clad,
    The vengeance of the Gael.
Silent all night the Northmen haled
    Their dead adown the bleeding wharf :—
Far north at dawn the Pirates sailed ;
    But on thy shore, Clontarf,

Old Eire once more, with wan cheeks wet,
　　Gave thanks that He who shakes the skies
Had burst His people's bond, and yet
　　Decreed that Sacrifice:
For God is One that gives and takes;
　　That lifts the low, and fells the proud;
That loves His land of Eire, and makes
　　His rainbow in His cloud.

Thus sang to Eire her Bard of old;
　　Thus sang to trampled kerne and serf,
While, sunset-like, her age of gold
　　Came back to green Clontarf.

HOPE IN DEATH.

I.

DESCEND, O Sun, o'er yonder waste,
　　O'er moors and meads and meadows:
Make gold a world but late o'ercast;
　　With purple tinge the shadows!
Thou goest to bless some happier clime
　　Than ours; but sinking slowly
To us thou leav'st a hope sublime
　　Disguised in melancholy.

II.

A Love there is that shall restore
　　What Death and Fate take from us;
A secret Love whose gift is more
　　Than Faith's authentic promise:

A Love that says, ' I hide awhile,
　　For sense, that blinds, is round you : '
O well-loved dead ! ere now the smile
　　Of that great Love has found you !

THE DECREE.

I.

HATE not the Oppressor !　He fulfils
　　Thy destiny decreed—no more :
What cometh, that the Eternal wills :
　　Be ours to suffer and adore.
O Thou the All-Holy, Thou the All-Just !
　　Thou fling'st Thy plague upon the blast :
We hide our foreheads 'mid the dust
　　In penance till the wrath be past.

II.

The nations sink, the nations rise
　　On the dread fount of endless Being,
Bubbles that burst beneath the eyes
　　Of Him the all-shaping and all-seeing.
Thou breath'st, and they are made !　Behold,
　　Thy breath withdrawn, they melt, they cease :—
Our fathers were Thy saints of old,
　　O grant at last their country peace !

SAINT BRIGID OF THE LEGENDS.

A SOFT child-saint, she lit the shade
    With brightness more than human :
Her little hand was soft, they said,
    As any breast of woman.

Through ways bemired to haunts of woe
    She sped, nor hindrance heeded :
Yet still her foot retained its snow ;
    No stream her white robe needed.

It chanced one eve she moved, foot-bare,
    Among the kine sweet-breathing,
With boughs, the insect tribe to scare,
    Their hornèd foreheads wreathing.

Slowly on her their dark eyes grave
    They rolled in sleepy pleasure,
Like things by music charmed, and gave
    Their milk in twofold measure.

That hour there passed a beggar clan
    Through sultry fields on faring :
' Come drink,' she cried, ' from pail and pan ! '—
    That small hand was unsparing.

In wrath her Mother near them drew :
    Those pails that late held nothing,
Like fountains tapped foamed up anew,
    And buzzed with milk-floods frothing !

O Saint, the favourite of the poor,
    The afflicted, weak, and weary !
Like Mary's was that face she bore :
    Men called her ' Erin's Mary.'

In triple vision God to her
  Revealed her country's story :
She saw the cloud its greatness blur,
  She saw, beyond, the glory !

Kildare of Oaks ! thy quenchless Faith,
  Her gift it was : she taught it !
The shroud Saint Patrick wore in death,
  'Twas she, 'twas she that wrought it !

Thus sang they on the sunburnt land
  Among the stacks of barley ;
And singing, smiled, by breezes fanned
  From Erin's dream-land early.

SAINT COLUMBA'S STORK.

A MINSTREL SONG.

COLUMBA raised in wrath a war ;
  Heart-stricken then for penance prayed :
' See thou thy native land no more : '—
  The Hermit spake : the Saint obeyed.

He sailed : he reached an island green :
  Alone he clomb its grassy steep :
Though dimly, Eire could still be seen :
  Once more he launched into the deep.

Iona's soil at last he trod.
  There, there once more, they say he mixed
His hymns of Eire with hymns of God,
  Standing with wide eyes southward fixed.

Three years went by.   One stormy morn
   He grasped a Monk that near him stood :
' Go down to yonder beach forlorn
   O'er which the northward sea-mists scud.

' There, bleeding thou shalt find ere long
   A Stork from Eire that loves her well,
Sore wounded by the tempest's wrong :
   Uplift and bear her to thy cell.

' Three days that Stork shall be thy guest :
   The fourth o'er yonder raging main
The exile, strong through food and rest,
   Will seek her native Eire again.'

The Monk obeyed.   That Stork he found,
   And fed, three days.   Those three days o'er
The exile, soaring, gazed around,.
   Then winged her to her native shore.

The Harper ended.   Loud and shrill
   They raised their shout, and praised that Stork,
And praised the Saint that, exiled, still
   Could sing for Eire ; for God could work.

THE GRAVES.

In the Cambrian valleys with sea-murmurs haunted
   The grave-yards at noontide are fresh with dawn-
      dew ;
On the virginal bosom white lilies are planted
   'Mid the monotone whisper of pine-tree and yew.

In the dells of Etruria, where all day long warbles
  The night-bird, the faithful 'mid cloisters repose :
And the long cypress shadow falls black upon
    marbles
  That cool aching hearts like the Apennines'
    snows.

In Ireland, in Ireland the wind ever sighing
  Sings alone the death-dirge o'er the just and the
    good ;
In the abbeys of Ireland the bones are round lying
  Like blocks where the hewer stands hewing the
    wood.

THE LONG DYING.

The dying tree no pang sustains ;
  But, by degrees relinquishing
Companionship of beams and rains,
  Forgets the balmy breath of Spring :

From off th' enringèd trunk that keeps
  His annual count of ages gone,
Th' embrace of Summer slowly slips :
  Still stands the giant in the sun :

His myriad lips, that suck'd of old
  The dewy breasts of heaven, are dry ;
His roots remit the crag, the mould ;
  Yet painless is his latest sigh :

He falls ; the forests round him roar ;—
  Ere long on quiet bank and copse
Untrembling moonbeams rest ; once more
  The startled babe his head down-drops :—

But ah for one who never drew
　From age to age a painless breath!
And ah the old wrong ever new!
　And ah the many-centuried death!

A BARD'S LOVE.

I.

I THOUGHT it was thy voice I heard ;—
　Ah no! the ripple burst and died ;
Among cold reeds the night-wind stirr'd ;
The yew-tree sigh'd ; the earliest bird
　Answer'd the white dawn far descried.

II.

I thought it was a tress of thine
　That grazed my cheek, and touch'd my brow ;—
Ah no! in sad but calm decline
'Twas but my ever grapeless vine
　Slow-waving from the blighted bough.

III.

O Eire, it is not ended!　Soon,
　Or late, thy flower renews its bud!
In sunless quarries still unhewn
Thy statue waits ; thy sunken moon
　Shall light once more the autumnal flood!

IV.

Memory for me her hands but warms
　O'er ashes of thy greatness gone ;

Or lifts to heaven phantasmal arms,
Muttering of talismans and charms,
  And grappling after glories flown.

v.

Tired brain, poor worn-out palimpsest!
  Sleep, sleep! man's troubles soon are o'er :—
When in dark crypts my relics rest
Star-high shall flash my Country's crest,
  Where birds of darkness cannot soar!

UNREVEALED.

GREY Harper, rest!—O maid, the Fates
  On those sad lips have press'd their seal!
Thy song's sweet rage but indicates
  That mystery it can ne'er reveal.

Take comfort! Vales and lakes and skies,
  Blue seas, and sunset-girded shore,
Love-beaming brows, love-lighted eyes,
  Contend like thee.   What can they more?

SHANID'S KEEP.

I.

A CONQUEROR stood upon Shanid's brow
  And, 'Build me aloft,' he cried,
' A castle to rule o'er the meads below
  From the hills to the ocean's side!'

In green Ardineer, far down, alone
   A beggar girl sang her song,
A sorrowful dirge for a roof o'erthrown
   And a fire stamped out by wrong.

II.

The beggar girl's song in the wind was drowned :
   A moment it lived : no more :
The Conqueror's castle went back to the ground,
   Went back after centuries four :
The great halls crumbled from roof to moat ;
   The grey Keep alone remains :
But echoes still of the sad song float
   All over the lonely plains.

———————

.

SAINT BRIGID OF THE CONVENTS.

. SHE looked not on the face of man :
   Nor husband hers, nor brother :
But where she passed the children ran
   And hailed that Maid their mother !

In haste she fled soft mead and grove,
   For Virtue's region hilly :
They called her, 'mid the birds, the Dove,
   Among the flowers, the Lily.

In woods of Oriel—Leix's vales—
   Her convent homes she planted ;
And Erin's cloistered nightingales
   Their nocturns darkling chanted.

By many a Scottish moorland wide,
  By many an English river,
Men loved of old their ' good Saint Bride ; '
  But Erin loves for ever !

A sword went forth : thy fanes they burn'd !
  Sweet Saint, no angers fret thee !—
There are that ne'er thy grace have spurn'd :
  There are that ne'er forget thee !

Thus sang they while the autumnal glade
  Exchanged green leaf for golden ;
And later griefs were lighter made
  By thought of glories olden.

IN FAR LANDS.

I SEE, I see the domes ascend,
  O Seville, o'er thy Guadalquiver :
I see thy breeze-touched cypress bend ;
  I hear thy moonlit palm-grove shiver :

I know that honour here to those
  Who suffered for the Faith is given ;
I know, I know that earthly woes
  Are secret blessings crowned in heaven :

But ah ! against Dunluce's crags
  To watch our green sea-billows swelling !
And ah ! once more to hear the stags
  In Coona's stormy oakwoods belling !

SAINT COLUMBA'S FAREWELL.

A MINSTREL SONG.

THE exiles gazed on headlands theirs no more,
    Lough Swilly's mountain portals dimly seen :
' Sing us that song Columba sang of yore : '
    Then sang the Minstrel, 'mid the sad, serene.

Farewell to Aran Isle, farewell !
    I steer for Hy : [1] my heart is sore :—
The breakers burst, the billows swell
    'Twixt Aran Isle and Alba's [2] shore.

Thus spake the Son of God, ' Depart ! '
    O Aran Isle, God's will be done !
By Angels thronged this hour thou art :
    I sit within my bark alone.

O Modan, well for thee the while !
    Fair falls thy lot, and well art thou !
Thy seat is set in Aran Isle :
    Northward to Alba turns my prow.

O Aran, Sun of all the West !
    My heart is thine !   As sweet to close
Our dying eyes in thee as rest
    Where Peter and where Paul repose !

O Aran, Sun of all the West !
    My heart in thee its grave hath found :
He walks in regions of the blest
    The man that hears thy church-bells sound !

[1] Iona.   [2] Scotland.

O Aran blest, O Aran blest !
  Accursed the man that loves not thee !
The dead man cradled in thy breast—
  No demon scares him : well is he.

Each Sunday Gabriel from on high
  (For so did Christ our Lord ordain)
Thy Masses comes to sanctify,
  With fifty Angels in his train.

Each Monday Michael issues forth
  To touch with blood each sacred fane :
Each Tuesday cometh Raphael
  To bless the hearth and bless the grain.

Each Wednesday cometh Uriel,
  Each Thursday Sariel, fresh from God ;
Each Friday cometh Ramael
  To bless thy stones and bless thy sod.

Each Saturday comes Mary,
  Comes Babe in arm, 'mid heavenly hosts !
O Aran, near to heaven is he
  That hears God's Angels bless thy coasts !

The Minstrel sang, and ceased ; while women's tears
  Shone, sunset-brightened, on pure cheeks and
    pale ;
And dreadful less became in children's ears
  The hoarse sea-dirges, and the rising gale.

ARBOR NOBILIS.

I.

LIKE a cedar our greatness arose from the earth ;
  Or a plane by some broad-flowing river ;
Like arms that give blessing its boughs it put forth :
  We thought it would bless us for ever.
The birds of the air in its branches found rest ;
  The old lions couched in its shadow ;
Like a cloud o'er the sea was its pendulous crest ;
  It murmur'd for leagues o'er the meadow.

II.

Was a worm at its root?   Was it lightning that
    charr'd
What age after age had created ?
Not so !   'Twas the merchant its glory that marr'd,
  And the malice that, fearing it, hated.
Its branches lie splintered ; the hollow trunk groans
  Like a church that survives desolations ;
But the leaves, scatter'd far when the hurricane
    moans,
  For the healing are sent of the nations !

SAINT COLUMBA OF THE LEGENDS.

A WEEK ere yet her Saint was born
  Columba's mother prayed alone,
(Thus sang the Bard on Ascension Morn),
  Then the Angel of Eire before her shone.

He raised a Veil snow-white, yet red
  With Roses wrought around and around :
And ' These are the Wounds of Love,' he said,
  ' That heal the wounded, and wound hearts sound.'

He dropped that Veil on her head ; and lo !
  A wind from God outstretched it wide ;
And a golden glory suffused its snow ;
  And the heart of its Roses grew deeplier dyed.

Like a cloud of dawn on the breeze it flew ;
  Yet it clung to her holy head the while ;
It spanned the woods, and the headlands blue ;
  It circled and girdled with joy, the Isle !

And this was a sign that, come what might,
  In gloom or glory, in good or ill,
Columba's Gospel with love and light
  Should clasp and comfort his Erin still :

A sign, and a pledge, and a holy troth
  That hath not failed her, and never can ;
For God to Columba sware an oath
  That Eire should be dear to the God made Man ;

More dear with the centuries onward rolled,
  When her bread should be shame, and grief her
    wine ;
And mantled more closely with fold on fold
  Of healing radiance and strength divine.

Thus sang to the vanquished the Bard Maelmire,
  As the tide swelled up on the grassy shore,
And the smooth sea filled with the sunset's fire :
  He sang ; and the weepers wept no more.

THE HERMIT'S COUNSEL.

I.

THUS spake the hermit : Count it gain,
    The scoff, the stab, the freezing fear :
Expiate on earth thine earthly stain ;
    The fire that cleanseth, find it here !
Nearest we stand to heavenly light
    When girt by Purgatorial glooms :
That Church which crowns the Roman height,
    Three centuries trod the Catacombs !

II.

But when thy God His hand withdraws,
    And all things round seem glad and fair,
Unchallenged Faith, impartial laws,
    And wealth, and honour, then beware !
Beware lest sin in splendour deck'd
    Make null the years of holy sighs,
And God's great People, grief-elect,
    Her birthright scorning, miss the prize.

EVENING MELODY.

FRESH eve, that hang'st in yon blue sky,
    On breeze-like pinions swaying,
And leav'st our earth reluctantly ;
    Departing, yet delaying !

Along the beach the ripples rake ;
  Dew-drench'd the thicket flushes :
And last year's leaves in bower and brake
  Are dying 'mid their blushes.

Is this the world we knew of yore,
  Long bound in wintry whiteness,
Which here consummates more and more
  Its talismanic brightness ?

To music wedded, well-known lines
  Let forth a hidden glory :
Thus, bathed in sunset, swells and shines,
  Lake, wood, and promontory.

New Edens pure from Adam's crime
  Invite the just to enter ;
The spheres of wrongfull Life and Time
  Grow lustrous to their centre.

Rejoice, glad planet !   Sin and Woe,
  The void, the incompleteness,
Shall cease at last ; and thou shalt know
  The mystery of thy greatness !

CARO REQUIESCET.

Look forth, O Sun, with beam oblique
  O'er crags and lowlands mellow ;
The dusky beech-grove fire, and strike
  The sea-green larch-wood yellow :

All round the deep, new-flooded meads
    Send thy broad glories straying;
Each herd that feeds 'mid flowers and weeds
    In golden spoils arraying:

Flash from the river to the bridge,
    Red glance with glance pursuing;
Fleet from low sedge to mountain ridge,
    Whatever thou dost undoing:

Kiss with moist lip those vapoury bands
    That swathe yon slopes of tillage;
Clasp with a hundred sudden hands
    The gables of yon village:

But O, thus sharpening to a point,
    O, brightening thus while dying,
Ere yet thou diest the graves anoint
    Where my beloved are lying!

Ye shades that mount the moorland dells,
    Ascend, the tree tops dimming;
But leave those amethystine hills
    Awhile in glory swimming!

THE SECRET OF POWER.

DARK, dark that grove at the Attic gate
    By the sad Eumenides haunted,
Where the Theban King in his blindness sat,
    While the nightingales round him chanted!

In a grove as dark of cypress, and bay
    Upgrown to a forest's stature,

In vision I saw at the close of day
    A Woman of godlike feature.

She stood like a Queen, and her vesture green
    Shone out as a laurel sun-lighted;
And she sang a wild song like a mourner's *keen*
    With an Angel's triumph united.

She sang like one whose grief is done;
    Who has solved Life's dread enigma;—
A beam from the sun on her brow was thrown,
    And I saw there the conquering Stigma.

EVENING MELODY.

O THAT the pines which crown yon steep
    Their fires might ne'er surrender!
O that yon fervid knoll might keep,
    While lasts the world, its splendour!

Pale poplars on the breeze that lean,
    And in the sunset shiver,
O that your golden stems might screen
    For aye yon glassy river!

That yon white bird on homeward wing
    Soft-sliding without motion,
And now in blue air vanishing
    Like snow-flake lost in ocean,

Beyond our sight might never flee,
    Yet forward still be flying;
And all the dying day might be
    Immortal in its dying!

Pellucid thus in saintly trance,
  Thus mute in expectation,
What waits the earth ?   Deliverance ?
  Ah no !   Transfiguration !

She dreams of that ' New Earth ' divine,
  Conceived of seed immortal ;
She sings ' Not mine the holier shrine,
  Yet mine the steps and portal ! '

THE ' OLD LAND.'

I.

Ah, kindly and sweet, we must love thee perforce !
  The disloyal, the coward alone would not love thee :
Ah, Mother of heroes ! strong Mother ! soft nurse !
  We are thine while the large cloud swims onward
    above thee !
By thy hills ever-blue that draw heaven so near ;
  By thy cliffs, by thy lakes, by thine ocean-lull'd
    highlands ;
And more—by thy records disastrous and dear,
  The shrines on thy headlands, the cells in thine
    islands !

II.

Ah, well sings the thrush by Lixnaw and Traigh-li !
  Ah, well breaks the wave upon Umbhall and
    Brandon !
Thy breeze o'er the upland blows clement and free,
  And o'er fields, once his own, which the hind
    must abandon.

A caitiff the noble who draws from thy plains
   His all, yet reveres not the source of his great-
      ness ;
A clown and a serf 'mid his boundless domains
   His spirit consumes in the prison of its strait-
      ness ;

III.

Through the cloud of its pathos thy face is more
   fair :
   In old time thou wert sun-clad ; the gold robe
      thou worest !
To thee the heart turns as the deer to her lair
   Ere she dies—her first bed in the gloom of the
      forest.
Our glory, our sorrow, our Mother ! Thy God
   In thy worst dereliction forsook but to prove
      thee :—
Blind, blind as the blindworm ; cold, cold as the clod
   Who seeing thee see not, possess but not love
      thee !

TO ETHNEA READING HOMER.

Ah, happy he who shaped the words
   Which bind thee in their magic net ;
Who draws from those old Grecian chords
   The harmonies that charm thee yet !

Who waves from that illumined brow
   The dark locks back ;—upon that cheek
Pallid erewhile as Pindan snow
   Makes thus the Pindan morning break !

'Tis he that fringes lids depress'd
 With lashes heavier for a tear,
And shakes that inexperienced breast
 With womanhood.   Upon the bier

Lies cold in death the hope of Troy;
 Thou hear'st the elders sob around,
The widow'd wife, the orphan'd boy,
 The old grey King, the realm discrown'd.

Hadst thou but lived that hour, by thee
 Well wept had been the heroic dead;
The heroic hands well kissed; thy knee
 Had propp'd the pallid princely head!

From thee Andromache had caught
 Dirges more sweet; and she who burn'd
With self-accusing grief shame-fraught,
 A holier woe from thee had learn'd!

Ah child!   Thy Troy in ruin lies
 Like theirs!   Her princes too are cold:
Again Cassandra prophesies,
 Vainly prophetic as of old.

Brandon to Ida's cloudy verge
 Responds.   Tirawley's kingless shore
Wails like the Lycian when its marge
 Saintly Sarpedon trod no more.

Not Gods benign, like Sleep and Death
 Who bore that shepherd-monarch home,
But famine's tooth and fever's breath
 Our exiles hunt o'er ocean's foam.

Peace reigns in heaven.   The Fates each hour
 Roll round earth's wheel through darkness vast:

Alone survives the Poet's power,
  A manlike Art that from the past

Draws forth that line whose sanguine track
  The wicked fear, the weak desert;
That clue which leads through centuries back
  The patriot to his Country's heart.

OMENS OF THE END.

'The Parliament of England seem to have considered
the permanent debility of Ireland as their best security for
her connection with the British crown; and the Irish Parliament to have rested the security of the colony upon
maintaining a perpetual and impassable barrier against the
ancient inhabitants of the country.'—*Speech of Lord Chancellor Clare.*

SOOTHSAYER of the Imperial State,
What saw'st thou in the skies of late?
  I saw a white cloud like a hand:
  It held aloft a Harp, not brand.

Soothsayer of the Imperial State,
What saw'st thou in the streams of late?
  A pale hand rising from a brook:
  It raised a seal'd yet bleeding Book.

Soothsayer of the Imperial State,
What saw'st thou on the seas of late?
  I saw ascending Liberty:
  Knowledge makes strong, and Commerce free.

Soothsayer of the Imperial State,
What saw'st thou 'mid the tombs of late?

I saw Religion upward burst,
Her last crown lordlier than her first.

Soothsayer of the Imperial State,
What saw'st thou in the streets of late ?
I saw old foes shake hands and say,
' One country have we—ours to-day.'

Then up with the banner, and on with the steed !
By the red streets of Wexford—
    (*Soothsayer*)   My master, no need !
We conquer'd them never : our arms they defied :
Here's money : seduce them ! here's falsehood :—
    divide !

GRATTAN.

I.

GOD works through man, not hills or snows !
    In man, not men, is the godlike power ;
The man, God's potentate, God foreknows ;
    He sends him strength at the destined hour :
His Spirit He breathes into one deep heart :
His cloud He bids from one mind depart :
A Saint !—and a race is to God re-born !
A Man !   One man makes a nation's morn !

II.

A man, and the blind land by slow degrees
    Gains sight !   A man, and the deaf land hears !
A man, and the dumb land like wakening seas
    Thunders low dirges in proud, dull ears !

A man, and the People, a three days' corse,
Stands up, and the grave-bands fall off perforce ;
One man, and the nation in height a span
To the measure ascends of the perfect man.

III.

Thus wept unto God the land of Eire :
    Yet there rose no man and her hope was dead :
In the ashes she sat of a burn'd-out fire ;
    And sackcloth was over her queenly head.
But a man in her latter days arose ;
A Deliverer stepp'd from the camp of her foes :
He spake ; the great and the proud gave way,
And the dawn began which shall end in day !

THE SECRET JOY.

O, BLITHESOME at times is life perforce
    When Death is the gate of Hope not Fear ;
Rich streams lie dumb ; over rough stones course
    The runlets that charm the ear.

' Her heart is hard ; she can laugh,' they say ;
    ' That light one can jest who has cause to sigh ! '
Her conscience is light ; and with God are they
    She loves : they are safe—and nigh.

God's light shines brightest on cheeks grief-pale !
    The song of the darkling is sad and dark :—
That proud one boasts of her nightingale !
    O Eire, keep thou thy lark !

INSIGHT.

SHARP stretch the shades o'er the sward close-bitten
  Which the affluent meadows receive but half;
Truth lies clear-edged on the soul grief-smitten,
  Congeal'd there in epitaph.

A vision is thine by the haughty lost ;
  An Insight reserved for the sad and pure :
On the mountain cold in the grey hoar frost
  Thy Shepherd's track lies sure !

SONG.

THE Little Black Rose shall be red at last !
  What made it black but the East wind dry,
And the tear of the widow that fell on it fast ?
  It shall redden the hills when June is nigh !

The Silk of the Kine shall rest at last !
  What drave her forth but the dragon-fly ?
In the golden vale she shall feed full fast
  With her mild gold horn, and her slow dark eye.

The wounded wood-dove lies dead at last :
  The pine long-bleeding, it shall not die !
—This song is secret.   Mine ear it pass'd
  In a wind o'er the stone-plain of Athenry.

THE CLUE.

To one in dungeons bound there came
  The last long night before he died
An Angel garlanded with flame
  Who raised his hand and prophesied :

' Thy life hath been a dream : but lo !
  This night thine eyes shall see the truth :—
That which thou thoughtest weal was woe ;
  And that was joy thou thoughtest ruth.

' Thy Land hath conquer'd through her loss ;
  With her God's chief of Creatures plain'd,
The same who scaled of old the Cross
  When Mary's self beneath remain'd.[1]

' Thou fought'st upon the righteous side :
  Yet, being dust, thou wroughtest sin :
Once—twice—thy hand was raised in pride :
  The Promised Land thou may'st not win ;

' But they, thy children, shall.' Next morn
  Around the Patriot-martyr press'd
A throng that cursed him. He in turn,
  The sentenced, bless'd them—and was bless'd.

ODE ON THE FIRST REPEAL OF THE PENAL LAWS.

A.D. 1778.

I.

The hour has struck ! at last in heaven
  The golden shield an Angel smites !

[1] Dante's description of Holy Poverty.

On Erin's altars thunder-riven
  A happier Destiny alights.
'Tis done that cannot be undone
The lordlier ages have begun ;
The flood that widens as it flows
Is loosed ; fulfilled the Triple Woes !

II.

Once more the Faith uplifts her forehead
  Star-circled to the starry skies :
Fangless at last, a snake abhorred,
  Beneath her foot Oppression lies :
Above the waning moon of Time
The Apparition stands sublime,
From hands immaculate, hands of light,
Down scattering gifts of saintly might.

III.

Long for her martyrs Erin waited :
  They came at last.   Rejoice this hour
Ye tonsured heads, or consecrated,
  That sank beneath the stony shower !
Thou Land for centuries dark, and dumb,
Arise and shine ! thy light is come !
Return ; for they are dead, their knife
Who raised, and sought the young child's life.

IV.

Again the wells of ancient knowledge
  Shall cheer the thirsty lip and dry :
Again waste places, fane and college,
  The radiance wear of days gone by !

Once more shall rise the Minster porch;
Once more shall laugh the village church
O'er plains that yield the autumnal feast
Once more to industry released!

v.

Once more the far sea-tide returneth
    And feeds the rivers of the Land:
Once more her heart maternal yearneth
    With hopes the growth of memories grand.
Immortal longings swell her breast
Quickened from dust of Saints at rest:
Once more six centuries bud and flower
To share the triumph of this hour!

VI.

Who was it called thee the Forsaken?
    A consort judged? a Wife put by?
He at whose nod the heavens are shaken,
    'Tis He Who hails thee from on high.
' I loved thee from of old: I saved:
Upon My palms thy name is graved:
With blood were sealed the bridal vows;
For lo, thy Maker is thy Spouse!'

VII.

Who, who are those like clouds of morning
    That sail to thee o'er seas of gold?
That fly, like doves, their exile scorning,
    To windows known and loved of old?
To thee the Isles their hands shall raise;
Thy sons have taught them songs of praise;
And Kings rebuild thy wall, or wait
Beneath thy never-closing gate.

VIII.

As from the fig-tree, tempest-wasted,
  The untimely fruitage falleth crude,
So dropp'd around thee, blighted, blasted,
  Age after age thy sentenced brood.
To thee this day thine own are given:
Yet what are these to thine in heaven?
They left thee in thy years of pain:
Thy cause they pleaded—not in vain.

IX.

Those years are o'er: made soft by distance
  Old wars like war-songs soon will seem,
The aggression dire, the wild resistance
  Put on the moonlight of a dream.
Ah, gentle Foes! If *wholly* past—
That Norman foe was friend at last!
Like him, the ill deed redress, recall—
In Erin's heart is room for all.

THE CAUSE.

I.

THE Kings are dead that raised their swords
  In Erin's right of old;
The Bards that dash'd from fearless chords
  Her name and praise lie cold:
But fix'd as fate her altars stand;
  Unchanged, like God, her Faith;
Her Church still holds in equal hand
  The keys of life and death.

II.

As well call up the sunken reefs
    Atlantic waves rush o'er
As that old time of native chiefs
    And Gaelic songs restore!
Things heavenly rise: things earthly sink:
    God works through Nature's laws;
Sad Isle, 'tis He that bids thee link
    Thine Action with thy Cause!

MEMORY.

'They are past, the old days: let the past be for-
    gotten:
    Let them die, the old wrongs and old woes that
    were ours,
Like the leaves of the winter, down-trampled and
    rotten,
    That light in the spring-time the forest with
    flowers.'

So sings the sweet voice! But the sad voice
    replieth;
    'Unstaunch'd is the wound while the insult re-
    mains;
The Tudor's black banner above us still flieth;
    The Faith of our fathers is spurned in their fanes!

'Distrust the repentance that clings to its booty!
    Give the people their Church and the priesthood
    its right:
Till then, to remember the past is a duty,
    For the past is our Cause, and our Cause is our
    might.'

ALL-HALLOWS; OR, THE MONK'S DREAM.

A PROPHECY.

I.

I TROD once more that place of tombs :
　　Death-rooted elder, full in flower,
Oppress'd me with its sad perfumes,
　　Pathetic breath of arch and tower :
The ivy on the cloister wall
　　Waved, gusty with a silver gleam :
The moon sank low : the billows' fall
　　In moulds of music shaped my dream.

II.

In sleep a funeral chant I heard,
　　A 'De profundis' far below ;
On the long grass the rain-drops stirr'd
　　As when the distant tempests blow :
Then slowly, like a heaving sea,
　　The graves were troubled all around ;
And two by two, and three by three,
　　The monks ascended from the ground.

III.

From sin absolved, redeem'd from tears
　　There stood they, beautiful and calm,
The brethren of a thousand years,
　　With lifted brows and palm to palm !
On heaven they gazed in holy trance ;
　　Low stream'd their beards and tresses hoar :
And each transfigured countenance
　　The Benedictine impress bore.

IV.

By Angels borne the Holy Rood
   Encircled thrice the church-yard bound ;
They paced behind it, paced in blood,
   With bleeding feet, but foreheads crown'd ;
And thrice they breathed that hymn benign,
   Which angels sang when Christ was born ;
And thrice I wept, ere tower or shrine
   Had caught the first white beam of morn.

V.

Down on the earth my brows I laid ;
   In these, His saints, I worshipp'd God :
And then return'd that grief which made
   My heart since youth a frozen clod :
' O ye,' I wept, ' whose woes are past,
   Look round on all these prostrate stones !
To these can Life return at last ?
   Can Spirit lift once more these bones ? '

VI.

The smile of him the end who knows
   Went, luminous, o'er them as I spake ;
Their white locks shone like mountain snows
   O'er which the orient mornings break :
They stood : they pointed to the West :
   And lo ! where darkness late had lain
Rose many a kingdom's citied crest
   Reflected in a kindling main !

VII.

' Not only these, the fanes o'erthrown,
   Shall rise,' they said, ' but myriads more ;

The seed, far hence by tempests blown,
　　Still sleeps on yon expectant shore.
Send forth, sad Isle, thy reaper bands!
　　Assert and pass thine old renown:
Not here alone—in farthest lands
　　For thee thy sons shall weave the crown.'

VIII.

They spake; and like a cloud down sank
　　The just and filial grief of years;
And I that peace celestial drank
　　Which shines but o'er the seas of tears.
Thy Mission flashed before me plain,
　　O thou by many woes anneal'd!
And I discern'd how axe and chain
　　Had thy great destinies sign'd and seal'd!

IX.

That seed which grows must seem to die:
　　In thee, when earthly hope was none,
The heaven-born hope of days gone by,
　　By martyrdom matured, lived on;
Conceal'd, like limbs of royal mould
　　In some Egyptian pyramid,
Or statued shape 'mid cities old
　　Beneath Vesuvian ashes hid.

X.

For this cause by a power divine
　　Each temporal aid was frustrated:
Tyrone, Tirconnell, Geraldine—
　　In vain they fought; in vain they bled:
Successive, 'neath th' usurping hand
　　Sank ill-starr'd Mary, erring James:
Nor Spain nor France might wield the brand
　　Which, for her own, Religion claims!

XI.

Arise, long stricken ! mightier far
    Are they who fight for God and thee
Than those that head the adverse war !
    Sad prophet ! lift thy face and see !
Behold, with eyes no longer wrong'd
    By mists the sense exterior breeds,
The hills of heaven around thee throng'd
    With fiery chariots and with steeds !

XII.

The years baptized in blood are thine ;
    The exile's prayer from many a strand ;
The woes of those this hour who pine
    Poor aliens in their native land ;
Angels and Saints from heaven down-bent
    Watch thy long conflict without pause ;
And the most Holy Sacrament
    From all thine altars pleads thy cause !

XIII.

O great through Suffering, rise at last
    Through kindred Action tenfold great !
Thy future calls on thee thy past
    (Its *soul* survives) to consummate !
Let women weep ; let children moan :
    Rise, men and brethren, to the fight :
One cause hath Earth, and one alone :
    For it, the cause of God, unite !

XIV.

Let others trust in trade and traffic !
    Be ours, O God, to trust in Thee !

Cherubic Wisdom, Love Seraphic,
  Beseem that land the Truth makes free.
The earth-quelling sword let others vaunt;
  Such toys allure the youth, the boy:
Be ours for loftier wreaths to pant,
  The Apostles' crown of Faith and Joy!

XV.

Hope of my country!   House of God!
  All-Hallows!   Blessed feet are those
By which thy courts shall yet be trod
  Once more as ere the spoiler rose!
Blessed the winds that waft them forth
  To victory o'er the rough sea foam:
That race to God which conquers earth—
  Can God forget that race at home?

HYMN.

ECCLESIA DEI.

I.

WHO is She that stands triumphant
  Rock in strength upon the Rock,
Like some city crown'd with turrets
  Braving storm and earthquake shock?
Who is she her arms extending;
  Blessing thus a world restored;
All the anthems of creation
  Lifting to creation's Lord?

Hers the Kingdom, hers the Sceptre !
  Fall, ye nations, at her feet !
Hers that Truth whose fruit is freedom ;
  Light her yoke ; her burden sweet.

II.

As the moon its splendour borrows
  From a sun unseen all night,
So from Christ, the Sun of Justice,
  Draws His Church her sacred light.
Touch'd by His her hands have healing,
  Bread of Life, absolving Key :
Christ Incarnate is her Bridegroom ;
  The Spirit hers ; His Temple she.
    Hers the Kingdom, hers the Sceptre !
      Fall, ye nations, at her feet !
    Hers that Truth whose fruit is freedom ;
      Light her yoke ; her burden sweet !

III.

Empires rise and sink like billows ;
  Vanish and are seen no more ;
Glorious as the star of morning
  She o'erlooks their wild uproar :
Hers the Household all-embracing,
  Hers the Vine that shadows earth ;
Blest thy children, mighty Mother !
  Safe the stranger at thy hearth.
    Hers the Kingdom, hers the Sceptre !
      Fall, ye nations, at her feet !
    Hers that Truth whose fruit is freedom ;
      Light her yoke ; her burden sweet !

IV.

Like her Bridegroom, heavenly, human,
 Crown'd and militant in one,
Chanting Nature's great Assumption
 And the Abasement of the Son,
Her magnificats, her dirges
 Harmonise the jarring years;
Hands that fling to heaven the censer
 Wipe away the orphan's tears.
  Hers the Kingdom, hers the Sceptre!
   Fall, ye nations, at her feet!
  Hers that Truth whose fruit is freedom;
   Light her yoke; her burden sweet!

ELECTA.

I.

THE Hour must come. Long since, and now
 The shaft decreed is on the wing:
Loosed from the Eternal Archer's bow
 The flying fate shall pierce the ring:
The Hour that comes to seal the right;
 The Hour that comes to judge the wrong;
To lift the vales, and thunder-smite
 Those cliffs the full-gorged eagles throng.

II.

Rejoice, Elect of Isles! Rejoice
 Pale image of the Church of God!
Like her afflicted, lift thy voice
 Like her, and hail, and hymn the rod!

Thou warr'st on earth : at each new groan
  In heaven thy guardian claps his hands ;
And glitters o'er the expectant Throne
  A crown inwoven of angel bands !

SONG.

I.

WHILE autumn flashed from woods of gold
  Her challenge to the setting sun,
And storm-clouds, breaking, seaward rolled
  O'er brightening waves, their passion done,
The linnets on a rain-washed beech
  So thronged I saw not branch for bird :
My skill is scant in forest speech ;
  But thus they sang, or thus I heard.

II.

' 'Tis all a dream—the wrong, the strife,
  The scorn, the blow, the loss, the pain !
Immortal Gladness, Love and Life
  Alone are lords by right and reign :
The Earth is tossed about as though
  Young Angels tossed a cowslip ball :
But, rough or level, high or low,
  What matter ? God is all in all.'

IRISH AIRS.

I.

On darksome hills thy songs I hear :—
   Nor growths they seem of minstrel art
Nor wanderers from Urania's sphere,
   But voices from thine own deep heart !
They seem thine own sad oracles
   Not uttered by thy sons but thee,
Like waters forced through stony cells
   Or winds from cave and hollow tree.

II.

From thee what forced them ?   Futile quest !
   What draws to widowed eyes the tears ?
The milk to Rachel's childless breast ?
   The blood to wounds unstaunched of years ?
Long cling the storm-drops—cling yet shake—
   On cypress spire and cedar's fan :
Long rust upon the guilty brake
   The heart-drops of the murdered man.

THE CHANGE.

I.

Was it Truth; was it Vision ?   The old year was
   dying ;
Clear rang the last chime from the turret of stone;
The mountain hung black o'er the village low-lying;
   O'er the moon, rushing forward, loose vapours
   were blown;

When I saw an angelical choir with bow'd faces
  Wafting on, like a bier, upon pinions outspread
An angel-like Form that of death had no traces :—
  Without pain she had died in her sleep; but was
    dead.

II.

Was it Truth; was it Vision? The darkness was
    riven ;
  Once more through the infinite breast of pure
    night
From heaven there looked downward, more beauteous
    than heaven,
  A visage whose sadness was lost in its light :—
' Why seek'st thou, my son, 'mid the dead for the
    living ?
  Thy Country is risen, and lives on in thy Faith ;
I died but to live ; and now, Life and Life-giving,
  Where'er the Cross triumphs I conquer in death.'

SEMPER EADEM.

I.

THE moon, freshly risen from the bosom of ocean,
  Hangs o'er it suspended, all mournful yet bright;
And a yellow sea-circle with yearning emotion
  Swells up as to meet it, and clings to its light :
The orb unabiding grows whiter, mounts higher ;
  The pathos of darkness descends on the brine :
O Erin ! the North drew its light from thy pyre ;
  Thy light woke the nations ; the embers were
    thine !

II.

'Tis sunrise! The mountains flash forth; and, new-
    redden'd,
    The billows grow lustrous, so lately forlorn;
From the orient with vapours long darken'd and
    deaden'd
    The trumpets of Godhead are pealing ' the morn!'
He rises, the Sun, in his might re-ascending;
    Like an altar beneath him lies blazing the sea!
O Erin! Who proved thee returns to thee, blending
    The future and past in one garland for thee!

EPILOGUE.

WITH spices and urns they come: ah me, how sorrow
    can babble!
    Nothing abides save Love; and to Love comes
    gladness at last:
Sad was the legend and sweet; but its truth was
    mingled with fable;
    Dire was the conflict and long; but the rage of
    the conflict is past.

They are past, the three great Woes; and the days
    of the dread Desolation;
    To amethyst changed are the stones blood-stain'd
    of the temple-floor:
A Spiritual Power she lives who seem'd to die as a
    Nation;
    Her story is that of a Soul:—and the story of
    Earth is no more.

Endurance it was that won ; Suffering, than Action
thrice greater ;
  For Suffering humbly *acts*. Away with sigh and
  with tear !
She has gone before you and waits : She has gifts
for the blinded who hate her ;
  And that bright Shape by the death-cave in music
  answers, 'Not here.'

SONNETS

BY THE LATE

HON. STEPHEN E. SPRING RICE

I.

WITH slow and thoughtful step I went my way
  Through new-mown meadows, crowded pastures
    green,
On the 'Hawk's Cliff,' in thickets deep, unseen,
Without a friend to pass the summer's day.
I read of murdered Strafford as I lay,
  Of timid, faithless Charles, of Pym serene
  Though mourning for the friend whose youth had
    been
Brightened, like his, with Freedom's purest ray.
Did Friendship earn from Charles no better fate?
  Could not strong Friendship something then avail,
And Justice from her claims on Pym abate?
  —Then rather let me listen to the gale
Ruffling the sunlit foliage, and create
  A world of friends unseen than trust to those who
    fail.

Curragh Chase, *August* 17, 1837.

II.

THE BLACK TARN UNDER MANGERTON.

WITH quicker coming breath and shorter stride
  We reached at length the level, purple height
  Which seemed from far unto our straining sight
The crown of that calm monarch's silent pride;
But, when we paused, we heard a petty tide
  Hoarse, low, monotonous; and, dark as night,
  A sullen lake lay shadowed by the might
Of rugged cliffs that bound its further side.
How fit an emblem of the mind whose share
  Of life is solitude and selfish thought,
Gloomy, and murmuring on a barren strand!
Mine be a bay by eager breezes fanned,
  And not by tempest into anger wrought,
Though Ocean's pulse is ever throbbing there!

  January 22, 1838.

III.

EARLY FRIENDSHIP.

THE half-seen memories of childish days
  When pains and pleasures lightly came, and
    went ;
  The sympathies of boyhood rashly spent
In fearful wanderings through forbidden ways ;
The vague, but manly, wish to tread the maze
  Of life to noble ends ; whereon intent,
  Asking to know for what man here is sent,
The bravest heart must often pause, and gaze—
The firm resolve to seek the chosen end
  Of manhood's judgment, cautious and mature :
Each of these viewless bonds binds friend to friend
  With strength no selfish purpose can secure ;—
My happy lot is this, that all attend
  That friendship which first came, and which shall
    last endure.

IV.

DRUDGERY.

PLEASANT it is, at close of weary day,
　　When all is out of sight that vexed the mind
　　To dull routine or petty task confined,—
Pleasant with intermitting chat to say
' This easy converse fully doth repay
　　The morning's labour.'　Search! and you shall
　　　find
　　That only toil upon some work assigned
Can fit foundation for such leisure lay.
My friends are gone; these things I think and feel,
　　As o'er the dewy grass a path I make :
Some distant waggon with its labouring wheel
　　Betrays the silence which it seems to break;
Slow, heavy perfumes o'er the garden steal;
　　The flickering branches in the moonbeam shake.

V.

TITIAN'S PICTURE OF BACCHUS AND ARIADNE.

YOUNG Ariadne, by her lover led
  Through narrow mountain pass, or woodland
    glade
Rich with a thousand flowers, loved the shade
That o'er her modest steps a veil outspread :
Now, with slow tears she mourns that lover fled :
  Her golden hair, half fallen from the braid,
  Hath but a wavering protection made
For the fair brow; and from her glossy head
The sunbeams glance. Alone she walks the shore ;—
When suddenly is thronged that barren place,
And youthful Bacchus, like a bursting wave
Leaps from his panther car with headlong grace.
—And will his godlike raptures please her more
Than calmer joys her mortal lover gave ?

August 20, 1843.

VI.

MARY SAYING HER PRAYERS.

1

WILFUL and dull and sullen seems that child;
　　But who in that soft countenance can find
　　An index to the thoughts that fret her mind?
By no long-cherished hope was she beguiled?
Has no uncertain vision gleamed and smiled,
　　Then faded from her eyelids?　Had the wind,
Circling the world, no messages consigned
To her young heart this morning sweet and mild,
When with the dawn it touched upon her brow?
　　By recollections flickering, undefined,
Perhaps she may be haunted even now;
By dim and shapeless aspirations vexed,
　　With infantile experiences entwined;
By half-seen truths surprised, alarmed, perplexed.

August 15, 1846.

VII.

2

Slow serious phrases, tender words and few
　The mother whispered in a voice subdued,
　Gently submitting to the wayward mood
Which from her loving watchfulness she knew
Would fade away, and by observance due
　Be soon succeeded; no abrupt or rude
　Commandment was she forward to intrude;
The instinct of affection, ever true
　To loftiest conceptions of the mind,
Prompted such patience and respect for those
　Who tho' on earth and to our care consigned
Are yet angelic.　Seeing them, she knows
　What loveliness might shine in humankind
If still unstained by sin, unworn by woes.

August 28, 1846.

VIII.

OLD AND MODERN LEARNING.

THE learning of old times was as a stream
  Through many an untrod glen that held its way,
Smooth-flowing, clear, and silent as a dream
  To the calm precincts of a cloister grey;
In which the sculptured fount would doubtless seem
  A Station fit, where holy men each day
Might read the gracious Word, and muse, and pray,
  'Send us the living water, Lord Supreme!'
The learning of these days doth rush along
  By humblest hut and proudest palace bowers,
Like a broad torrent, troubled, loud, and strong;
  Each sloping bank, throughout the circling hours,
Is crowded by an eager, restless throng—
  They crush to dust the few remaining flowers.

IX.

Love is historic; rests upon the past;
  Still lingers lovingly on old detail;
  Still, like the holy bells, rings out a tale
For ever new, from earliest to last:
Love is prophetic; climbing still the mast
  Discerns of distant hope the signal pale,
  And on the straining spar extends the sail
Withheld by colder counsels from the blast.
Mysterious delight in what is lost!
  Wild half fruition of what may be won
By struggling perseverance, tempest-toss'd!
Yet love in silence wrapt and deep repose,
  Whilst one short hour its hasty course can run,
May find more joy than many a lifetime knows!

X.

THINK not man's fallen nature can accept,
   Or, if accepting, value at their worth
   Rites that lack splendour; slave of grief or mirth
By fleshly lusts he is in bondage kept.
Far less believe that splendid rites give birth
   To heartfelt sorrow, such as his, who 'wept
   And smote upon his breast,' for this man stept
With downcast eyes, not heeding aught on earth.
Man must employ in worship every power,
   Will, reason, understanding, heart, and sense;
   And should he on some dull or fond pretence
Neglect but one, then from devotion's flower
   He cuts a leaf that drank the heavenly dew,
   Or root, that purity from baseness drew.

XI.

IF, task'd beyond my strength, I crave delay
　　And weakly wish that to another hand
　　Had been committed what divine command
Has sent to mine; if on th' appointed way
I pause, and, thoughtless of my purpose, stray;
　　If, wearied with the men, the clime, the land
　　Which I call mine, I seek another strand,
That on the wings of chance I lightly may
Outstrip the homely cares which day by day
　　Hum in my ears; if by myself I stand
Accused of all these faults, and cannot say
That I less subject am unto their sway
　　Now than of old—you needs must understand
How rashly upon me new duties would you lay.

XII.

SOFT sighing wind that comest to dispel
   The rigid bond that holds the buds so long
   As almost to provoke a sense of wrong
In those who now have sadly watched them swell
Slowly, for weeks ; O, would that I could tell
   How deep the joy thou bringest, and how strong !
   O that I too could blossom into song,
And hail thee loosen'd from thy southern cell
Whilst all surrounding Nature seems to smile
   And bare her breast at thy sunbright approach !
O, wherefore hast thou tarried so long while ?
   Dear spirit ! tenderly must I reproach
Thee, dallying upon the Italian shore,
Or launching thence across the purple, smooth sea
   floor.

XIII.

No sweeter pleasure can this life supply
  Than what my darling children daily bring
  To me, well wearied of that noisy thing
We call society : without a sigh—
Nay, gladly—I would cast ambition by,
  Content to hear their eager questioning
  (The chirping of young birds that cannot sing),
To weigh for them the words of my reply,
  And righteously instruct them—I should rest,
Like the worn ship in harbour there below,
  Which, safe from struggling on the Ocean's breast,
Floats in the silent water—what a glow
  The setting sun casts on her tricolor crest!
She hears far off waves toss and tempests blow.

JARDIN MARENGO, ALGIERS :
    January 28, 1855.

XIV.

SYMPATHY DISPENSED WITH.

AND if indeed I wear my soul away,
 And pour my heart out upon barren stones,
 And vainly try to vivify dead bones,
And through dry deserts hunt a worthless prey ;
If, disappointed, thus from men I stray,
 And strive to find a meaning in the tones,
 The half-heard whispers and the sullen moans,
In which unfeeling Nature seems to say,
But says most falsely, that in her doth dwell
 A sympathetic beating of the heart,
Should then myself against myself rebel,
 And dream of a self-centred life apart,
Myself shall blame myself : all may be well :
 Love, without self-love soothes the bitterest smart.

February 8, 1857.

XV.

THE HEART KNOWETH ITS OWN BITTERNESS.

WE sat together underneath a lime,
  Whose netted branches wove an emerald night;
  And in short sentences—in low and light
Whispers—recalled the stories of old time:
Until some word, I know not what, some rhyme
  Dragged out a hidden grief, that lived—in spite
  Of creeping lichen years—such years as might
Well humble all that once was thought sublime.
My grief it was, and will be : *she* but sees
  A strangeness which she cannot understand ;
A nameless tower overgrown with trees ;
  A heap of stones encumbering the land ;
A hearth now haunted by the wintry breeze,
  Long, long ago, by love and fancy fanned.

January 19, 1858.

XVI.

'THE spacious Shenan, spreading like a sea,'
　Lies far below, beyond the lawn and wood,
　That, tender green, this, rich in purple bud ;
And, hidden from the sight by bush and tree,
I hear a tinkling streamlet fall and flee
　Through the deep glen to seek that distant flood ;
　Soft airs escape from the hill-side and scud,
With gentle touches, bird-like, wild, and free,
Across that glassy bosom.　All is peace.
　Would that with me such calm might ever dwell !
That I might live content, nor seek release
　From cares appointed ; never feel the swell
Of vague ambition ; dream of no increase ·
　In wealth or power ; well loved, and loving well !

MOUNT TRENCHARD : *April* 6, 1860.

XVII.

SICK DREAMS ALL.

(Written in sickness.)

THE spirit worn with sickness walks thro' vales
  Of shadowy meaning, elbowed by a flow
  And ceaseless throng of ghastly forms, that show
Some fleeting token, which, tho' light, assails
The memory, and rends aside its veils ;
  Or through some ebon vault, set deep below,
  With outstretched hands and stumbling step and
      slow,
The sick man's fancy wanders ; or he sails
Upon a smooth broad sea ; some unseen hand
  Directs the helm and gives a steady run ;
His languid eye perceives no distant land ;
  He knows not of his journey ; if begun
But now, or ending, cannot understand ;
  But sails toward a drooping blood-red sun.

April 1861.

XVIII.

THE DREAM OF A LIFE.

(Written in sickness.)

I WANDER in a thick-set wood alone—
　Tall, naked boles of trees around me crowd,
　And overhead their branches weave a shroud
For the dead earth : ever I hear the moan
Of the sharp winter wind, or else the groan
　Of some old tree that in past-tempests bowed
　And shaken to the root betrays aloud
Its coming fall.　I find no friendly stone
　That measures distance in this dreary wild ;
　No path is obvious to my drooping eyes ;
Days, weeks, and years have gone since on me smiled
　Unbroken light above ; I sit, and rise ;
Lie down or wander aimless : hope is gone ;
Escape from this dark forest there is none.

　June 1861.

XIX.

' HOLD UP, OLD HORSE ! '

THE exile pacing o'er the Russian plain
  To that far East where he must waste his life,
  Exhausted with the long and passionate strife
Whose failure earned this fate, can not retain
Or fix the thoughts which flit across his brain ;
  His memory with formless clouds is rife,
  Of youth and home—of children and of wife—
Lost in a haze of dull and leaden pain :
  So I, ere half my day is spent, outworn,
And stepping surely towards an early end,
  But dimly see the promise of my morn,
  Though far unlike that wretched one forlorn ;—
Lovers and friends my failing steps attend ;
And I can welcome all that God may send.

March 4, 1864.

XX.

SPRING.

Long wished-for, bursts in gladness the new year,
  Sweetness and beauty freely sheds around,
  And hides anew the sullen withered ground
With tender verdure, whilst from far and near
The song of birds crowds thick upon the ear,
  Perplexing sense with multitudinous sound ;
  No jealous laws are felt that tie and bound
The bounteousness of Nature, no sad fear
Of late born frosts her genial step delays :
As friend to friend his hoarded thought betrays,
  Long chilled and frozen by the mastering need
Of sympathy, and finds both that and praise,
  So spring is welcome in each flower and weed,
Lavish in love, and fearless in her ways.

May 12, 1864.

XXI.

TO LINA.

THE night is soft as under southern skies;
   The garden is deserted, save by me;
   Whilst ever and anon a gleam I see
Flash from the house, perplexing my old eyes;
For one short moment on the lawn it lies,
   Then into ghostly being brings a tree
   Unseen before—the murmur of the sea
Steals through the branches. But a glad surprise
Absorbs all these delights, and gives its own;
   From the sweet south leaps out a gracious wind,
   Fresh, strong, and soothing, stirring in the mind
Old thoughts and new, by its elastic tone;—
   Such and so sudden was, on seeing you,
   My joy to-day; ah! moments dear and few!

August 4, 1864.

XXII.

LEFT ALONE.

The sea-gulls glancing o'er the glittering wave
  Are now my sole companions: and indeed,
  When questioned, I replied I had no need
Of others. Vain my boast! ah! vainly brave
From past experience, when warm pulses gave
  An inner strength that either took no heed
  Of outward circumstance, or let it lead
By seeming chance to thoughts or gay or grave.
But now a leaden heart has lost its spring
  And must renew its impulse from without.
  Whenso my darling children crowd about,
And their swift thoughts wheel by upon the wing,
  Strong in their strength, I follow in their flight:
  One after one they pass; and then comes dreary
    night.

GIBRALTAR BAY, ON BOARD THE 'SIDON:'
November 25, 1864.

XXIII.

EDIFICATION.

(On the Baptism of an Infant in St. Peter's.)

I<small>F</small> this vast building had been reared for nought
   But as a temple where this solemn rite
Might be completed, still the hands that wrought
   Its stately walls, the intellectual might
Of its great architect, the wealth that brought
   Art's choicest treasures had been used aright,
Clothing with fitting dignity the thought
   That on man's heart God's Spirit doth alight.
Yet it may happen that this helpless child
   Should far surpass the wonder here achieved,
Leading a life of virtue, pure and mild,
   By this world's shallow splendour undeceived,
May build in many hearts shrines undefiled
   With bright examples from his life received.

XXIV.

THE BABY ON THE RUG.

THE sky that was in purity divine
  When the fresh dawn crept down upon the bay,
  Is harried now with clouds, nor comes a ray
Of hope ;—of peace and happiness no sign.
Against the silver sky, a brighter line
  The sea-horizon drew, and with the day
  Grew brighter still, and broader, till the sway
Of those swift clouds seemed all things to consign
  To gloom and trouble.   Turn, O turn and see
  A purity untroubled by a cloud ;
A sweeter smile than from the glittering sea :—
  Though this angelic nature may be bowed
By grief and pain, I dare to prophesy
All soiling sin will from its presence fly.

  SPEZIA : *December* 26, 1864.

MISCELLANEOUS POEMS

ODE TO THE DAFFODIL.

1

O LOVE-STAR of the unbeloved March,
  When, cold and shrill,
Forth flows beneath a low, dim-lighted arch
  The wind that beats sharp crag and barren hill,
  And keeps unfilmed the lately torpid rill !

2

      A week or e'er
Thou com'st thy soul is round us everywhere ;
  And many an auspice, many an omen,
  Whispers, scarce noted, thou art coming.
Huge, cloudlike trees grow dense with sprays and
    buds,
  And cast a shapelier gloom o'er freshening grass,
And through the fringe of ragged woods
  More shrouded sunbeams pass.
Fresh shoots conceal the pollard's spike
  The driving rack out-braving ;
The hedge swells large by ditch and dike ;
And all the uncoloured world is like
  A shadow-limned engraving.

3

Herald and harbinger ! with thee
Begins the year's great jubilee !
　Of her solemnities sublime
(A sacristan whose gusty taper
Flashes through earliest morning vapour),
　Thou ring'st dark nocturns and dim prime.
Birds that have yet no heart for song
　Gain strength with thee to twitter;
And, warm at last, where hollies throng,
　The mirrored sunbeams glitter.
With silk the osier plumes her tendrils thin :
　Sweet blasts, though keen as sweet, the blue lake
　　wrinkle ;
And buds on leafless boughs begin
　Against grey skies to twinkle. .

4

　　　To thee belongs
　A pathos drowned in later scents and songs !
Thou com'st when first the Spring
　On Winter's verge encroaches;
When gifts that speed on wounded wing
　Meet little save reproaches !
Thou com'st when blossoms blighted,
　Retracted sweets, and ditty,
From suppliants oft deceived and spited
　More anger draw than pity !
Thee the old shepherd, on the bleak hill-side,
　Far distant eyeing leans upon his staff
Till from his cheek the wind-brushed tear is dried :
　In thee he spells his boyhood's epitaph.
To thee belongs the youngling of the flock,
　When first it lies, close-huddled from the cold,

Between the sheltering rock
   And gorse-bush slowly overcrept with gold.

5

Thou laugh'st, bold outcast bright as brave,
When the wood bellows, and the cave,
And leagues inland is heard the wave !
   Hating the dainty and the fine
   As sings the blackbird thou dost shine !
Thou com'st while yet on mountain lawns high up
   Lurks the last snow ; while by the berried breer
As yet the black spring in its craggy cup
   No music makes or charms no listening ear :
Thou com'st while from the oak stock or red beech
Dead Autumn scoffs young Spring with splenetic
     speech ;
While in her vidual chastity the Year
With frozen memories of the sacred past
Her doors and heart makes fast,
And loves no flower save those that deck the bier :—
     Ere yet the blossomed sycamore
     With golden surf is curdled o'er ;
     Ere yet the birch against the blue
     Her silken tissue weaves anew :
Thou com'st while, meteor-like 'mid fens, the weed
   Swims, wan in light ; while sleet-showers whitening
     glare ;
Weeks ere by river brims, new furred, the reed
   Leans its green javelin level in the air.

6

Child of the strong and strenuous East !
Now scattered wide o'er dusk hill bases,
Now massed in broad, illuminate spaces ;
   Torchbearer at a wedding feast

Whereof thou mayst not be partaker,
But mime, at most, and merrymaker;
Phosphor of an ungrateful sun
That rises but to bid thy lamp begone :—
                         Farewell! I saw
Writ large on woods and lawns to-day that Law
Which back remands thy race and thee
To hero-haunted shades of dark Persephone.
To-day the Spring has pledged her marriage vow:
　　Her voice, late tremulous, strong has grown and
　　　　steady :
To-day the Spring is crowned a queen : but thou
　　Thy winter hast already!
Take my song's blessing, and depart,
　　Type of true service—unrequited heart.

A FAREWELL.

I.

Round me thy great woods sigh
In their full-foliaged glory; but I die :
　　Ah, blame me not; although,
Tired and o'er-spent, I never pray'd to go.
　　In thine old towers I leave
A cradled pledge to take his mother's part;
　　To vex thee not, nor grieve,
Yet lay, at times, my hand about thy heart.

II.

Nearer—this dying past—
Bend nearer down that noble head at last;

Lower and yet more low
Till o'er my brow a tear has leave to flow.
　　Then the brief seizure quell;
And say that all is over; all is well:
　　Say I lived—and died—
For this, and am in silence satisfied.

- - -

SONG.

LOVE laid down his golden head
　　On his mother's knee;
'The world runs round so fast,' he said,
　　'None has time for me.'

Thought, a sage unhonoured, turn'd
　　From the on-rushing crew;
Song her starry legend spurn'd;
　　Art her glass down threw.

Roll on, blind world, upon thy track
　　Until thy wheels catch fire!
For that is gone which comes not back
　　To seller nor to buyer!

- - -

A PICTURE OF HERODIAS' DAUGHTER
BY LUINI.

ALAS, Salome! Couldst thou know
　　How great man is—how great thou art—

What destined worlds of weal or woe
  Lurk in the shallowest human heart,

From thee thy vanities would drop
  Like sins in noble anger spurn'd
By one who finds, beyond all hope,
  The passion of his youth return'd.

Ah, sunbright face whose brittle smile
  Is cold as sunbeams flash'd on ice !
Ah, lips how sweet yet hard the while !
  Ah, soul too barren even for vice !

Vanity's glittering mask !   Those eyes
  No beam the less around them shed
Albeit in that red scarf there lies
  The dancer's meed the prophet's head.

VANITY.

I.

FALSE and fair ! Beware, beware !
  There is a tale that stabs at thee !
The Arab seer, he stripp'd thee bare,
  He told thy secret, Vanity !
By day a mincing foot is thine ;
Thou runn'st along the spider's line :
Ay ! but heavy sounds thy tread
By night, among the uncoffin'd dead !

II.

Fair and foul ! Thy mate, the ghoul,
  Beats, bat-like, on thy latticed gate ;

Around the graves the night-winds howl;
  'Arise,' they cry, '*thy* feast doth wait!'
Dainty fingers thine, and nice,
With thy bodkin picking rice!
Ay! but when the night's o'erhead
  Limb from limb they rend the dead!

CHAUCER.

ESCAPED from the city, its smoke, its glare,
  'Tis pleasant (showers over, and birds in chorus)
To sit in green alleys and breathe cool air
  Which the violet only has breathed before us!

Such healthful solace is ours, forsaking
  The glass-growth of modern and modish rhyme
For the music of days when the Muse was breaking
  On Chaucer's pleasance like dawn's sweet prime.

Hands rubb'd together smell still of earth:
  The hot-bed verse has a hot-bed taint;
'Tis sense turn'd sour, its cynical mirth:
  'Tis pride, its darkness: its blush, 'tis paint!

His song was a feast where thought and jest
  Like monk and franklin alike found place,
Good will's Round Table! There sat as guest
  Shakespearian insight with Spenser's grace.

His England lay laughing in Faith's bright morn!
  Life in his eye look'd as rosy and round
As the cheek of the huntsman that blows on the
    horn
  When the stag leaps up, and loud bays the hound.

King Edward's tourney, fair Blanche's court,
    Their clarions, their lutes in his verse live on :
But he loved better the birds' consort
    Under oaks of Woodstock while rose the sun.

The cloister, the war-field tented and brave,
    The shout of the burghers in hostel or hall,
The embassy grave over ocean's wave,
    And Petrarch's converse—he loved them all.

In Spring, when the breast of the lime-grove gathers
    Its roseate cloud ; when the flush'd streams sing,
And the mavis tricks her in gayer feathers ;
    Read Chaucer then ; for Chaucer is Spring !

On lonely evenings in dull Novembers
    When rills run choked under skies of lead,
And on forest-hearths the year's last embers
    Wind-heap'd and glowing, lie, yellow and red,

Read Chaucer still ! In his ivied beaker
    With knights, and wood-gods, and saints em-
        boss'd,
Spring hides her head till the wintry breaker
    Thunders no more on the far-off coast.

ODE, WRITTEN BESIDE THE LAGO VARESE.

(SEE SIR HENRY TAYLOR'S POEM, ENTITLED ' LAGO
VARESE.')

    STILL rise around that lake well sung
      New growths as boon and good
    As when, by sunshine saddened, long
      Beside its margin stood

That northern youth, and o'er it breathed a lay
Which praised things beauteous, mourning their
    decay.

  As then, great Nature, 'kind to sloth,'
   Lets drop o'er all the land
  Her gifts, the fair and fruitful both,
   Into the sleeper's hand :
On golden ground once more she paints as then
Starr'd cistus bower, and convent-brighten'd glen.

  Still o'er the flashing waters lean
   The mulberry and the maize,
  And roof of vines whose purple screen
   Tempers those piercing rays,
Which here forego their fiercer shafts, and sleep,
Subdued, in crimson cells, and verdurous chambers
    deep.

  And still in many a sandy creek
   Light waves run on and up,
  While the foam-bubbles winking break
   Around the channell'd cup :
Against the rock they toss the bleeding gourd,
Or fret on marble stair and skiff unmoor'd.

  Fulfill'd thus far the Poet's words :
   And yet a truth, that hour
  By him unsung, upon his chords
   Descends, their ampler dower.
Of Nature's cyclic life he sang, nor knew
That frailer shape he mourn'd should bloom per-
    petual too.

  There still—not skilful to retract
   A glance as kind as keen—

By the same southern sunset back'd
   There still that Maid is seen :
Through song's high grace there stands she ! from
   her eyes
Still beam the cordial mirth, the unshamed sur-
   prise !

   Not yet those parted lips remit
      A smile that grows and grows :
   The Titianic morning yet
      Breaks from that cheek of rose :
Still from her locks the breeze its sweetness takes :
Around her white feet still the ripple fawns and
   rakes.

   And, bright'ning in the radiance cast
      By her on all around,
   That shore lives on, while song may last,
      Love-consecrated ground ;
Lives like that isthmus, headland half, half isle,
Which smiled to meet Catullus' homeward smile.

   O Sirmio ! thou that shedd'st thy fame
      O'er old Verona's lake,
   Henceforth Varese without blame
      Thine honours shall partake :
A Muse hath sung her, on whose front with awe
Thy nymphs had gazed as though great Virtue's self
   they saw !

   What Shape is that, though fair severe,
      Which fleets triumphant by
   Imaged in yonder mirror clear,
      And seeks a hardier sky,
With locks succinct beneath a threat'ning crest—
Like Juno in the brow, like Pallas in the breast ?

A Muse that flatters nothing base
    In man, nor aught infirm,
' Sows the slow olive for a race
    Unborn.'   The destined germ,
The germ alone of Fame she plants, nor cares
What time that secular tree its deathless fruitage
    bears ;

    Pleased rather with her function sage—
        To interpret Nature's heart ;
    The words on Wisdom's sacred page
        To wing, through metric art,
With life ; and in a chariot of sweet sound
Down-trodden Truth to lift, and waft, the world
    around.

    Hail, Muse, whose crown, soon won or late,
        Is Virtue's, not thine own !
    Hail, Verse, that tak'st thy strength and state
        From Thought's auguster throne !
Varese too would hail thee !   Hark that song—
Her almond bowers it thrills and rings her groves
    along !

    October 4, 1856.

ODE.

THE GOLDEN MEAN.

Fortune ! unloved of whom are those
    On whom the Virtues smile,
Forbear the land I love, and choose,
    Choose still some meaner isle !
Thy best of gifts are gilded chains ;
The gold wears off ; the bond remains.

Thus much of good, nor more, is thine,
　　That, clustering round the wand
Thou lift'st, with honey smear'd and wine,
　　In that unqueenly hand,
Close-limed are trapp'd those sun-bred flies
Which else had swarm'd about the wise.

The vanities of fleeting time
　　To powers that fleet belong;
They fear and hate the sons sublime
　　Of science and of song,
And those that, scorn'd as weak, o'errule
The strong, and keep the world at school.

For how could Song her tenderer notes
　　Elaborate for the ear
Of one on vulgar noise who doats;
　　Of one through deserts drear
On rushing in that race distraught
Whose goad is hate, whose goal is naught?

And how could Science trust that line
　　(Her labyrinth's sacred clue)
Of subtly-woven thought, more fine
　　Than threads of morning dew,
To those unhallow'd hands and coarse,
The drudges base of greed or force?

Faith to the sensual and the proud
　　Whom this world makes her prey,
But glimmers with the light allow'd
　　To tapers at noonday;
When garish joys have ta'en their flight
Like stars she glorifies the night.

Nor less the Heroic Life extracts
 From circumstance adverse
Her food of sufferings and of acts ;
 While pain, a rugged nurse,
On the rough breasts of wintry seas
Rocks it 'mid stormy lullabies.

Hail, Poor Estate !   Through thee man's race
 Partake, by rules controll'd,
The praise of them discalced who pace,
 And them that kneel white-stoled ;
Where thou hast honours due, hard by
Obedience stands and chastity.

Hail, too, O Bard, nor poor nor rich,
 Whom one blue gleam of sea
Binds to our British Cuma's beach ;
 Our gold we store in thee ;
To thee not wealth but worlds belong,
Like Delos raised ; such might hath song !

Through thee to him who climbs that down
 Arch'd onward toward the west,
White cliff, green shore, and stubble brown
 In Idyl grace are dress'd ;
Beside low doors, a later Ruth,
Thy Dora sits—serene as truth.

Thy song can girdle hill and mead
 With choirs more pure, more fair
(Their locks with wild flower dressed, and weed)
 Than ever Hellas bare :
Theocritus, we cry, once more
Treads his beloved Trinacrian shore!

O long with freedom's gale refresh'd,
  With mild sea-murmurs lull'd,
O long by thee, in cares unmesh'd,
  Those healthier flowers be cull'd
Rich Egypt knew not, nor the wain
That creak'd o'er deep Bœotian plain !

They lit Arcadian peaks : they breathed
  (Light soils have airs divine)
O'er Scio's rocks with ivy wreathed,
  Stern Parnes' brow, and thine,
Pentelicus, whose marble womb
With temples crown'd all-conquering Rome.

Teach us in all that round us lies
  To see and feel, each hour,
More than Homeric majesties,
  And more than Phidian power :
Teach us the coasts of modern life
With lordlier tasks are daily rife

Than theirs who plunged the heroic oar
  Of old by Chersonese :
But bid our Argo launch from shore
  Unbribed by golden Fleece :
Bid us Dædalean arts to scorn
Which prostituted ends suborn !

That science—slave of sense—which claims
  No commerce with the sky,
Is baser thrice than that which aims
  With waxen wing to fly !
To grovel, or self-doom'd to soar—
Mechanic age, be proud no more !

LUGANO: *October* 7, 1856.

LINES COMPOSED NEAR SHELLEY'S HOUSE AT LERICI, ON ALL SOULS' DAY, 1856.

DEDICATED TO J. W. FIELD, IN MEMORY OF A DAY
PASSED WITH HIM AT LERICI.

I.

AND here he paced! These glimmering pathways
    strewn
With faded leaves his light swift footstep crush'd ;
The odour of yon pine was o'er him blown :
    Music went by him in each wind that brush'd
Those yielding stems of ilex ! Here, alone,
    He walk'd at noon, or silent stood and hush'd
When the ground-ivy flashed the moonlight sheen
Back from the forest carpet always green.

II.

Poised as on air the lithe elastic bower
    Now bends, resilient now against the wind
Springs up, like Dryads that one moment cower
    And rise the next with loose locks unconfined :
Through the dim roof like gems the sunbeams shower;
    Old cypress trunks the aspiring bay-trees bind,
And soon will have them wholly underneath,
Types eminent of glory conquering death.

III.

Far down on weedy shelves and sands below
    The respirations of a southern sea
Beat with susurrent cadence, soft and slow :
    Round the grey cave's fantastic imagery,

In undulation eddying to and fro,
    The purple waves on roll or backward flee ;
While, dew'd at each rebound with gentlest shock,
The myrtle leans her green breast on the rock.

IV..

And here he stood! upon his face that light,
    Stream'd from some furthest realm of luminous
        thought,
Which clothed his fragile beauty with the might
    Of suns for ever rising !   Here he caught
Visions divine.   He saw in fiery flight
    ' The hound of Heaven,' with heavenly vengeance
        fraught,
· Run down the slanted sunlight of the morn—' [1]
Prometheus frown on Jove with scorn for scorn.

V.

He saw white Arethusa, leap on leap,
    Plunge from the Acroceraunian ledges bare
With all her torrent streams, while from the steep
    Alpheus bounded on her unaware :
Hellas he saw, a giant fresh from sleep,
    Break from the night of bondage and despair.
Who but had cried, as there he stood and smiled,
' Justice and Truth have found their winged child ! ' [2]

VI.

Through cloud and wave and star his insight keen
    Shone clear, and traced a God in each disguise,
Protean, boundless.   Like the buskin'd scene
    All Nature rapt him into ecstasies :

---

[1] ' Prometheus Unbound.'   [2] ' Revolt of Islam.'

In him, alas! had Reverence equal been
  With Admiration, those resplendent eyes
Had wander'd not through all her range sublime
To miss the one great marvel of all time.

VII.

The winds sang loud; from this Elysian nest
  He rose, and trod yon spine of mountains bleak,
While stormy suns descending in the west
  Stain'd as with blood yon promontory's beak :
That hour, responsive to his soul's unrest,
  Carrara's marble summits, peak to peak,
Sent forth their thunders like the battle-cry
Of nations arming for the victory.

VIII.

Visions that hour more fair, more false, he saw
  Than those the mythologic heaven that throng ;
Mankind he saw exempt from Faith and Law,
  Move godlike forth, with science wing'd and song ;
He saw the Peoples spurn religious awe,
  Yet tower aloft through inbred virtue strong.
Ah Circe! not for sensualists alone
Thy cup! It dips full oft in Helicon !

IX.

Mankind he saw one equal brotherhood,
  All things in common held as light and air !
' Vinum dæmonum ! ' Just, and wise, and good—
  Were man all this, such freedom man might bear !
The slave creates the tyrant! In man's blood
  Sin lurks, a panther couchant in his lair :
Nature's confession came before the Creed's ;
Authority is still man's first of needs.

X.

All things in common ; equal all ; all free !
  Not fancies these, but gifts reserved in trust :
A spiritual growth is Liberty ;
  Nature, unnatural made through hate and lust,
Yields it no more, or chokes her progeny
  With weeds of foul desire or fell disgust.
Convents have all things common : but on Grace
They rest.   Inverted systems lack a base.

XI.

The more obedience to a law divine
  Tempers the chaos of man's heart, the less
Becomes his need of outward discipline
  The balance of injustice to redress :
' Wild Bacchanals of Truth's mysterious wine ' [1]
  Must bear the Mænad's waking bitterness.
Anticipate not heaven.   Not great thy worth
Heaven without holiness, and heaven on earth !

XII.

Alas ! the errors thus to truth so near
  That sovereign truths they are, though misap-
    plied,
Errors to pure but passionate natures dear,
  Errors by aspirations glorified,
Errors with radiance crown'd like Lucifer
  Ere fall'n, like him to darkness changed through
    pride,
These of all errors are the heart and head :
The strength of life is theirs ; yet they are dead !

[1] Shelley's ' Ode to Liberty.'

XIII.

That Truth Reveal'd, by thee in madness spurn'd,
　Plato, thy master in the walks of light,
Had knelt to worship ! For its day he yearn'd
　Through the long hungry watches of the night :
Its dawn in Thought's assumptions he discern'd
　Silvering hoar contemplation's star-loved height ;
The God-Man came ! Thy pagan phantasy,
Feigning a Man-God, storm'd against His sky.

XIV.

Sorrowing for thee, with sorrow joy is mix'd,
　With triumph shame ! Our hopes themselves are
　　sad ;
But fitful lustres break the shades betwixt ;
　So gleams yon olive bower, in mourning clad,
And yet at times with showery gleams transfix'd,
　That opal among trees which, grave or glad,
Its furtive splendour, half reveal'd or wholly,
Shoots ever from a base of melancholy.

XV.

Our warfare is in darkness. Friend for foe
　Blindly, and oft with swords exchanged, we strike :
Opinion guesses : Faith alone can know
　Where actual and illusive still are like.
Thine was that strength which fever can bestow ;
　The madness thine of one that, fever-sick,
'Beats a sad mother in distemper'd sleep : ' [1]
Perhaps death woke thee, on her breast to weep !

----

[1] From 'Prometheus Unbound.'

XVI.

Thee from that Mother sins ancestral tore !
　No heart hadst thou, from Faith's sole guide
　　remote,
With statutable worship to adore,
　Or learn a nation-licensed Creed by rote ;
No heart to snatch thy gloss of sacred lore
　From the blind prophet of the public vote.
Small help from such in life, or when thy pyre
Cast far o'er Tuscan waves its mirror'd fire !

XVII.

Hark ! She thou knew'st not mourns thee ! Slowly
　　tolls,
　As sinks the sun, yon church-tower o'er the sea :
Abroad once more the peal funereal rolls,
　And Spezia now responds to Lerici :
This day is sacred to Departed Souls ;
　This day the Dead alone are great ; and we
Who live, or seem to live, but live to plead
For the departed myriads at their need.

XVIII.

Behold, the long procession scales the rock ;
　In the red glare dusk banners sadly wave :
Behold, the lambs of the immaculate flock
　Fling flowers on noted and on noteless grave :
O Cross ! sole Hope that dost not woo to mock !
　Some, some that knew thee not thou liv'st to save
All spirits not wholly—by their own decree—
From infinite Love exiled, and lost to thee !

———————

I.

WRITTEN AT VEVEY, SEPTEMBER 15, 1856.

FROM terraced heights that rise in ranks
  Thick set with almond, fig, and maize,
O'er waters blue as violet banks,
  I hear the songs of boyhood's days.

Up walnut slopes, at morn and eve,
  And downward o'er the pearly shore,
From Clarens on they creep; nor leave
  Uncheer'd cold Chillon's dungeon-floor.

Fair girls that please a mother's pride,
  Bright boys from joy of heart that sing,
The voice of bridegroom and of bride,
  Through clustered vines how clear they ring!

For me they blot these southern bowers:
  The ghosts of years gone by they wake:
They send the drift of northern showers
  Low-whispering o'er a narrower lake.

Once more upon the couch he lies
  Who ruled his halls with stately cheer;
Waves slow the lifted hand; with eyes
  And lips rewards the strains most dear.

And ah! from yon empurpled slope
  What fragrance swells that arch beneath!
Geranium, jasmine, heliotrope—
  They stay my breath: of her they breathe!

Flower-lover ! wheresoe'er thou art
  May flowers and sunshine greet thee still ;
And voices vocal to the heart ;
  No sound approach of sad or ill !

II.

WRITTEN NEAR SPEZIA, OCTOBER 19, 1856.

In boyhood's flush when first I strayed
  'Mid those delicious, classic climes,
Troubling each river-bank and glade
  With petulance of forward rhymes,

Of thee the oft recurrent thought
  Was yet but casual, and could pass,
A brightness every shade might blot,
  An image faithless to its glass :

But now that thou art gone, behold,
  Where'er I roam, whate'er I see,
Of all I feel, the base or mould
  Is one unchanging thought of thee.

Thousands with blank regard pass by
  All-gracious Nature's open doors :
The barren heart, the beamless eye,
  Ah not for these her priceless stores !

But thou, the nursling of the Muse—
  On hearts as pure, as still as thine,
All beauty glistening lies like dews
  Upon the smooth leaf of the vine !

Even now on yonder hill-girt plain,
  Sea-lulled, and hollowed like a vase,

I see thee gaze, and gaze again,
  With bright and ever-brightening face;

And hear thee say, ' More fair that vale,
  With happy hearths and homesteads strewn,
Than Alpine summits darkly pale
  Where loveless grandeur reigns alone.'

III.

WRITTEN IN ISCHIA, FEBRUARY 1, 1859.

HERE in this narrow island glen
  Between the dark hill and the sea,
Remote from books, remote from men
  I sit; but O how near to thee!

I bend above thy broidery frame;
  I smell thy flowers; thy voice I hear:
Of Italy thou speak'st: that name
  Woke long thy wish; at last thy tear!

Hadst thou but watch'd that azure deep;
  Those rocks with myrtles mantled o'er;
Misenum's cape, yon mountains' sweep;
  The smile of that Circean shore!

But seen yon crag's embattled crest,
  Whereon Colonna mourn'd alone,
An eagle widow'd in her nest,
  Heart strong and faithful as thine own!

This was not in thy fates.   Thy life
  Lay circled in a narrower bound:
Child, sister, tenderest mother, wife—
  Love made that circle holy ground.

Love bless'd thy home—its trees, its earth,
   Its stones—that ofttimes trodden road,
Which link'd the region of thy birth
   With that till death thy still abode.

From the loud river's rocky beach,
   To that clear lake the woodlands shade,
Love stretch'd his arms.   In sight of each,
   The place of thy repose is made.

IV.

WRITTEN NEAR SPEZIA, 1864.

SINCE last with thee, my guide unseen,
   I loved, where thou hadst loved, to stray,
Eight years have passed ; and, still heart-green,
   They tell me that my head is grey.

Again I mark yon nectared plain :
   Again I pace the rhythmic shore :
But o'er my gladness triumphs pain ;
   I muse on things that are no more.

With thee how fares it ?   Endless youth
   Is thine in regions still and pure :
In climes of Beauty and of Truth
   Some place is thine, serene, secure.

From thee the obscuring mist at last
   Is lifted ; loosed the earthly bond :
The gloomy gates of death are passed,
   And thine th' eternal Peace beyond :

Not lonely peace !   Thine earlier lost
   And latest, by thy side or knee,

With thee from that celestial coast
　　Look down as when they waited thee,

Singing those hymns that, earthward borne,
　　To these dull ears at last make way
From realms where life is always morn,
　　And climes where Godhead is the day.

TO A BIBLE.

SHE read thee to the last, beloved Book!
　　Her wasted fingers 'mid thy pages stray'd ;
　　Upon thy promises her heart was stay'd;
Upon thy letters linger'd her last look
Ere life and love those gentlest eyes forsook :
　　Upon thy gracious words she daily fed ;
　　And by thy light her faltering feet were led
When loneliness her inmost being shook.
O Friend, O Saviour, O sustaining Word,
　　Whose conquering feet the Spirit-land have trod,
Be near her where she is, Incarnate Lord!
　　In the mysterious silence of the tomb
　　Where righteous spirits wait their final doom,
Forsake her not, O Omnipresent God!

E.

SPRING.

WINTER, that hung around us as a cloud,
　　Rolls slowly backward ; from her icy sleep
Th' awaken'd earth starts up and shouts aloud,
　　　　The waters leap

From rock to rock with a tumultuous mirth,
　　With Bacchanalian madness and loud song ;
From the fond bosom of the teeming earth
　　　　All young things throng ;

And hopes rise bubbling from the deepest fountain
　　Of man's half-frozen heart.　Faith trustingly
Rests its broad base on God, as doth a mountain
　　　　Upon the sea.

Affections pure, and human sympathies
　　The summer sun of charity relumes,
That fire divine that warms and vivifies,
　　　　But not consumes.

Love, vernal music, charity, hope, faith,
　　Warm the cold earth, fair visions from on high,
Teaching to scorn and trample fear of death ;
　　　　For nought can die.

　　　　　　　　　　　　　S. E. DE VERE

STANZAS.

ALTHOUGH I know that all my love,
　　My true love, is in vain ; yet I
Must loose the strained cord that holds
My bursting heart within its folds,
　　　　And love or die.

Dear is the breath of early Spring
　　To the low-crouching violet ;
The grateful river smiles upon
The glories of the sinking sun ;
　　　　But dearer yet

Than breath of Spring to the young flower,
   Or sun-burst to the clouded sea,
One glance of pity from thine eye,
The music of thy faintest sigh,
     Sweet love, to me.

This dreary world is very cold :
   A heavy sorrow presses down
My famish'd heart. One tear-drop shed
In memory of the faithful dead,
     When I am gone.

                      S. E. DE VERE.

CHARITY.

THOUGH all the world reject thee, yet will I
Fold thee, with all thine errors, in my heart,
And cherish even thy weakness ! Who can say
That he is free from sin ; or that to him
Belongs to speak the judgments of the Lord,
To vindicate the majesty of Heaven ?
Behold the Master ! prostrate at His feet,
Shuddering with penitential agony,
Magdalen ! O those mild forgiving eyes,
Mercy and pity blossoming in Love !
O lips full founts of pardon and of blessing !
Shall I, a sinner, scorn a sinner, or
Less love my brother seeing he is weak ?
Shall not my heart yearn to his helplessness
Like the fond mother's to her idiot boy ?
O cruel mockery, to call that love
Which the world's frown can wither ! Hypocrite !
False friend ! Base selfish man ! fearing to lift

Thy soiled fellow from the dust !   From thee
The love of friends, the sympathy of kind
Recoil like broken waves from a bare cliff,
Waves that from far seas come with noiseless step
Slow stealing to some lonely ocean isle ;—
With what tumultuous joy and fearless trust
They fling themselves upon its blackened breast,
And wind their arms of foam around its feet,
Seeking a home ; but finding none, return
With slow, sad ripple, and reproachful murmur.
No ! No ! True Charity scorns not the love
Even of the guiltiest, but treasures up
The precious gift within its heart of hearts,
Freely returning love where wanted most,
Like flowers that from the generous air imbibe
The essences of life, and give them forth
Again in odours.   Spirit of Love Divine
That filledst with tenderness the reverent eyes
Of Mary as she gazed upon her Babe,
Soften our stony nature ; make us know
How much we need to be forgiven ; build up
True Charity on humbleness of heart.

S. E. DE VERE.

ODE.

THE ASCENT OF THE APENNINES.

MAY 1859.

I.

I MOVE through a land like a land of dream,
Where the things that are, and that shall be, seem
Wov'n into one by a hand of air,
And the Good looks piercingly down through the
        Fair !

No form material is here unmated;
  Here blows no bud, no scent can rise,
No song ring forth, unconsecrated
  To meaning or model in Paradise!
Fallen, like man, is elsewhere man's earth;
Human, at best, in her sadness and mirth;
Or if she aspires after something greater,
  Lifting her hands from her native dust,
  In God she beholds but the Wise, the Just;
The Saviour she sees not in the Creator:
But here, like children of Saints who learn
  The things above ere the things below,
Who choirs angelic in clouds discern
  Ere the butterfly's wing from the moth's they
    know,
True Nature as ashes all beauty reckons
  That claims not hereafter some happier birth;
She calls from the height to the depth; she beckons
  From the nomad waste to a heavenly hearth:
'The Curse is cancell'd,' she cries; 'thou dreamer,
Earth felt the tread of her great Redeemer!'

II.

Ye who ascend with reverent foot
  The warm vale's rocky stairs,
Though lip be mute, in heart salute
  With praises and with prayers
The noble hands, now dust, that reared
  Long ages since on crag or sward
Those Stations that from their cells revered
  Still preach the Saviour-Lord!
Ah! unseductive here the breath
  Of the vine-bud that blows in the breast of morn;

That orange bower, yon jasmine wreath,
    Hide not the crown of thorn !
Here none can bless the spring, and drink
    Those waters from the dark that burst,
Nor see the sponge and reed, and think
    Of the Three Hours' unquenched thirst.
The Tender, the Beauteous receives its comment
    From a truth transcendent, a life divine ;
And the coin flung loose of the passing moment
    Is stamped with Eternity's sign !

III.

Alas those days of yore
When Nature lay vassal to pagan lore !
Baia—what was she ?   A sorceress still
To brute transforming the human will !
Nor pine could whisper, nor breeze could move
    But a breath infected ran o'er the blood
Like gales that whiten the aspen grove
    Or gusts that darken the flood.
Along blue ocean's level
The beauteous base ones held their revel,
Dances on the sea-sand knitting,
    With shouts the sleeping shepherd scaring,
Like Oreads o'er the hill-side flitting,
    Like Mænads thyrsus-bearing.
The Siren sang from the moonlit bay,
    The Siren sang from the redd'ning lawn,
Until in the feastful cup of day
    Lay melted the pearl of dawn.
Unspiritual intelligence
Changed Nature's fane to a hall of sense,
That rings with the upstart spoiler's jest,
And the beakers clash'd by the drunken guest !

IV.

Hark to that convent bell!
False pagan world, farewell;
From cliff to cliff the challenge vaults rebounded!
Echo, her wanderings done,
Heart-peace at last hath won,
The rest of love on Faith not Fancy founded;
' By the parch'd fountain let the pale flower die,'
She sings, ' True Love, true Joy, triumphant reign
    on high ! '

V.

The plains recede; the olives dwindle;
  I leave the chestnut slopes behind;
The skirts of the billowy pine-woods kindle
  In the evening lights and wind:
Not here we sigh for the Alpine glory
  Of peak primeval and death-pale snow;
For the cold grey green, and the glacier hoary,
  Or blue caves that yawn below:
The landscape here is mature and mellow;
  Fruit-like, not flower-like :—hills embrown'd;
Ridges of purple and ledges of yellow
  From runnel to rock church-crown'd:
'Tis a region of mystery, hush'd and sainted:
  Serene as the pictures of artists old
When Giotto the thoughts of his Dante painted :—
  The summit is reach'd! Behold!
Like a sky condensed lies the lake far down;
  Its curves like the orbit of some fair planet;
A fire-wreath falls on the cliffs that frown
  Above it, dark walls of granite;
The hill-sides with homesteads and hamlets glow;
With wave-washed villages zoned below:

Down drops by the island's woody shores
The banner'd barge with its gleam of oars.
No solitude here, no desert cheerless
   Is needed pure thoughts or hearts to guard ;
'Tis a ' populous solitude,' festal, fearless,
   For men of good-will prepared.
The hermit may hide in the wood, but o'er it
   Three times each day the chimes are rolled :
The black crag woos the cloud, but before it
   The procession winds on white-stoled.
Farewell, O Nature !   None meets thee here
But his heart goes up to a happier sphere !
He sees, from the blossom of sense unfolded
   By the Paraclete's breath, its divine increase,
Rose-leaf on rose-leaf in sanctity moulded,
   The flower of Eternal Peace ;
The home and the realm of man's race above ;
The Vision of Truth, and the Kingdom of Love !

VI.

There shall the features worn and wasted
   Let fall the sullen mask of years :
There shall that fruit at last be tasted
   Whose seed was sown in tears :
There shall that amaranth bloom for ever
   Whose blighted blossom droop'd erewhile
   In this dim valley of exile,
And by the Babylonian river.
The loved and lost once more shall meet us ;
Joys that never were ours shall greet us ;
Delights for the love of the Cross foregone
Fullfaced salute us, ashamed of none.
Heroes unnamed the storm that weathered
   There shall sceptred stand and crown'd ;

Apostles the wilder'd flocks that gather'd
  Sit throned with nations round.
There, heavenly sweets from the earthly bitter
  Shall rise like odour from herbs down-trod;
There, tears of the past like gems shall glitter
  On trees that gladden the mount of God.
The deeds of the righteous, on earth despised,
By the lightning of God immortalised
Shall crown like statues the walls sublime
  Of all the illuminate, mystic City,
Memorial emblems that conquer Time,
  Yet tell his tale.   That Pity
Which gave the lost one strength to speak,
  That Love in guise angelic stooping
O'er the grey old head, or the furrow'd cheek,
  Or the neck depress'd and drooping,
Shall live for aye, at a flash transferr'd
From the wastes of earth to the courts of the Word;
The Thoughts of the Just, the frustrate schemes,
  Shall lack not a place in the wondrous session;
The Prayers of the Saints, their griefs, their dreams,
  Shall be manifest there in vision;
For they live in the Mind Divine, their mould,
  That Mind Divine the unclouded mirror
Wherein the glorified Spirits behold
  All worlds, undimm'd by error.

VII.

Fling fire on the earth, O God,
  Consuming all things base!
Fling fire upon man, his soul and his blood,
  The fire of Thy Love and Grace:

That his heart once more to its natal place
Like a bondsman freed may rise,
Ascending for ever before Thy face
From the altar of Sacrifice !

And thou, Love's comrade, Hope,
That yield'st to Wisdom strength, to Virtue scope,
That giv'st to man and nation
The on-rushing plumes of spiritual aspiration,
Van-courier of the ages, Faith's swift guide,
That still the attain'd foregoest for the descried ;
On, Seraph, on, through night and tempest winging !
On heavenward, on, across the void, vast hollow !
And be it ours, to thy wide skirts close clinging
Blindly, like babes, thy conquering flight to follow :
What though the storm of Time roar back beside us ?
Though this world mock or chide us ?
We shall not faint or fail until at last
The eternal shore is reach'd, all peril past !

A MOTHER'S SONG.

I.

O TIME, whose silent foot down treads
The kingly towers and groves,
Who lay'st on loftiest, loveliest heads,
The hand that no man loves,
Take all things else beneath the skies,
But spare one infant's laughing eyes !

II.

O Time, who build'st the coral reef,
Whom dried-up torrents fear,

And rocks far hurled, like storm-blown sheaf,
   From peak to glacier drear,
Waste all things else; but spare the while
The lovelight of one infant's smile!

III.

Where sunflowers late from Summer's mint
   Brought back the age of gold,
Through thee once more the sleet showers dint
   The black and flowerless mould:
But harm not, Time, and guard, O Nature,
What is not yours—this living creature!

IV.

From God's great love a Soul forth sprang
   That ne'er till then had being:
The courts of heaven with anthems rang:
   He bless'd it, He the All-seeing!
Nor suns nor moons, nor heaven nor earth,
Can shape a Soul or match in worth.

V.

No thought of thee when o'er the leas
   A child I raced delighted;
No thought when under garden trees
   A girlish troth I plighted:
We knew not what the church bells said
That giddy morn the girl was wed:
Of thee they babbled, pretty maid!

A CHRISTIAN POETESS.

ADELAIDE PROCTER.

SHE stooped o'er earth's poor brink, light as a breeze
That bathes, enraptured, in clear morning seas,
And round her, like that wandering Minstrel, sent
Twofold delight—music with freshness blent:
Ere long in night her snowy wings she furled,
Waiting the sunrise of a happier world,
And God's New Song.   O Spirit crystalline,
What lips shall better waft it on than thine?

IN MEMORY OF EDWIN EARL OF DUNRAVEN.

ONCE more I pace thy pillared halls,
    And hear the organ echoes sigh
In blissful death, on storied walls:
    But where art thou? not here; nor nigh.

Once more the rapt spring-breezes send
    A flash o'er yonder winding flood,
And with the garden's fragrance blend
    A fresher breath from lawn and wood.

Friend! where art thou?   Thy works reply;
    The lowly School; the high-arched Fane:
Who loves his kind can never die:
    Who serves his God, with God shall reign.

ADARE, 1873

A SONG OF AGE.

I.

WHO mourns ?   Flow on, delicious breeze !
Who mourns, though youth and strength go by ?
Fresh leaves invest the vernal trees,
Fresh airs will drown my latest sigh :
This frame is but a part outworn
Of earth's great Whole that lifts more high
A tempest-freshened brow each morn
To meet pure beams and azure sky.

II.

Thou world-renewing breath, sweep on,
And waft earth's sweetness o'er the wave !
That earth will circle round the sun
When God takes back the life He gave !
To each his turn !   Even now I feel
The feet of children press my grave,
And one deep whisper o'er it steal—
'The Soul is His Who died to save.'

SPENSER.

ONE peaceful spot in a storm-vex'd isle
Shall wear for ever the past's calm smile ;
Kilcolman Castle !   There Spenser sate ;
There sang, unweeting of coming fate.

The song he sang was a life-romance
Woven by Virtues in mystic dance
Where the gods and heroes of Grecian story
Themselves were virtues in allegory.

True love was in it, but love sublimed,
Occult, high-reason'd, bewitch'd, be-rhymed!
The knight was the servant of ends trans-human,
The women were seraphs, the bard half woman.

Time and its tumults, stern shocks, hearts wrung,
To him were mad words to sweet music sung,
History to him a rough Breviary quaint
Border'd round with gold Angel and azure Saint.

Creative indeed was that eye, sad Mary!
That hail'd in thy rival a queen of faery,
And in Raleigh, half statesman, half pirate, could see
But the shepherd of ocean's green Arcady.

Under groves of Penshurst his first notes rang:
As Sidney lived so his Spenser sang:
From the well-head of Chaucer one stream found
     birth,
Like an Arethusa, on Irish earth.

From the court he had fled, and the courtly lure:
One virgin muse in an age not pure
Wore Florimel's girdle, and mourn'd in song
(Disguised as Irena's) Ierne's wrong.

Roll onward, thou western Ilyssus, roll,
'Mulla,' far kenn'd by 'old mountain Mole!'
With thy Shepherds a Calidore loved to dwell;
And beside him an Irish Pastorel.

Dead are the wild-flowers she flung on thy tide,
Bending over thee, giftless—that well-sung bride: [1]
The flowers have pass'd by, but abideth the river;—
May its Genius, its Guardian, be near it for ever!

[1] 'Song made in lieu of many ornaments.'
Spenser's Epithalamium on his own Marriage.

SONG.

THE FLOWER OF THE TREE.

I.

O THE flower of the tree is the flower for me,
That life out of life, high-hanging and free,
By the finger of God and the south wind's fan
Drawn from the broad bough, as Eve from Man!
From the rank red earth it never upgrew:
It was woo'd from the bark in the glistening blue.

II.

Hail, blossoms green 'mid the limes unseen,
That charm the bees to your honey'd screen,
As like to the green trees that gave you birth
As true tongue's kindness to inward worth!
We see you not; but, we scarce know why,
We are glad when the air you have breathed goes by.

III.

O flowers of the lime! 'twas a merry time
When under you first we read old rhyme,
And heard the wind roam over pale and park,
(*We* not I) 'mid the lime-grove dark!
Summer is heavy and sad.   Ye bring
With your tardy blossoms a second Spring.

A FRAGMENT.

LIKE two smooth waves that o'er a foamless ocean
  On slide in sequence past a grassy lea,
Made beautiful by sunrise and with motion,   .
  Serener than unmoved tranquillity,
Or like two gusts that toward one bowery shore
  Successive sweep in fragrance, then go by,
Were those two Sisters.   They who wept of yore
  This day partake their happy rest on high,
  Happier—how much—in heaven for each poor
    earthly sigh.

EPITAPH.

GREAT Love, death-humbled, yields awhile to earth
Its Bright One, waiting there the immortal birth:
Rich Love, made poor, can trust one Hope alone,
Its best, its holiest, to the cold grave-stone:
Eternal Easter of that Hope, be born!
The pure make perfect; comfort the forlorn.

SONNETS

SONNETS.

———◆◆◆———

I.

COMPOSED AT RYDAL.

SEPT. 1860.

THE last great man by manlier times bequeath'd
To these our noisy and self-boasting days
In this green valley rested, trod these ways,
With deep calm breast this air inspiring breathed:
True bard, because true man, his brow he wreathed
With wild-flowers only, singing Nature's praise;
But Nature turn'd, and crown'd him with her bays,
And said, 'Be thou *my* Laureate.' Wisdom sheath'd
In song love-humble; contemplations high,
That built like larks their nests upon the ground;
Insight and vision; sympathies profound
That spann'd the total of humanity;
These were the gifts which God pour'd forth at large
On men through him; and he was faithful to his
    charge.

II.

TO WORDSWORTH, ON VISITING THE DUDDON.[1]—1

So long as Duddon 'twixt his cloud-girt walls
Thridding the woody chambers of the hills
Warbles from vaulted grot and pebbled halls
Welcome or farewell to the meadow rills;
So long as linnets pipe glad madrigals
Near that brown nook the labourer whistling tills,
Or the late-reddening apple forms and falls
'Mid dewy brakes the autumnal redbreast thrills,
So long, last poet of the great old race,
Shall thy broad song through England's bosom roll,
A river singing anthems in its place,
And be to later England as a soul.
Glory to Him Who made thee, and increase,
To them that hear thy word, of love and peace!

III.

TO WORDSWORTH, ON VISITING THE DUDDON.—2.

WHEN first that precinct sacrosanct I trod
Autumn was there, but Autumn just begun;
Fronting the portals of a sinking sun
The queen of quietude in vapour stood,
Her sceptre o'er the dimly-crimson'd wood
Resting in light.   The year's great work was done;
Summer had vanish'd, and repinings none
Troubled the pulse of thoughtful gratitude.
Wordsworth! the autumn of our English song
Art thou: 'twas thine our vesper psalms to sing:
Chaucer sang matins; sweet his note and strong;
His singing-robe the green, white garb of Spring:
Thou like the dying year art rightly stoled;
Pontific purple and dark harvest gold.

[1] See Wordsworth's Sonnet to the Poet Dyer.

IV.

SELF-DECEPTION.

LIKE mist it tracks us wheresoe'er we go,
Like air bends with us ever as we bend;
And, as the shades at noontide darkest grow,
With grace ascending so its snares ascend:
Weakness with virtue skill'd it is to blend,
Breed baser life from buried sins laid low,
Make void our world of God and good, yet lend
The spirit's waste a paradisal glow.
O happy children simple even in wiles!
And ye of single eye, thrice happy Poor!
Practised self-love, that cheat which slays with smiles,
Weaves not for you the inevitable lure.
Men live a lie: specious their latest breath:
Welcome, delusion-slayer, truthful Death!

V.

POETIC RESERVE.

NOT willingly the Muses sing of love:
But, ere their Songs descend to man's domain,
Through the dark chambers of the poet's brain
They pass, and passing take the stamp thereof:
And, as the wind that sweeps the linden grove
Wafts far its odour, so that sphere-born Strain
Learns from its mortal mould to mourn and plain,
Though the strong Muses sit like Gods above.
True poetry is doubly-dower'd—a brightness
Lit from above yet fuell'd from below;
A moon that rolls through heaven in vestal whiteness,
Yet, earthward stooping, wears an earthly glow.
Mysteries the Muse would hide the Bards reveal:
They love to wound: her mission is to heal.

VI.

ON A GREAT FUNERAL.

No more than this ?   The chief of nations bears
Her chief of sons to his last resting-place :
Through the still city, sad and slow of pace
The sable pageant streams : and as it nears
That dome, to-day a vault funereal, tears
Run down the grey-hair'd veteran's wintry face ;
Deep organs sob ; and flags their front abase ;
And the snapt wand the rite complete declares.
—Soul, that before thy Judge dost stand this day,
Disrobed of strength and puissance, pomp and power,
O Soul defrauded at thine extreme hour
Of man's sole help from man, and latest stay,
Swells there for thee no prayer from all that host ?
Is this blank burial but a Nation's boast ?

VII.

TO CHARLES ELIOT NORTON.—I.

On reading his 'Vita Nuova' of Dante.   March 28, 1860.

NORTON ! I would that oft in years to come
The destined bard of that brave land of thine [1]
Sole-seated 'neath the tempest-roughen'd pine,
In boyhood's spring when genius first doth plume
Her wing, 'mid forest scents and insects' hum
And murmurs from the far sea crystalline
May smell *this* blossom from the Tuscan vine,
May hear *this* voice from antique Christendom ;
For thus from love and purity and might
Shall he receive his armour, and forth fare
Champion elect in song, that country's knight
Who early burst the chains weak nations bear
Weeping.   'Mid trumpet-blasts and standards torn
To manhood, with loud cries, thy land was born !

[1] America.

VIII.

TO THE SAME.—2. JUNE 12, 1861.

' To manhood with loud cries thy land was born '—
Was born! is born! Her trumpets peal this hour
The authentic voice of Nationhood and Power!
The iron in her soul indignant worn
This day she tramples down. Her lips have sworn
To lift the dusky race in chains that cower;
And if once more the tempests round her lower
Her smile goes through them like the smile of morn!
Great Realm! The men that in thy sunnier day
Look'd on thee dubious or with brow averse,
Now thou hast put the evil thing away,
(Our sin and thine, Time's dread transmitted curse)
Send up their prayers to prop that lifted hand
Which gives to God a liberated Land!

IX.

THE AMERICAN STRUGGLE.—1.
THE PRINCIPLE. FEBRUARY 20, 1865.

SWORD! ere the sheath that hid thy light so long
That splendour quench, go thou like lightning forth,
High Bride of Justice, not of South or North,
And raise, as now the weak, and quell the strong!
Advance, till from the black man's hearth the song
Rises to God, and by the black man's hearth
Humanity hath leave in godly mirth
To sit, forgetful of her ancient wrong.
Then rest for ever; for to work like thine
While the world lasts no other can succeed
Equal, or second. Hang in heaven, a Sign,
But stoop no more to earth, or earthly need,
Nor ever leave thy starry home august,
Vassal of vulgar wars, and prone Ambition's lust.

X.

THE AMERICAN STRUGGLE.—2.

PRINCIPLE A POWER ; OR, LOGIC IN HISTORY. FEBRUARY 21, 1865.

Lo ! as an Eagle battling through a cloud
That from his neck all night the vapour flings,
And ploughs the dark, till downward from his wings
Sunrise, long waited, smites some shipwrecked crowd
Beneath a blind sea-cavern bent and bowed ;—
Thus through the storm of Men, the night of Things,
That Principle to which the issue clings
Makes fateful way, and spurns at last its shroud.
There were that saw it with a sceptic ken :
There were that saw it not through hate or pride :
But, conquering and to conquer, on it came,
No tool of man but making tools of men,
Till Nations shook beneath its advent wide,
And they that loosed the Portent rued the same.

XI.

ROBERT ISAAC WILBERFORCE.

' No way but this.'   There where the pleasant shade
Dropp'd from the ledges of the Alban hill
Creeps to the vast Campagna and is still,
The mightier shadow reach'd him ! Prayer was
But he to God his tribute just had paid,   [made :
And earn'd his rest.   The deep recall'd the rill :
A long life's labour with a perfect will
He on the altar of the Church had laid.
Child of the old English Learning sage and pure,
Authentic, manly, grave, without pretence,
From this poor stage of changeful time and sense
Released, sleep well, of thy reward secure :
Beside the Apostles' threshold thou dost lie,
Waiting, well-pleased, thy great eternity.

ROME : 1857.

XII.

' LE RÉCIT D'UNE SŒUR.'—1.

WHENCE is the music ? minstrel see we none ;
Yet soft as waves that, surge succeeding surge,
Roll forward, now subside, anon emerge,
Upheaved in glory o'er a setting sun,
Those beatific harmonies sweep on !
O'er earth they sweep from heaven's remotest verge
Triumphant hymeneal, hymn, and dirge,
Blending in everlasting unison.
Whence is the music ?   Stranger ! these were they
That, great in love, by love unvanquished proved :
These were true lovers, for in God they loved :
With God, these Spirits rest in endless day,
Yet still for Love's behoof, on wings outspread
Float on o'er earth, betwixt the Angels and the
    Dead !

XIII.

' LE RÉCIT D'UNE SŒUR.'—2.

ALEXANDRINE.

BETWEEN two graves, a sister's grave and one
Wherein the husband of her youth was laid,
In countenance half a Spirit, half a Nun,
She stood : a breeze that branch of jasmine swayed
In her slight hand upholden : ' Peace ! ' she said :
A smile all gold to meet the sinking sun
Came forth : the pale, worn face transfigured shone
Sun-like beneath the sorrowing widow-braid.
She raised that branch, away her tears to wipe—
' How happy seemed our life twelve years ago !
I weep him still, but gaily weep at last !
Like some sweet day-dream looks that earthly past :
Of genuine joy the pledge it was, the type :
Now, now alone the joy itself I know ! '

XIV.

A WINTER NIGHT IN THE WOODS.

WHEN first the Spring her glimmering chaplets wove
This way and that way 'mid the boughs high hung,
We watched the hourly work, while thrushes sung
A song that shook with joy their bowered alcove:
Summer ere long o'erarched with green the grove,
And deepening shades to flower-sweet alleys clung:
Then last—one dirge from many a golden tongue—
The chiding leaves with chiding Autumn strove.
These were but Nature's preludes.   Last is first!
Winter, uplifting high both flail and fan,
With the great forests dealt as Death with man;
And therefore through their desolate roofs hath burst
This splendour veiled no more by earthly bars;
Infinite heaven, and the fire-breathing stars!

XV.

POLAND AND RUSSIA.—1.

WHEN, fixed in righteous wrath, a Nation's eye
Torments some crowned Tormentor with just hate,
Nor threat, nor flattery may that gaze abate:
Unshriven the unatoning years go by:
For, as that starry Archer [1] in the sky
Unbends not his bright bow, though early and late
The Syren sings, and folly weds with fate,
Even so that sure though silent Destiny
Which keeps fire-vigil in God's judgment-heaven
Upon the countenance of the Doomed looks forth
Consentient with a Nation's gaze on earth:
To those twinned Powers a single gaze is given:
The earthly Fate reveals the Fate on high—
A Brazen Serpent raised, that says not, 'live,' but
    'die!'

[1] Sagittarius.

XVI.

POLAND AND RUSSIA.—2.

THE Strong One with the Weak One reasons thus :
'Through sin of thine our eagle wings are clipt :
Through frost of thine our summer branch is nipt :
Thy wounds accuse : thy rags are mutinous :
The nations note thine aspect dolorous
Like some starved shape that cowers in charnel crypt,
Or landscape in eclipse perpetual dipt,
And, ignorant, cavil, not at thee but us ! '
Then answer makes that worn voice, stern and slow :
' Am I a dog the scourger's hand that licks,
And fattens ?   Blind reproof but spurns the pricks.
That which I am thou mad'st me ! long ago
My face thou grav'dst to be a face of woe,
Fixed as the fixed face of a Crucifix.'

XVII.

GALATEA AND URANIA; OR, ART AND FAITH.

' DREAD Venerable Goddess, whom I fear,
Gaze not upon me from thy starry height !
I fear thy levelled shafts of ruthless light,
Thine unfamiliar radiance and severe :
Thy sceptre bends not ! stern, defined, and clear
Thy Laws : thy face intolerantly bright :   •
Thine is the empire of the Ruled and Right :
Never hadst thou a part in smile or tear !
I love the curving of the wind-arched billow ;
The dying flute tone, sweeter for its dying :
To me less dear the Pine tree than the Willow,
The mountain than the shadows o'er it flying.'
Thus Galatea sang, (whilst o'er the waters
Urania leant :) and cowered 'mid Ocean's foam-white
    daughters.

XVIII.

COMMON LIFE.

ONWARD between two mountain warders lies
The field that man must till. Upon the right,
Church-thronged, with summit hid by its own height,
Swells the vast range of the Theologies :
Upon the left the hills of Science rise
Lustrous but cold : nor flower is there, nor blight :
Between those ranges twain through shade and light
Winds the low vale wherein the meek and wise
Repose. The knowledge that excludes not doubt
Is there ; the arts that beautify man's life :
There rings the choral psalm, the civic shout,
The genial revel, and the manly strife :
There by the bridal rose the cypress waves :
And there the all-blest sunshine softest falls on graves.

XIX.

MODERN DESPONDENCY.

WRITTEN IN DEVONSHIRE.

SOFT land, and gracious as some nectarous fruit
In whose warm bosom Autumn's heart is glad,
Thou hadst of old thy bards, whose lyre and lute
Well praised thy joyous woodlands blossom-clad :
Thou hadst thy blithesome days! If ours be sad,
May thy blue bays and orchards never mute
That sadness charm—slay causeless sorrow's root—
Loveless Self-Will, the Pride that maketh mad!
Wed, blameless Nature, wed with Grace Divine
Once more, like sweet harps blent with sweeter voices,
Thy powers : then sing, till child and man rejoices
Betwixt those ' Double Seas ' of England ! Shine,
Sun of past years ! Disperse those modern glooms
At least from golden Devon's Tors and Combes !

XX.

PONTEFRACT CASTLE, AND TREASON'S BEQUEST.

WIND-WASTED castle without crown of towers!
Dread dungeon keep, watching the dying day!
A crownless king, great Edward's grandson,[1] lay
Wasting in thee, and counting prisoned hours:
A century passed: The Faith's embattled Powers
Thus far advanced; here stood, a stag at bay:
The eighth Henry trembled in his blood-stained
    bowers;—
Thou saw'st that 'Pilgrimage of Grace' decay!
Two Woes thou saw'st; the fall of England's Crown,
That drowned in blood her old Nobility;
Then, baser plague, the old Temples trampled down
By Despots new! Twice-doomed! the fount in thee
I mark of that Red Sea which rolls between
England that is, and England that hath been!

XXI.

INDUSTRY.

VIRTUE defamed for sordid, rough, and coarse,
Unworthy of the glimpses of the moon,
Praise of the clown alone whose heavy shoon [source,
Kneads the moist clay, nor spares the pure stream's
In thee how strong is grace! how fair is force!
How generous art thou, and to man how boon!
Not thine the boastful plain with carnage strewn,
Nor chambers, wassail-shamed, where late Remorse
Sits, the last guest! From ocean on to ocean,
From citied shore to hills far-forested,
The increase of earth is thine, in rest or motion;
The crown is thine on every Sage's head;
The ship, the scythe, the rainbow among flowers:
Thine too the song of girls exulting 'mid their bowers.

---

[1] Richard II.

XXII.

TO THE MOST FAIR.

FAIR, noble, young!　Of thee I thought to sing,
(If so Love willed, and the ever-virgin Muse
Who cannot grace accord unless Love choose,
Were pleased from Love's first bath, Castalia's Spring,
One flower, or sparkling drop, on me to fling)
For ofttimes thus some clan barbaric strews
Their earth and wood, the little island's dues,
Before his feet whom conquest made its King:
So dreamed I, when, a mourner sad and stern,
The Muses' Mother fixed on me her eyes—
Memory—nor slow their meaning to discern
Like a child stung I dropped the forfeit prize:
Some holier hand from out the immortal river
The destined reed must draw, and hymn thy praise
　　　for ever!

XXIII.

IN MEMORY OF THE LATE SIR JOHN SIMEON.—1.

FEAST OF THE PURIFICATION, 1873.

THIS day we keep our Candlemas in snow:
Wan is the sky; a bitter wind and drear
Wrinkles the bosom of yon blackening mere:
Of these I reck not, but of thee, and O!
Of that bright Roman morn, so long ago,
When, children new of her, that Church more dear
To liegeful hearts with each injurious year,
We watched the famed Procession circling slow.
Once more I see it wind with lights upholden
On through the Sistine, on and far away:
Once more I mark beneath its radiance golden
Thy forehead shine, and, with it kindling, say,
'Rehearsals dim were those, O friend: this hour
Surely God's light it is that on thee rests in power!'

XXIV.

IN MEMORY OF THE LATE SIR JOHN SIMEON.—2.

AGAIN we met.   We trod the fields and farms
Of that fair isle, thy happy English home ;
We gazed upon blue sea, and snowy foam
Clipt in the jutting headland's woody arms :
The year had reached the fulness of her charms :
The Church's year, from strength to strength in-
    creased,
Its zenith held that great Assumption feast
Whose sun with annual joy the whole earth warms.
That day how swiftly rushed from thy full heart
Hope's glorying flood !   How high thy fancy soared,
Kenning, though far, once more thine England's crest
A light to Christendom's old heaven restored !
' In a large room ' thy heart its home had found :
The land we trod that day to thee was holy ground.

XXV.

IN MEMORY OF THE LATE SIR JOHN SIMEON.—3.

THE world external knew thee but in part :
It saw and honoured what was least in thee ;
The loyal trust, the inborn courtesy ;
The ways so winning, yet so pure from art ;
The cordial reverence, keen to all desert,
All save thine own ; the accost so frank and free ;
The public zeal that toiled, but not for fee,
And shunned alike base praise, and hireling's mart :
These things men saw ; but deeper far than these
The under-current of thy soul worked on
Unvexed by surface-ripple, beam, or breeze,
And unbeheld its way to ocean won :
Life of thy life was still that Christian Faith
The sophist scorns.   It failed thee not in death.

XXVI.

THE POETRY OF THE FUTURE.
An anticipation addressed to a young authoress.

Go forth, fair Book! Go, countenanced like that man
Upon whose brow all Eden's light was stayed;
Beauteous as Truth, go forth to cheer and aid,
Breathing of greatness ours ere sin began;
With angel-wing from eyes earth-wearied fan
Convention's mist; revive great hopes that fade;
Bid nature rule where reigned but masquerade;
Bear witness to that joy divine which ran
Down to creation's heart, while, bending o'er it,
The great Creator saw that all was good,
That mightier joy, when, dying to restore it,
He rose Who washed it in His conquering blood :
Go forth, a seer in minstrel raiment clad;
Say to the meek, 'Be strong;' the poor, 'Be glad!'

XXVII.

THE RUINS OF EMANIA, NEAR ARMAGH.

Why seek we thus the living 'mid the dead?
Beneath that mound, within yon circle wide,
Emania's palace, festive as a bride
For centuries six, had found its wormy bed
When Patrick lifted here his royal head,
And round him gazed. Perhaps the Apostle sighed
Even then, to note the fall of mortal pride :
Full fourteen hundred years since then have fled !
Then, too, old Ulster's hundred kings were clay ;
Then, too, the Red Branch warriors slept forlorn ;
Autumn, perhaps, as now, a pilgrim grey,
Counted her red beads on the berried thorn,
Making her rounds; while from the daisied sod
The undiscountenancéd lark upsoared, and praised
     her God.

XXVIII.

DUNLUCE CASTLE, COUNTY OF ANTRIM.

O ! of the fallen most fallen, yet of the proud
Proudest; sole-seated on thy tower-girt rock;
Breasting for ever circling ocean's shock;
With blind sea-caves for ever dinned and loud;
Now sunset-gilt; now wrapt in vapoury shroud;
Till distant ships—so well thy bastions mock
Primeval nature's style in joint and block—
Misdeem *her* ramparts, round thee bent and bowed,
For thine, and on *her* walls, men say, have hurled
The red artillery stored designed for thee:
Thy wars are done!   Henceforth perpetually
Thou restest, like some judged, impassive world
Whose sons, their probatory period past,
Have left that planet void amid the vast.

XXIX.

HORN HEAD, COUNTY OF DONEGAL.

SISTER of Earth, her sister eldest-born,
Huge world of waters, how unlike are ye!
Thy thoughts are not as her thoughts: unto thee
Her pastoral fancies are as things to scorn:
Thy heart is still with that old hoary morn
When on the formless deep, the procreant sea,
God moved alone: of that Infinity,
Thy portion then, thou art not wholly shorn.
Scant love hast thou for dells where every leaf
Boasts its own life, and every brook its song;
Thy massive floods down stream from reef to reef
With one wide pressure; thy worn cliffs along
The one insatiate Hunger moans and raves,
Hollowing its sunless crypts and sanguine caves.

XXX.

THE CENTENARY OF AMERICAN LIBERTY.

A CENTURY of sunrises hath bowed
Its fulgent forehead 'neath the ocean-floor
Since first upon the West's astonished shore,
Like some huge Alp, forth struggling through the
    cloud,
A new-born nation stood, to Freedom vowed:
Within that time how many an Empire hoar
And young Republic, flushed with wealth and war,
Alike have changed the ermine for the shroud!
O 'sprung from earth's first blood,' O tempest-nursed,
For thee what Fates? I know not. This I know,
The Soul's great freedom, gift, of gifts the first,
Thou first on man in fulness didst bestow;
Hunted elsewhere, God's Church with thee found rest:
Thy future's Hope is she—that queenly Guest.

XXXI.

FOUNTAINS ABBEY.

THE hand of Time is heavy; yet how soft
Its touch can be, yon mouldering chancel knows!
The ruin too can ' blossom like the rose;'
Nor e'er from orchard bower, or garth, or croft,
More sweetly sang the linnet than aloft
She sings from that green tower! The sunset glows
Behind it; and yon stream that, darkling, flows
From arch to arch, reflects it oft and oft,
Humbly consenting 'mid the gloom to smile,
And take what transient gladness may befall.
Rejoice thou, too, O venerable Pile,
With loftier heart answering a holier call:
Like those, thy buried saints, make strong thy trust,
Waiting the Resurrection of the Just.

XXXII.

ON READING AN UNTRUE CHARGE.

BEAUTIFUL Land! They said, ' He loves thee not! '
But in a church-yard 'mid thy meadows lie
The bones of no disloyal ancestry,
To whom in me disloyal were the thought
Which wronged thee. For my youth thy Shakspeare
    wrought;
For me thy minsters raised their towers on high;
Thou gav'st me friends whose memory cannot die :—
I love thee, and for that cause left unsought
Thy praise. Thy ruined cloisters, forests green,
Thy moors where still the branching wild deer roves,
Dear haunts of mine by sun and moon have been
From Cumbrian peaks to Devon's laughing coves.
They love thee less, be sure, who ne'er had heart
To take, for truth's sake, 'gainst thyself thy part.

SHORT POEMS EPIGRAMS, &c.

z 2

SHORT POEMS, ETC.

ON A GREAT PLAGIARIST.

PHŒBUS drew back with just disdain
  The wreath: the Delphic Temple frowned:
The suppliant fled to Hermes' fane,
  That stood on lower, wealthier ground.

The Thief-God spake, with smile star-bright:
  ' Go thou where luckier poets browse
The pastures of the Lord of Light,
  And do—what I did with his cows.'[1]

THE TRUE HARP.

SOUL of the Bard! stand up, like thy harp's majestical
    pillar!
  Heart of the Bard, like its arch in reverence bow
    thee and bend!

'He stole, killed, and ate the whole of Apollo's herd
before he was a day old!'—See Homer's *Hymn to Mercury.*

Mind of the Bard, like its strings be manifold,
    changeful, responsive :
This is the harp God smites, the harp, man's
    master and friend !

SELF-LOVE.

LIGHT-WINGED Loves ! they come ; they flee :
    If we were dead they'd never miss us :
Self-Love ! with thee is Constancy—
    Thine eyes to *one* were true, Narcissus !

THE SERIOUS 'VIVE LA BAGATELLE.'

BRIGHT world ! you may write on my heart what you
    will,
    But write it with pencil not pen :
Your hand hath its skill : but a hand finer still
    Will whiten your tablet again.

To the moment its laugh, and its smile to the flower !
    Not niggard we give them ;—but why ?
Old Time must devour the year as the hour :
    Our trust is Eternity.

A CHRISTIAN MAID.

HER coral lip a sunbeam smote :
    Behind her shapely head

The white veil refluent seemed to float
  Like clouds in ether spread :
She looked so noble, sweet, and good,
  Love clapped his hands for glee,
And cried, ' This, this is Womanhood—
  The rest but female be ! '

So modest, yet confiding too,
  So tender to bestow
On each that loving honour due
  To all things, high or low,
Her soft self-reverence part had none
  In consciousness or pride,
A reflex of that worship won
  From her by all beside.

So creaturely in all her ways,
  So humbly great she seemed—
O Grecian lays, O Pagan praise,
  Of such ye never dreamed !
Through sunshine on she moved as one
  Innocuously possest
(Thy lot reversed, O Babylon !)
  By some angelic guest.

Buoyant as bird in leafy bower,
  As calm she looked as those
Who long have worn the nuptial flower
  Upon their matron brows :
Yet ten years hence, when girl and boy
  May mount her lap at will,
That virgin grace, that vestal joy
  Now hers will haunt her still !

A GIRL'S SONG.

UNKIND was he, the first who sang
  The spring-time shamed, the flower's decay !
What woman yet without a pang
  Could hear of Beauty's fleeting May ?
O Beauty ! with me bide, and I
A maid will live, a maid will die.

Could I be always fair as now,
  And hear, as now, the Poets sing
' The long-lashed eyes, the lustrous brow,
  The hand well worthy kiss and ring,'
Then, then some casual grace were all
That e'er from me on man should fall !

I sailed last night on Ina's stream :
  Warm 'mid the wave my fingers lay ;
The cold-lipped Naiad in my dream
  Kissed them, and sighed, and slipped away—
Ah me ! down life's descending tide
Best things, they say, the swiftliest glide.

YOUNG AND OLD.

DANCING, glancing, cheerily
  Thro' the mottled olive shades,
Singing, laughing, merrily,
  Gallant youths, and loving maids ;
Such is youth.   Beware, beware ;
Scorpions lurk 'neath blossoms fair !

Fainting, faltering, wearily
  Thro' the tangled forest's gloom ;
Gazing sadly, drearily,
  Round a desolated home ;
Such is age, last hour of night
Heralding the coming light.

Be true, be patient, steadily
  Fix aloft thy longing eyes ;
Accept thy burden readily ;
  Wait in faith the glad sunrise :
The wings of Christ's baptismal dove
Have cleared the path for truth and love
Thro' cloud and storm to God above.

S. E. DE VERE.

December, 1875.

FEBRUARY.

WHAT dost thou, laggard Daffodil,
  Tarrying so long beneath the sod ?
Hesper, thy mate, o'er yonder hill
  Looks down and strikes with silver rod
The pools that mirrored thee last year,
Yet cannot find thee far or near.

Pale Primrose ! for a smile of thine
  Gladly to earth these hands would pour
An ivied urn of purple wine,
  Such as at Naxos Bacchus bore,
Watching with fixed black eyes the while
That pirate bark draw near his isle !

Shake down, dark Pine, thy scalp of snow :
   False witch, stripped bare, grim Ash-tree tall !
Ye ivy masses that now swing slow
   Now shudder in spasms on the garden wall,
Shake down your load and the black mould strew ;
The rosemary borders and banks of rue.

The Robin, winter's Nightingale,
   Hung mute to-day on the blackthorn brake :
We heard but the water-fowl pipe and wail
   Fluting aloud on the lake ;
Who hears that bell-note so clear and free,
Though inland he stands, beholds the sea.

As the moon that rises of saffron hue
   Ascending, changes to white,
So the year, with the Daffodil rising new,
   On Narcissus will soon alight :
Rise up, thou Daffodil, rise ! With thee
The year begins, and the spring-tide glee !

'THE POSITIVE PHILOSOPHY;'

OR, THE EPICUREAN'S 'DOWNWARD WAY.'

Ye Twelve Olympians crowned for aye,
   Hurl back the Furies and the Fates !
Nightmares of Conscience, hence, away,
   Beyond your famed Tartarean Gates !

Ye laughing Gods of wood-recess
   That din the dusk with bounding hoof,
Drive back those Sceptred Twelve no less :
   Their starry stillness means Reproof.

Ye children, scare with cowslip ball
   Those Woodgods last! With idle breath
They mock that King who draggeth all
   Into his own dread silence—Death.

Faith darkens, Love distempers, life :
   The chaplets fade on Fancy's brow :
Come, Iris, with thy painless knife :
   The last of Gods, and best, art thou !

SAD MUSIC.

DESCEND into the depths forlorn
   Of this obscured and silent soul,
O Song ! With touch like beam of morn,
   Our spirits greet, and make them whole !

Blot thou base worlds, and make us see
   Those pitying Presences which stand
Round sensuous life perpetually,
   And beckon to the Spirit-land.

Teach us to feel the Truths we know :
   The shores we tend to—draw them nigh :
The things that leave us—bid them go
   With modulated movement by.

Song sad and sweet, the power be thine
   Breeze-like o'er life's suspended wreath
To sprinkle freshening dews benign,
   And waft us toward the gates of Death

With happier grace than his who reared
The mild Caducean wand, and led
O'er Lethe's wave, no longer feared,
The pensive Shades of Heroes dead.

ON VISITING A HAUNT OF COLERIDGE'S.

FROM Lynton, where the double streams
Through forest-hung ravines made way,
And bounded into seas late grey
That shook with morning's earliest beams,
I wandered on to Porlock bay ;

And thence, for love of him who sang
His happiest songs beside their rills,
To ' seaward Quantock's heathy hills ' [1]
Advanced, while lane and hedge-grove rang,
And all the song-birds ' had their wills.'

There, like a sweet face dimmed with pain,
The scene grew dark with mist and shower:
Its yellow leaf the autumnal bower
Moulted full fast; and as the rain
Washed the last fragrance from the flower

I heard the blue-robed schoolboy's tongue
Thrilling Christ's Hospital once more
With mythic chant and antique lore,
While round their Bard his playmates hung,
Wondering, and sighed, the witchery o'er.

[1] See Coleridge's ' Recollections of Love.'

I saw him tread soft Devon's coombes—
　　Ah! thence he drew that southern grace
　　Which in his songs held happy place
Amid their mystic northland glooms,
　　Like some strange flower of alien race.

That Bard who like a gleam, or strain
　　Of music, crossed at morn and eve
　　Those hills, who sang of Genevieve
And that weird Pilgrim from the main,
　　Not less at Truth's command could leave

Song's sheltered haunt the steeps to climb
　　Where, high o'er cloud and precipice,
　　Mind, throned among the seas of ice,
Watches from specular tower sublime
　　Far visions kenned through freezing skies,

Outlines of Thought, like hills through mist
　　That stretch athwart the Infinite
　　In dread mathesis lines of light—
Such Thoughts the Muse's spell resist;
　　Above her mark they wing their flight!

The songs he gave us, what were they
　　But preludes to some loftier rhyme
　　That would not leave the spheral chime,
The concords of eternal Day,
　　And speak itself in words of Time?

O ever-famished Heart!　O hands
　　That still ' drew nectar in a sieve ! '
　　At birth of thine what witch had leave
To bind such strength in willow bands,
　　The web half-woven to unweave?

O for those Orphic songs unheard
  That lived but in the Singer's thought !
  Who sinned ?   Whose hand the ruin wrought?
Unworthy was the world or Bard
  To clasp those Splendours all but caught ?

What Bard of all who e'er have sung
  Since that lark sang when Eve had birth,
  Song's inmost soul had uttered forth
Like thee ? from Song's asperge had flung
  Her lesser baptism o'er the earth ?

The world's base Poets have not kept
  ʹSong's vigil on her vestal height,
  Nor scorned false pride and foul delight,
Nor with the weepers rightly wept,
  Nor seen God's visions in the night !

Profane to enthrone the Sense, and add
  A gleam that lies to shapes that pass,
  Ah me ! in song as in a glass
They might have shown us glory-clad
  His Face Who ever is and was !

They might have shown us cloud and leaf
  Lit with the radiance uncreate ;
  Love, throned o'er vanquished Lust and Hate ;
Joy, gem-distilled through rocks of Grief ;
  And Justice conquering Time and Fate !

But they immodest brows have crowned
  With violated bud and flower :
  Courting the high Muse 'par amour,'
Upon her suppliants she hath frowned,
  And sent them darkness for a dower.

Better half-sight and tear-dimmed day
  Than dust-defiled, o'er-sated Touch !
  Better the torn wing than the crutch !
Better who hide their gift than they
  Who give so basely and so much.

Thy song was pure : thy heart was high :
  Thy genius in its strength was chaste :
  And if that genius ran to waste,
Unblemished as its native sky
  O'er diamond rocks the river raced !

Great Bard !   To thee in youth my heart
  Rushed as the maiden's to the boy,
  When love, too blithesome to be coy,
No want forebodes and feels no smart,
  A selfless love self-brimmed with joy !

Still sporting with those amaranth leaves
  That shape for others coronals,
  I ask not on whose head it falls
That crown the Fame Pandemian weaves—
  Thee, thee the Fame Uranian calls !

For wildered feet point thou the path
  Which mounts to where triumphant sit
  The Assumed of Earth, all human yet,
From sun-glare safe, and tempest's wrath,
  Who sing for love ; nor those forget,

The Elders crowned that, singing, fling
  Their crowns upon the Temple floor ;
  Those Elders ever young, though hoar,
Who count all praise an idle thing
  Save His who lives for evermore !

AUTUMNAL ODE.

DEDICATED TO MY SISTER.

OCTOBER 1867.

I.

MINSTREL and Genius, to whose songs or sighs
  The round earth modulates her changeful sphere,
That bend'st in shadow from yon western skies,
  And lean'st, cloud-hid, along the woodlands sere,
  Too deep thy notes too pure for mortal ear!
    Yet Nature hears them: without aid of thine
    How sad were her decline!
From thee she learns with just and soft gradation
  Her dying hues in death to harmonise;
  Through thee her obsequies
A glory wear that conquers desolation.
Through thee she singeth, 'Faithless were the sighing
Breathed o'er a beauty only born to fleet:
A holy thing and precious is the dying
Of that whose life was innocent and sweet.'
From many a dim retreat
  Lodged on high-bosomed, echoing mountain lawn,
  Or chiming convent 'mid dark vale withdrawn,
From cloudy shrine or rapt oracular seat
Voices of loftier worlds that saintly strain repeat.

II.

It is the Autumnal Epode of the year:
  The nymphs that urge the seasons on their round,
They to whose green lap flies the startled deer
  When bays the far-off hound,
They that drag April by the rain-bright hair,
(Though sun-showers daze her and the rude winds
    scare)

O'er March's frosty bound,
They by whose warm and furtive hand unwound
    The cestus falls from May's new-wedded breast,
Silent they stand beside dead Summer's bier,
    With folded palms, and faces to the West,
And their loose tresses sweep the dewy ground.

III.

A sacred stillness hangs upon the air,
    A sacred clearness. Distant shapes draw nigh:
Glistens yon Elm grove, to its heart laid bare,
    And all articulate in its symmetry,
    With here and there a branch that from on high
Far flashes washed in wan and watery gleam:
Beyond, the glossy lake lies calm—a beam
Upheaved, as if in sleep, from its slow central stream.

IV.

This quiet, is it Truth, or some fair mask?
    Is pain no more? Shall Sleep be lord, not Death?
Shall sickness cease to afflict and overtask
    The spent and labouring breath?
Is there 'mid all yon farms and fields, this day,
    No grey old head that drops? No darkening eye?
Spirits of Pity, lift your hands, and pray—
    Each hour, alas, men die!

V.

The love songs of the Blackbird now are done:
    Upon the o'er-grown, loose, red-berried cover
The latest of late warblers sings as one
        That trolls at random when the feast is over:
        From bush to bush the dusk-bright cobwebs hover,
            Silvering the dried-up rill's exhausted urn;

No breeze is fluting o'er the green morass :
Nor falls the thistle-down : in deep-drenched grass,
    Now blue, now red, the shifting dew-gems burn.

VI.

Mine ear thus torpid held, methinks mine eye
    Is armed the more with visionary power :
    As with a magnet's force each redd'ning bower
Compels me through the woodland pageantry :
Slowly I track the forest's skirt : emerging,
    Slowly I climb from pastoral steep to steep :
I see far mists from reedy valleys surging :
    I follow the procession of white sheep
    That fringe with wool old stock and ruined rath,
How staid to-day, how eager when the lambs
Went leaping round their dams !
I cross the leaf-choked stream from stone to stone,
    Pass the hoar ash-tree, trace the upland path,
The furze-brake that in March all golden shone
    Reflected in the shy kingfisher's bath.

VII.

No more from full-leaved woods that music swells
    Which in the summer filled the satiate ear :
A fostering sweetness still from bosky dells
    Murmurs ; but I can hear
A harsher sound when down, at intervals,
The dry leaf rattling falls.
Dark as those spots which herald swift disease
The death-blot marks for death the leaf yet firm :
Beside the leaf down-trodden trails the worm :
    In forest depths the haggard, whitening grass
Repines at youth departed.   Half-stripped trees
    Reveal, as one who says, ' Thou too must pass,'

Plainlier each day their quaint anatomies.
Yon Poplar grove is troubled ! Bright and bold
Babbled his cold leaves in the July breeze
As though above our heads a runnel rolled :
   His mirth is o'er : subdued by old October
   He counts his lessening wealth, and, sadly sober,
Tinkles his minute tablets of wan gold.

VIII.

Be still, ye sighs of the expiring year !
   A sword there is : ye play but with the sheath !
Whispers there are more piercing, yet more dear
   Than yours, that come to me those boughs be-
      neath ;
And well-remembered footsteps known of old
   Tread soft the mildewed mould.
O magic memory of the things that were ;
   Of those whose hands our childish locks carest,
Of one so angel-like in tender care,
   Of one in majesty so godlike drest ;
O phantom faces painted on the air
   Of friend or sudden guest :—
I plead in vain :
The woods revere, but cannot heal my pain :
Ye sheddings from the Yew-tree and the Pine,
   If on your rich and aromatic dust
      I laid my forehead, and my hands put forth
In the last beam that warms the forest floor,
No answer to my yearnings would be mine,
To me no answer through those branches hoar
   Would reach in noontide trance or moony gust !
      Her secret Heaven would keep, and mother
      Earth
Speak from her deep heart—' Where thou know'st
   not, trust ! '

A A 2

IX.

That pang is past.   Once more my pulses keep
    A tenor calm, that knows nor grief nor joy ;
Once more I move as one that died in sleep,
    And treads, a Spirit, the haunts he trod, a boy,
And sees them like-unlike, and sees beyond :
Then earthly life comes back, and I despond.
Ah life, not life !   Dim woods of crimsoned beech
    That swathe the hills in sacerdotal stoles,
Burn on, burn on ! the year ere long will reach
    That day made holy to Departed Souls,
The day whereon man's heart, itself a priest,
    Descending to that Empire pale wherein
    Beauty and Sorrow dwell, but pure from Sin,
Holds with God's Church at once its fast and feast.
Dim woods, they, they alone your vaults should tread,
The sad and saintly Dead !
Your pathos those alone ungrieved could meet
    Who fit them for the Beatific Vision :
The things which, as they pass us, seem to cheat,
    To them would be a music-winged fruition,
    A cadence sweetest in its soft subsiding :
    Transience to them were dear ;—for theirs the
      abiding—
Dear as that Pain which clears from fleshly film
    The spirit's eye, matures each spirit-germ,
    Frost-bound on earth, but at the appointed term
Mirror of Godhead in the immortal realm.

X.

Lo there the regal Exiles !—under shades
    Deeper than ours, yet in a finer air—
Climbing, successive, elders, youths, and maids,
    The penitential mountain's ebon stair :

The earth-shadow clips that halo round their hair :
And as lone outcasts watch a moon that wanes,
Receding slowly o'er their native plains,
 Thus watch they, wistful, something far but fair.
  Serene they stand, and wait,
  Self-banished by the ever-open gate :
Awhile self-banished from the All-pitying Eyes,
Lest mortal stain should blot their Paradise.
Silent they pace, ascending high and higher
 The hills of God, a hand on every heart
That willing burns, a vase of cleansing fire
 Fed by God's love in souls from God apart :
Each lifted face with thirst of long desire
  Is pale ; but o'er it grows a mystic sheen,
  Because on them God's face, by them unseen,
Is turned, through narrowing darkness hourly nigher.

XI.

Sad thoughts, why roam ye thus in your unrest
 The bourne unseen ? Why scorn our mortal
  bound ?
Is it not kindly, Earth's maternal breast ?
 Is it not fair, her head with vine-wreaths crowned ?
Farm-yard and barn are heaped with golden store ;
 High piled the sheaves illume the russet plain ;
Hedges and hedge-row trees are yellowed o'er
 With waifs and trophies of the labouring wain :
Why murmur, ' Change is change, when downward
  ranging ;
Spring's upward change but pointed to the un-
  changing ? '
Yet, O how just your sorrow, if ye knew
The true grief's sanction true !

'Tis not the thought of parting youth that moves us;
   'Tis not alone the pang for friends departed :
The Autumnal pain that raises while it proves us
   Wells from a holier source and deeper-hearted !
For this a sadness swells above our mirth;
   For this a bitter runs beneath the sweetness;
     The throne that shakes not is the Spirit's right ;
     The heart and hope of Man are infinite ;
Heaven is his home, and, exiled here on earth,
   Completion most betrays the incompleteness !

XII.

Heaven is his home.—But hark! the breeze in-
   creases :
   The sunset forests, catching sudden fire,
   Flash, swell, and sing, a million-organed choir :
Roofing the West, rich clouds in glittering fleeces
     O'erarch ethereal spaces and divine
     Of heaven's clear hyaline.
No dream is this !   Beyond that radiance golden
   God's Sons I see, His armies bright and strong,
The ensanguined Martyrs here with palms high
   holden,
   The Virgins there, a lily-lifting throng !
The Splendours nearer draw.   In choral blending
   The Prophets' and the Apostles' chant I hear;
I see the Salem of the Just descending
   With gates of pearl and diamond bastions sheer.
The walls are agate and chalcedony :
   On jacinth street and jasper parapet
The unwaning light is light of Deity,
   Not beam of lessening moon or suns that set.
That indeciduous forestry of spires
   Lets fall no leaf ! those lights can never range :

Saintly fruitions and divine desires
   Are blended there in rapture without change.
—Man was not made for things that leave us,
   For that which goeth and returneth,
For hopes that lift us yet deceive us,
   For love that wears a smile yet mourneth;
Not for fresh forests from the dead leaves springing,
   The cyclic re-creation which, at best,
Yields us—betrayal still to promise clinging—
   But tremulous shadows of the realm of rest:
      For things immortal Man was made,
    God's Image, latest from His hand,
      Co-heir with Him, Who in Man's flesh arrayed
    Holds o'er the worlds the Heavenly-Human wand:
His portion this—sublime
To stand where access none hath Space or Time,
Above the starry host, the Cherub band,
To stand—to advance—and after all to stand!

NOTES

NOTES.

Preface, p. xxvi. *The interior life of a nation.*

A NATION has its inward life no less than an individual, and from this its outward life also is characterised. For what does a nation effect by war, but either the securing of its existence or the increasing of its power? We honour the heroism shown in accomplishing these objects; but power, nay, even existence, are not ultimate ends; the question may be asked of every created being why he should live at all, and no satisfactory answer can be given, if his life does not, by doing God's will, consciously or unconsciously tend to God's glory and to the good of his brethren. And if a nation's annals contain the record of deeds ever so heroic, done in defence of the national freedom or existence, still we may require that the freedom or the life so bravely maintained should be also employed for worthy purposes; or else even the names of Thermopylæ and of Morgarten become in after years a reproach rather than a glory.'—Dr. ARNOLD'S *Lectures on Modern History*, p. 11.

Page 55. *In Benchor the holy, in Aran the blest.*

The testimony of the Venerable Bede respecting the sanctity of the Irish race after its conversion, and its missions in England and Scotland, especially those of the monks from Iona, is not only interesting in itself, but singularly touching from the picture which it presents of friendship between two nations in later times so constantly at variance. He tells us how King Oswald of Northumbria, who had himself at an earlier period found a refuge in Ireland, sent thither for missionaries—how St. Aidan came at his prayer—how, while the Saint preached, the King interpreted his discourses—how Aidan was made Bishop of Lindisfarne and was succeeded there by St. Finan and St. Colman, also Irish monks. He tells us how the Irish monk, Columba, was the first preacher of Christianity among the Picts to the north of the mountains. He tells us how, at a later time, Adamnan, one of St. Columba's successors at Iona, and, thirteen years afterwards, the Irish clergy at Iona, and many elsewhere, adopted that later Roman time for celebrating Easter, which had been introduced into England by the Anglo-Saxon mission of Augustine, but had at first been resisted as an innovation both by the Irish clergy, and by such priests of the early British church (founded, as he records, by missionaries sent from Pope Eleutherus) as survived the sword of the Saxons. His expressions on this subject are striking. This correction, in the Irish, of those two points relating to discipline in which alone they erred, he says, 'appears to have been accomplished by a wonderful dispensation of the Divine goodness, to the end that the *same nation* which had willingly and without envy communicated to the *English people* the knowledge of the true Deity, should afterwards, by means of the English nation, be brought, where they were defective, to the true rule of life. Even as, on the contrary, the Britons, who would not acquaint the English with the knowledge of the Christian faith, now, when the English people enjoy the true faith, and are thoroughly instructed in its rules, continue inveterate in their errors, *expose their heads without a crown, and keep the solemnity of Christ without the society of the Church.*' The mode of making the tonsure was the second point in dispute.

Bede is copious in his references also to the continental missions of the Irish, as well as to the multitudes of English and others who retired to Ireland 'either for the sake of divine studies, or of a more continent life.' The early Irish usage, as regards the time for celebrating Easter, was not, as has been inaccurately stated, the Oriental usage, but the one originally practised at Rome, whence, as Bede tells us, Palladius was sent to the Irish 'that believed in Christ, to be their bishop, A.D. 431.' The Irish were at first reluctant to change even a matter of discipline which they associated with their earlier saints; but this opposition, as Bede tells us, gave way gradually to argument, to a desire to be at one mind with the rest of the Church, and to their respect for the Holy See. He says that the 'Scoti which dwell in the south of Ireland had long since, by the admonition of the Apostolic See, learned to observe Easter according to the canonical customs.' The Irish he calls by their name of 'Scoti,' for so many centuries theirs, and the record, as was supposed, of their *Scythian* descent.

There is no other example of a nation devoting itself to spiritual things with an ardour and a success comparable to that which distinguished Ireland. During the first three centuries after her conversion to Christianity she resembled one vast monastery. Statements so extraordinary that if they came from Irish sources only they might be supposed to have originated in national vanity, have reached us in such numbers from the records of foreign nations under whose altars the relics of Irish saints and founders repose, that upon this point there remains no difference of opinion among the learned. For ordinary readers the subject is illustrated perhaps most briefly by modern historians. According to Montalembert more than two-thirds of England in the Saxon time were converted to Christianity by the Irish monks, or reconverted after a relapse into Paganism.[1] He remarks that the great English Saint, Wilfrid, had been a pupil of the Irish monks at Lindisfarne ('la résidence des seize premiers évêques de la Northumbrie.') He tells us how Aidan, the Irish bishop, made of Lindisfarne an eastern Iona, how he redeemed the young Saxon children from slavery and instructed them in the Christian faith. His details respecting the conversion of Scotland are not less interesting. 'Tout le monde s'accorde à lui (St. Columba) attribuer la conversion des Pictes du Nord et l'introduction ou le rétablissement de la foi chez les Pictes du Midi et les

---

[1] *Les Moines d'Occident*, vol. iv. p. 121.

Scots de l'Ouest.' To this period he ascribes the foundation of the monasteries at Old Melrose, Abercorn, Tynning-
ham, and Coldigham ; and to an Irish origin he refers the
Round Towers of Brechin and Abernethy, and those foundations, consisting of huge stones joined without cement, found
at St. Kilda, and elsewhere among the Hebrides.

Mr. Moore enumerates many monuments of early Irish
missions, as the tomb of the Irish priest Caidoc, in the
monastery of Centula in Ponthieu, and the hermitage of St.
Fiacre, to which Anne of Austria, in the year 1641, made
her pilgrimage on foot. He records the labours of St. Fursa
among the East Angles, and afterwards in France, and of
his brothers Ultan and Foillan in Brabant ; of St. Livin in
Ghent ; of St. Fridolin beside the Rhine. He refers to the
two Irishmen successively bishops of Strasburg, St. Arbo-
gast, and St. Florentius to the two brothers Erard and
Albert, whose tombs were long shown at Ratisbon ; to St.
Wiro, to whom Pepin used to confess, barefooted ; to St.
Kilian, the great apostle of Franconia, who consummated
his labours by martyrdom, and who is still honoured at
Wurzburg as its patron saint. He c ommemorates Catal-
dus, patron of Tarentum, and at one period an ornament of
the celebrated school of Lismore, and Virgilius, or Feargal,
denounced to the Pope by Boniface as a heretic for having
anticipated at that early period the discovery of the 'anti-
podes,' and maintained 'that there was another world, and
other men under the earth.' This great man propagated
the Gospel among the Carinthians. He records the selection
by Charlemagne of two Irishmen, Clement and Albinus, one
of whom he placed at the head of a seminary founded by
him in France, while the other presided over a similar insti-
tution at Pavia; a third Irishman, Dungal, being especially
consulted by the same prince on account of his astronomical
knowledge. This celebrated teacher carried on a controversy
with Claudius, Bishop of Turin, who had revived the heterodox
opinions of Vigilantius against the veneration of the saints.
He bequeathed to the monastery of Bobbio his library, the
greater part of which is still preserved at Milan.

The progress of Ireland's Christianity is briefly but com-
prehensively narrated also in Mr. Haverty's *History of*

Ireland :—' Among the great ecclesiastical schools or monasteries founded in Ireland about this time (the fifth century),
were those of St. Ailbe of Emly, of St. Benignus of Armagh,
of St. Fiech of Sletty, of St. Mel of Ardagh, of St. Mochay
of Antrim, of St. Moctheus of Louth, of St. Ibar of Beg-Erin,
of St. Asicus of Elphin, and of St. Olcan of Derkan.'—P. 78.
' The most celebrated of them, founded early in the sixth
century, were Clonard in Meath, founded by St. Finan or
Finian ; Clonmacnoise, on the banks of the Shannon, in
the King's County, founded in the same century by St.
Kiaran, called the Carpenter's Son ; Bennchor, or Bangor, in
the Ards of Ulster, founded by St. Comgall in the year 558,
and Lismore in Waterford, founded by St. Carthach, or
Mochuda, about the year 633.   These and many other Irish
schools attracted a vast concourse of students, the pupils of
a single school often numbering from one to three thousand,
several of whom came from Britain, Gaul, and other countries, drawn thither by the reputation for sanctity and learning which Ireland enjoyed throughout Europe.'—P. 91.
' Scarcely an island round the coast, or in the lakes of
the interior, or a valley, or any solitary spot, could be found
which, like the deserts of Egypt and Palestine, was not
inhabited by fervent cœnobites and anchorites.'—P. 92.
After various quotations from eminent foreign authorities,
as Erie of Auxerre, and Tierry, Mr. Haverty proceeds :—
Stephen White (*Apologia*, p. 24) thus sums up the labours
of the Irish saints on the Continent :—" Among the names
of saints whom Ireland formerly sent forth there were, as I
have learned from the trustworthy writings of the ancients,
150 now honoured as patrons of places in Germany, of whom
36 were martyrs ; 45 Irish patrons in the Gauls, of whom 6
were martyrs ; at least 30 in Belgium ; 44 in England ; 13
in Italy ; and in Norway and Iceland 8 martyrs, beside
many others."   It has been calculated that the ancient Irish
monks had 13 monastic foundations in Scotland, 12 in
England, 7 in France, 12 in Armoric Gaul, 7 in Lotharingia,
11 in Burgundy, 9 in Belgium, 10 in Alsatia, 16 in Bavaria, 6
in Italy, and 15 in Rhetia, Helvetia, and Suavia, besides
many in Thuringia, and on the left margin of the Rhine
between Gueldres and Alsatia.'—P. 108.   Even after the

Danish invasion Ireland continued to found her religious establishments in foreign countries :—'A few Irish monks settled at Glastonbury, and for their support began to teach the rudiments of sacred and secular knowledge. One of the earliest and most illustrious of their pupils was the great St. Dunstan, who, under the tuition of these Irishmen, became skilful in philosophy, music, and other accomplishments. . . . St. Cadroc, the son of a king of the Albanian Scoti, was at the same time in Ireland, studying in the schools of Armagh.'—P. 154. Mr. Haverty gives also an interesting account of the Culdees of Ireland, 'religious persons resembling very much members of the tertiary orders of St. Dominic and St. Francis in the Catholic church at the present day, or one of the great religious confraternities of modern times.'— P. 110. He also explains those abuses, the cause of so much misconception, by which the great chiefs occasionally usurped and transmitted, though not in Holy Orders, the titles and estates of the richer bishoprics, the spiritual duties of which were vicariously discharged by churchmen, as has happened more frequently at a later time in the case of parishes appropriated by lay rectors.

Page 55. *In Alba were children ; we sent her a man.*

Recording this Irish settlement Sir Walter Scott writes thus (*History of Scotland*, vol. i. p. 7):—'In the fifth century there appear in North Britain two powerful and distinct tribes, who are not before named in history. These were the Picts and the Scots. . . . The Scots, on the other hand, were of Irish origin ; for, to the great confusion of ancient history, the inhabitants of Ireland, those at least of the conquering and predominating caste, were called Scots. A colony of these Irish Scots, distinguished by the name of Dalriads, or Dalreudini, natives of Ulster, had early attempted a settlement on the coast of Argyleshire ; they finally established themselves there under Fergus, the son of Eric, about the year 503, and, recruited by colonies from Ulster, continued to multiply and increase until they formed a nation which occupied the western side of Scotland.'— Vol. i. p. 11. 'A much more important struggle, then, than 'that between the Saxons and the Picts was maintained between the latter nation and the Scoto-Irish inhabiting, as we have seen, the western, as the Picts held the eastern, side of the Island. It was indeed evident that until these two large portions of North Britain should be united under one government the security of the country against foreign invaders was not to be relied on. After many desperate battles, much effusion of blood, and a merciless devastation of both countries, some measures seem to have been taken for settling a lasting peace betwixt these contending nations. Urgaria, sister of Ungus, King of Picts, was married to Aycha IV., King of Scots, and their son Alpine, succeeding his father as King of Scots, flourished from 833 to 836, in which last year he was slain, urging some contests in Galloway. The Pictish throne, thus thrown open for want of an heir male, was claimed by Kenneth, son and successor of Alpine, who, as descended from Urgaria, the sister of Ungus, urged his right of inheritance with an army. Wrad, the last of the Pictish monarchs, died at Forteviot, in 842, fighting in defence of his capital and kingdom, and the Pictish people were subdued. . . . So complete must have been the revolution, that the very language of the Picts is lost, and what language they spoke is a subject of doubt to antiquarians. . . . When Kenneth MacAlpine joined in his person the crowns both of the Picts and Scots, he became an adversary fit to meet and match with the warlike Saxons. The country united under his sway, was then called *for the first time* Scotland. . . . Kenneth MacAlpine was the twenty-ninth in descent from Fergus, son of Eric, first of the race.' Fergus entered Scotland (then Alba) A.D. 503, in support of the Dalriad Colony; but it was about the close of the second century that that colony was led from Antrim into Scotland by Carbry Riada, named Reuda by Bede, from whom the Dalriada derived their name.

Page 56. *Her kings are our blood, and she crowns them*
at Scone.

' Malcolm IV., at the age of twelve years, succeeded to his excellent grandfather, David I., in 1153. Being a Celtic prince, succeeding to a people of whom the great proportion were Celts, he was inaugurated at Scone with the peculiar ceremonies belonging to the Scoto-Irish race. In compliance with their ancient customs, he was placed upon a fated stone, dedicated to this solemn use, and brought for that purpose from Ireland, by Fergus, the son of Eric. An Iro-Scottish, or Highland bard, also stepped forward and chanted to the people a Gaelic poem, containing a catalogue of the young king's ancestors, from the reign of the same Fergus, founder of the dynasty.' (Sir W. Scott's *History of Scotland*, vol. i. p. 34.) He proceeds to record the removal, by Edward I. of the stone of Destiny from Scone to Westminster Abbey, where it still supports the chair of Edward the Confessor, used at coronations. From Kenneth, and the succeeding Scotch kings of Irish race, Robert Bruce was descended, and consequently the Stuarts, and our existing Royal House.

Mr. Moore quotes a host of early writers, most of them Scotch, who record the Irish immigration into Scotland, Innes, Pinkerton, Usher, Chalmers, Mackenzie, John Major, Hector Boece, Leslie, Buchanan, Bishops Lloyd and Stillingfleet, and amusingly illustrates the last attempt to mystify that event, or at least ignore it, namely, MacPherson's attempt to pass off, in his new version, Irish Ossianic fragments which of course had found their way wherever the Irish race made settlements, as poetry native to the Highlands. Sir W. Scott's tribute to Ossian, Fingal, and the other Irish heroes of their age, in his poem on visiting Ulster, is conclusive as to his opinion respecting this brilliant endeavour to change Irish ballads, still recited on the mountains and coasts of Western Ireland, into Scotch epics of the third century. It is remarkable that a man of MacPherson's genius did not perceive that Ossianic fragments were not likely to gain in verisimilitude by being invested with structural completeness, and with three qualities of all others the least characteristic of Gaelic poetry, viz. the stilted, the self-conscious, and the epigrammatic.

Page 57. *The blood of O'Ruark is on Lacy's wall.*

Tiernan O'Rourke was treacherously slain by Hugh de Lacy at a conference. In 1317 the De Lacys joined the standard of Edward Bruce. John de Lacy fell into the hands of the Lord Justice, and was sentenced to be pressed to death.

Page 61. *The Scythian Parricide.*

Parthalon. According to the legend he fled from his country, where he had been guilty of parricide, and founded the first colony in Ireland. It was swept off by pestilence after the lapse of 300 years.

Page 61. *I, Fintan the Bard, was living then.*

The bards claimed a sort of poetical immortality. They were superior to the injuries of time, and spoke as if they had witnessed what they recorded.

.

Page 61. *Hymn on the founding of the Abbey of St. Thomas.*

'The celebrated Abbey of St. Thomas the Martyr was founded in Dublin by Fitz-Adelm, by order of Henry II. The site was the place now called Thomas' Court. In the presence of Cardinal Vivian and St. Laurence O'Toole the Deputy endowed it with a carucate of land called Donore.' —HAVERTY'S *History of Ireland*, p. 222.

Page 63. *Dead is the Prince of the Silver Hand.*

This belongs to the legendary, not the historical, portion of the Irish annals. Before the establishment of the great Milesian or Gaelic race in Ireland, the monarchy of which expired with Roderick, the country had been successively possessed by two races, the Firbolgs and the Tuatha de Danann. Nuad 'of the Silver Hand' was the leader of the Tuatha de Danann, who are said by the bards to have landed in Ireland A.M. 3303. Eochy, the last of the Firbolgic kings, was slain by them; and a cairn still shown on the sea-coast near Sligo is said to be his grave.

The invasion of the Tuatha de Danann is thus recorded by a recent historian :—'According to the superstitious ideas of the bards, these Tuatha de Danann were profoundly skilled in magic, and rendered themselves invisible to the inhabitants until they had penetrated into the heart of the country. In other words, they landed under the cover of a fog or mist; and the Firbolgs, at first taken by surprise, made no regular stand until the new-comers had marched almost across Ireland, when the two armies met face to face on the plain of Moyturey, near the shore of Lough Corrib, in part of the ancient territory of Partry. Here a battle was fought, in which the Firbolgs were overthrown, "with the greatest slaughter," says an old writer, "that was ever heard of in Ireland at one meeting." . . . The scattered fragments of his (Eochy's) army took refuge in the northern isle of Aran, Rathlin Island, the Hebrides, the Isle of Man, and Britain. . . . The victorious Nuad lost his hand in this battle, and a silver hand was made for him by Credne Cerd, the artificer, and fitted on him by the physician Diencecht, whose son, Miach, improved the work, according to the legend, by infusing feeling and motion into every joint of the artificial hand, as if it had been a natural one.'—HAVERTY'S *History of Ireland*, p. 5.

Twenty-seven years later Nuad was killed in battle by Balor ' of the mighty blows,' a Fomorian. The sway of the Tuatha de Danann is said to have lasted for 197 years, when it was terminated by the immigration of the Milesian race. Dr. O'Donovan says (*Four Masters*, vol. i. p. 24):—' From the many monuments ascribed to this colony by tradition, and in ancient Irish historical tales, it is quite evident that they were a real people; and from their having been considered gods and magicians by the Gaedhil, or Scoti, who subdued them, it may be inferred that they were skilled in arts which the latter did not understand. . . . It appears from a very curious and ancient Irish tract, written in the shape of a dialogue between St. Patrick and Caoilte Mac Ronain, that there were very many places in Ireland where the Tuatha de Danann were then supposed to live as sprites or fairies, with corporeal and material forms, but endued with immortality. The inference naturally to be drawn from these stories is that the Tuatha de Danann lingered in the country for many centuries after their subjection by the Gaedhil, and that they lived in retired situations, where they practised abstruse arts, which induced the others to regard them as magicians.'

The Tuatha de Danann are chiefly remembered in con· nection with two circumstances. They are asserted to have carried into Ireland the far-famed 'Lia Fail,' or 'Stone of Destiny,' and they gave Ireland her name. The three names by which Ireland was called in early years—Eire, Banba, and Fodhla—were assigned to her in consequence of their belonging to the wives of the three last kings of the Tuatha de Danann race, each of whom reigned successively during a single year. These three queens were slain in the battle fought by the Milesians against the Tuatha de Danann at Tailtinn, or Teltown, in Meath ; the Irish queens being accustomed in the pagan times to lead their armies to battle. The Tuatha de Dananns seem to have easily kept the Firbolgs, a pastoral people, in subjection, being, though inferior to them in numbers, far superior in civilisation. 'It is pro- bable,' says Mr. Haverty, 'that by the Tuatha de Dananns mines were first worked in Ireland ; and it is generally believed that they were the artificers of those beautifully shaped bronze swords and spear-heads that have been found in Ireland, and of which so many fine specimens may be seen in the Museum of the Royal Irish Academy. . . . There is evidence to show that the vast mounds or artificial hills of Drogheda, Knowth, Dowth, and New Grange, along the banks of the Boyne, with several minor tumuli in the same neighbourhood, were erected as the tombs of Tuatha de Danann kings and chieftains ; and as such they only rank after the pyramids of Egypt for the stupendous efforts which were required to raise them. As to the Firbolgs, it is doubtful whether there are any monuments remain· ing of their first sway in Ireland ; but the famous Dun Angus, and other great stone forts in the islands of Aran, are well-authenticated remnants of their military struc- tures of the period of the Christian era, or thereabouts.'— P. 20.

Page 63. *Ere lived Milesius they ruled the land.*

According to Charles O'Connor the last of the three early invasions of Ireland, that of the Milesians, took place not

much earlier or later than B.C. 760, that is, at about the
period of the foundation of Rome. This computation seems
more probably correct than that of the *Four Masters*, or
that of the *Ogygia*, which refers it to a period more ancient.
Distinguishing between the main facts respecting this immigration, and the various adornments which they received
from the bardic fancy of later times, we arrive at these
results. The six sons of Milesius King of Spain, or of the
Gadelian portion of Spain, after his death, sailed to Ireland
accompanied by his widow Scota, in part to avenge the
death of Ith, a prince of the same race who had some time
previously landed on the coast of Donegal, and been put to
death as a pirate by the Tuatha de Danann. The names of
the brothers were Heber, Colpa, Amergin, Ir, Donn, and
Heremon. From their ancestor, Gaedhuil Glas, this race
had long been known by the name of Gaedhil, Gadelian, and
Gael; by the last of these names their descendants in Ireland were called, as well as by the name of Scoti. The following account of their earlier fortunes is given by Mr.
Haverty :—' The Tuatha de Danann confessed that they were
not prepared to resist them, having no standing army, but
said that if they again embarked, and could make good a
landing according to the rules of war, the country should be
theirs. Amergin, who was the Olav, or learned man and
judge of the expedition, having been appealed to, decided
against his own people, and they accordingly re-embarked
at the southern extremity of Ireland, and withdrew the
distance of "nine waves" from the shore. No sooner had
they done so than a terrific storm commenced, raised (as
the bards affirmed) by the magic arts of the Tuatha de
Danann, and the Milesian fleet was completely scattered.
Several of the ships, among them those of Donn and Ir,
were lost off different parts of the coast. Heremon sailed
round by the north-east, and landed at the mouth of the
Boyne (called Inver Colpa from one of the brothers who was
drowned there), and others landed at Inver Scene, so called
from Scene Dubsaine, the wife of Amergin, who perished in
that river. In the first battle fought with the Tuatha de
Danann, at Slieve Mish, near Tralee, the latter were
defeated; but among the killed was Scota, the wife of

Milesius, who was buried in the place since called from her Glen-Scoheen.'—P. 13. The sway of the Milesians was soon acknowledged, and they formed alliances with the races which had preceded them in Ireland. The Firbolgs, from whom many of the race still existing in the west of Ireland are descended, were allowed to retain some of their ancient territories. The people of southern Ireland are regarded as chiefly the descendants of Heber, while many of the families of Leinster and Connaught, the Hi Nials of Ulster, &c., claim descent from Heremon.

Page 64. *The Faithful Norman.*

Maurice de Prendergast.

Page 66. *They fought ere sunrise at Tor Conainn.*

This battle, recorded in the legendary lore of Ireland, is the chief memorial of two early races supposed to have existed there before the Firbolg period,—that of the Nemedians, said to have come from the borders of the Euxine, and that of the Fomorians. The latter race are thought to have been pirates from Scandinavia. Their memory is preserved in the 'Giant's Causeway,' the Irish name of which is Cloghanna-Fomharaigh, or 'Stepping Stones of the Fomorians.' Nearly the whole Nemedian army having been drowned by the sea in this battle, which was fought on the coast of Donegal, about A.M. 3066, the survivors of the Nemedian race escaped over the sea, and Ireland is said to have remained nearly a wilderness for 200 years, till the arrival of the Firbolgs. But such narratives belong rather to the romance than the history of Ireland.

Page 78. *'Twas a holy time when the Kings, long foemen.*

Malachi, who fought under the great Brian Borumha at Clontarf, where the Danish power in Ireland was overthrown for ever, had himself been King of all Ireland, but allowed himself to be deposed, A.D. 1003, and his rival to be elevated in his place.

Page 78. *'Thou shalt not be a Priest,'* he said.

Conall Creevan, a brother of Laeghaire, King of Ireland,
was one of St. Patrick's earliest converts, and became his devoted follower. He asked permission to become a Priest;
but the Saint commanded him to remain a soldier. The
shield marked with the sign of the Cross was ever after
called 'Sciath-Bachlach,' or the Shield of the Crosier. This
is stated by Dr. O'Donovan to be the earliest authentic notice
found of armorial bearings in Ireland.

Page 86. *The Dirge of Edward Bruce.*

The time when Ireland seems to have been most near to
becoming once more an independent kingdom was A.D.
1315.   The Irish Princes offered the throne to Edward
Bruce, who was descended, in the female line, from those
kings of Irish race who had so long ruled over Scotland.
He arrived in Ireland with an army of 6,000 men, landing at
Larne, and, on being joined by the Irish Chiefs, marched
nearly round the whole island, defeating the Lord Justice,
Butler, and subsequently Sir Roger Mortimer, who encountered him with 15,000 men. In 1317 he crossed the Boyne,
accompanied by his great brother, Robert Bruce, at the
head of 20,000 men, and marched as far as Limerick. A
terrible famine and pestilence prevented his doing more,
and his brother returned to Scotland. The next year,
October 14, he encountered, at Faughard, the army levied by
the Norman nobles, and commanded by Birmingham. In
the beginning of the battle an Anglo-Irish Knight, John
Maupas, rushed through a host of foes, and engaged in
single combat with Edward Bruce. Both warriors fell;
and the body of one was found lying on that of the other.

Page 87. *The tanist succeeds when the king is dust.*

According to the Irish law the king, far from being able
to alienate his kingdom, had but a life interest in the sovereignty. His son did not succeed to the crown. The sovereignty was vested in a particular family as representing

the clan or race. Within certain limits of kindred in that family the king was chosen by election; and at the same period his Tanist, or successor.

Page 87. *Brave Art MacMurrough! Arise, 'tis morn.*

The unconquerable king of Leinster. Though his terri- tories were surrounded by the Norman settlements, he maintained their independence against all the efforts of the Lords of the Pale and of the Lords Justices. King Richard II. marched against him to Kilkenny, but succeeded in nothing more than burning the villages in the forests. Richard swore by St. Edward that he would not depart out of Ireland till he had MacMurrough in his hands, dead or alive; but his attempt cost him his kingdom, as the Usurper, Henry IV., took advantage of his absence from England to dethrone him. The Irish king is thus described by a French chronicler, Creton, who accompanied Richard:—' From a mountain between two woods we saw MacMurrough de- scending, accompanied by multitudes of the Irish, and mounted upon a horse without a saddle, which cost him, it was reported, 400 cows. His horse was fair, and, in his de- scent from the hill to us, ran as swiftly as any stag, hare, or the swiftest beast I have seen. In his right hand he bore a long spear, which, when near the spot where he was to meet the Earl, he cast from him with much dexterity. The crowd that followed him then remained behind, while he advanced to meet the Earl near a small brook. He was tall of stature, well composed, strong, and active; his countenance fierce and cruel.' Richard II. effected little in Ireland beyond conferring the titles of Duke of Ireland and Marquess of Dublin upon Robert de Vere, Earl of Oxford, his favourite.

Page 88. *From the heart of the nation her king is grown.*

The Irish kings had never forfeited this high claim. Those princes who, in the southern half of Ireland, sub- mitted to Henry II., whether voluntarily or by compulsion, acknowledged him solely as a suzerain. Thus Leland says (*History of Ireland*, vol. i. p. 78):—' They stipulated to

become his vassals and tributaries. He was to protect them
in the administration of their petty governments according
to their own model.' He then quotes Sir John Davies : ' By
the Brehon law they governed their people; they made
their own magistrates and officers : they pardoned and
punished all malefactors within their several countries ; they
made war and peace, one with another, without controlment ; and this they did, not only during the reign of Henry
II., but afterwards in all times until the reign of Queen
Elizabeth.'   Thus again the author of ' Past and Present
Policy of England in Ireland ' remarks :—' The native chiefs
who submitted to Henry stipulated for the use of their
own laws.' Henry VIII. was the first English sovereign
who substituted the title of ' King ' for that of ' Lord ' of
Ireland.   By this change he both renounced the original
ground on which his possession of Ireland was founded, and
distinctly admitted that, in the days of his predecessors, the
Gaelic princes acknowledging an English sovereign were
true princes, just as were in France the Plantagenets who
did homage to the French King for their continental possessions.   Previous to Henry VIII.'s time the English sovereigns,
to use the language of Burke, ' called for obedience from the
people of Ireland, not on principles of subjection, but as
vassals, and mesne lords between them and the Popes.'
Towards the close of his reign, it is true that many of the
chief Irish princes, after having been long pressed by war,
accepted Earldoms at the king's hand, and surrendered their
rights of sovereignty.   They were simply trustees who had
betrayed their trust : for they ruled by law ; and they broke
both the laws and the oaths by which they were as solemnly
bound as their meanest clansmen. Henry VIII. no more
believed that they had a right thus to dispose of their prin-
cipalities than Henry II. believed in the Pope's temporal
right over all Christian islands. It was the people, thus
lawlessly transferred, who were deceived : and the decep-
tion, often not discovered for many years, was sometimes sternly avenged. At other times the ancient order
was simply restored. A MacCarthymore changed into an
Earl, was forced to resume his old Irish sway and recognise his Tanist. The Prince of Tyrone who accepted

King Henry's coronet had, at an earlier period, pronounced a curse upon any of his descendants who proved unfaithful to his country's traditions. 'With this he was often up-braided by his kinsmen and followers; and finding the Irish nation now more than ever estranged from the English government by their recent attempt to force them out of their religion, he chose this as the most favourable moment to throw off allegiance, and revert to the ancient conse-quence and independence of O'Nial.'[1]

The Prince of Thomond had at first replied to Henry's proposed exchange, that 'although he was the captain of his nation, he was yet but one man in it,' and could do nothing without consulting with those whose rights he was sworn to maintain. Shane O'Nial, son of 'Con the Lame,' who accepted King Henry's Earldom of Tyrone, having been summoned to a conference by the Lord Deputy, refused to attend him, and explained that the surrender of Con Bacagh was invalid, being against the Irish laws—that he himself was chieftain of Tyr-owen for life only; 'nor could have more by the law of Tanistry; nor could surrender but by consent of the laws of his country.' Soon after he went to London attended by a large guard, bearing battle-axes, with their curled hair flowing over their doublets of Irish saffron. To Elizabeth he made the same statement, 'which matters forasmuch as the Queen gave credit to, he was sent home again with honour.'[2] For want of accurate knowledge on this subject numerous wars, which were but resistance to aggression, have been styled 'rebellions.'

Page 92. *Lament for the Baron of Loughmoe.*

A noble piece of Irish music is thus named, and bears the date 1507. The poem in this series entitled 'Bonny Port-more' was suggested by an ancient Irish air called by that name.

Page 95. *The Statute of Kilkenny.*

It is thus described by Mr. Plowden:—'The substance of that singular statute is offered as a specimen of the

---

[1] Plowden's *Hist. of Ireland*, vol. i. p. 194. [2] Camden.

ferocious arrogance with which the English then treated the Irish. It was enacted that intermarriages with the natives, or any connection with them as fosterers, or in the way of gossipred, should be punished as High Treason; that the use of their name, language, apparel, or customs should be punished by the forfeiture of lands and tenements; that to submit to be governed by the Brehon laws was treason.' Lord Chancellor Clare comments on it thus:—'It was a declaration of perpetual war, not only against the native Irish, but against every person of English blood who had settled beyond the limits of the Pale. . . . It drew closer the confederacy it was meant to dissolve, and implicated the colony of the Pale in ceaseless warfare.'

A remarkable picture of Ireland in the fourteenth century is presented by a remonstrance addressed to Pope John XXII. by O'Neil, King of Ulster, and the other princes of that province.

Extracts from the Irish Remonstrance to Pope John XXII.

'We have now to inform your Holiness, that Henry, king of England, and the four kings his successors, have violated the conditions of the Pontifical Bull by which they were impowered to invade this kingdom; for the said Henry promised, as appears by the said Bull, to extend the patrimony of the Irish Church, and to pay to the Apostolical See annually one penny for each house: now this promise both he and his successors above mentioned, and their iniquitous ministers, observed not at all with regard to Ireland. On the contrary, they have entirely and intentionally eluded it, and endeavoured to force the reverse.

'As to the church lands, so far from extending them, they have confined them, retrenched them, and invaded them on all sides, insomuch that some cathedral churches have been by open force notoriously plundered of half their possessions: nor have the persons of our clergy been more respected; for in every part of the country we find Bishops and Prelates cited, arrested, and imprisoned without distinction; and they are oppressed with such servile fear by those frequent and unparalleled injuries, that they have not even the courage to represent to your Holiness the sufferings they are so wantonly condemned to undergo. But since they are so cowardly and so basely silent in their own cause they deserve not that we should say a syllable in their favour. The English promised also to introduce a better code of laws, and enforce better morals among the Irish people; but instead of this they have so corrupted our morals, that the holy and dove-like simplicity of our nation is, on account of the flagitious example of those reprobates, changed into the malicious cunning of the serpent.

'We had a written code of laws, according to which our nation was governed hitherto; they have deprived us of those laws, and of every law except one, which it is impossible to wrest from us; and for the purpose of exterminating us they have established other iniquitous laws by which injustice and inhumanity are combined for our destruction; some of which we here insert for your inspection, as being so many fundamental rules of English jurisprudence established in this kingdom.

'Every man, not an Irishman, can on any charge however frivolous prosecute an Irishman; but no Irishman, whether lay or ecclesiastic (the prelate alone excepted), can prosecute for any offence whatsoever, because he is an Irishman. If any Englishman should, as they often do, treacherously and perfidiously murder an Irishman, be he ever so noble or so innocent, whether lay or ecclesiastic, secular or regular, even though he should be a prelate, no satisfaction can be obtained from an English court of justice; on the contrary, the more worthy the murdered man was and the more respected by his own countrymen, the more the murderer is rewarded and honoured, not only by the English rabble, but even by the English clergy and bishops: and especially by those whose duty it is chiefly, on account of their station in life, to correct such abominable malefactors. Every Irishwoman, whether noble or ignoble, who marries an Englishman, is, after her husband's death, deprived of the third of her husband's lands and possessions on account of her being an Irishwoman. In like manner, whenever the English can violently oppress to death an Irishman, they will by no means permit him to make a will or any disposal whatsoever of his affairs; on the contrary, they seize violently on all his property, deprive the church of its rights, and perforce reduce to a servile condition that blood which has been from all antiquity free.

'The same tribunal of the English, by advice of the King of England and some English bishops, among whom the ignorant and ill-conducted Archbishop of Armagh was president, has made in the city of St. Kenniers (Kilkenny) the following absurd and informal statute,—that no religious community in the English Pale shall receive an Irishman as novice, under pain of being contumacious contemners of the King of England's laws. And as well before as after this law was enacted it was scrupulously observed by the English Dominicans, Franciscans, monks, canons, and all other religious orders of the English nation, who showed a partiality in the choice of their religious subjects the more odious inasmuch as those monasteries were founded by Irishmen, from which Irishmen are so basely excluded by Englishmen in modern times. Besides, where they ought to have established virtue, they have done exactly the contrary; they have exterminated our native virtues, and established the most abominable vices in their stead. . . .

'Let no person wonder then if we endeavour to preserve our lives, and defend our liberties as well as we can, against those cruel tyrants, usurpers of our just properties and murderers of our persons:—so far from thinking it unlawful, we hold it to be a meritorious act, nor can we be accused of perjury or rebellion, since neither our fathers nor we did at any time bind ourselves by any oath of allegiance to their fathers or to them; and therefore without the least remorse of conscience, while breath remains, we will attack them in defence of our just rights, and never lay our arms until we force them to desist.'

Page 97. *A cry comes up from wood and wold.*

In the reign chiefly of Edward I. The king was then too much occupied with his scheme for the conquest of Scotland to pay adequate attention to affairs in Ireland. He was, otherwise, of all English kings the one most likely to have granted the petition of the Irish that, their old Brehon law having been abrogated by England, the English law should be accorded to them in its place.

In the natural order of things, an amalgamation of races and of interests would then have taken place, such as took place in England between Saxon and Norman. This result was prevented by a prolonged outlawry more unjust than the original Norman Conquest of Ireland.

It is thus that Sir John Davies, Attorney-General in the reign of James I., and an authority not likely to be prejudiced in favour of the Irish, comments on this state of things :—' For the space of 350 years after the conquest first attempted, the English laws were not communicated to the Irish, nor the benefit and protection thereof allowed to them, though they earnestly desired and sought the same. As long as they were out of the protection of the law, so that every Englishman might oppress, spoil, and kill them without controlment, how was it possible they should be other than outlaws and enemies to the crown of England? If the king would not admit them to the condition of his subjects, how could they learn to acknowledge and obey him as their sovereign? . . . In a word, if the English would neither in peace govern them by the law, nor in war root them out by the sword, must they not needs be pricks in their eyes and thorns in their sides, till the world's end? '—DAV. *Disc.*

In justice to the English sovereigns it should be remembered that although they were of course responsible for what was done in Ireland by persons armed with their authority, several of them showed a disposition to govern legally. King John and King Henry III. were among these. The former caused a regular code of English laws to be deposited in the Exchequer of Dublin, under the king's seal, 'for the common benefit of the land.' In Henry III.'s reign a duplicate of the great Charter was sent to Ireland. Except as regards the Norman Barons these acts bore little fruit; but they evinced a good intention. It was not from the early English kings that the Irish outlawry of three centuries and a half originated, but from the Norman settlers, who eventually became themselves 'more Irish than the Irish,' in spite of the statute of Kilkenny. The ultimate result was more

fatal to English law than to Irish. The former by degrees
withered away: the latter grew up again from its roots.
Chief Baron Finglas, writing early in the reign of Henry
VIII., affirms that, except in parts of the counties round
Dublin which constituted the Pale, 'the English statutes
passed in Ireland are not observed eight days after passing
them; whereas those laws and statutes made by the Irish on
their hills they keep firm and stable, without breaking through
them for any favour or reward.'

Page 110. *Halls that roofed her outlawed Prelates blacken
like a blackening brand.*

In foreign countries as well as in Ireland, religion was
ever regarded as the chief cause for which the House of
Desmond had fought against Elizabeth. She had declared
war against the Catholic Faith in 1559, the second year of
her reign. A Parliament, so called, her tool, and professing
but to represent ten counties, passed a law sentencing every
person who maintained the spiritual supremacy of the Pope,
that is, every Catholic, to forfeit, for the first offence, all his
property, and for the third, to be deemed guilty of treason!
It also required all men to attend the churches where the
new liturgy was recited, under pain of fines. The Irish
Annalists inform us that this law was 'surreptitiously obtained by the art of Stanihurst, the then Speaker; who, at
an unusual hour, and on an unaccustomed day, procured the
Bill to be passed.' The fraud was no sooner discovered
than it was denounced; but the Lord Deputy engaged 'with
oaths and protestations, that the penalties of that act should
never be inflicted.' (Plowden, vol. i. p. 221.) In most
parts of the country it proved impossible to carry this statute
into effect, but where the Queen's authority prevailed the
Catholic clergy abandoned their cures; no Protestant ministers could be found to fill their place; the churches fell into
ruin, and the people were left without sacred rites, as we
learn from the letters of Sir Henry Sidney. The intruding
Bishop of Cork publicly burned the image of St. Dominick,
as if in emulation of the earlier outrages of Archbishop
Browne, who had burned what he styled 'the Idol of Trim,'

viz. a celebrated statue of the Blessed Virgin, as well as the Crucifix of the Abbey of Ballybogan, and the world-famed Crosier of St. Patrick, called 'the Staff of Jesus.' No brief list of martyrs is transmitted to us by the Irish historians. The House of Desmond was in those days the hope of the persecuted. It protected Leverons, Bishop of Kildare, and many a priest besides.

The war was, however, provoked also by another cause. Like Strongbow, the Geraldines had made conquests in Ireland before Henry II. had landed on her shores, and they boasted their special privileges, such as exemption from attendance in Parliament, and the duty of attending a chief governor. In Kerry they had ruled as Lords Palatine ; by them justice was executed, and with them rested the power of life and death. Elizabeth insisted on a fundamental innovation ; her courts of justice were to be held in Kerry, and her judges to go circuit. Such a revolution, at that crisis, meant the full execution of the Penal Laws, and the utter destruction of the House of Desmond. The one policy on which the Deputy, Sidney, had long insisted was the breaking up of the great estates. Of him Desmond had already had experience. His great position had rendered him the chief object of the Deputy's jealousy. He had been summoned to attend the latter in his visitation of Munster, and, having complied, was treacherously seized in Kilmallock. He and his brother, John of Desmond, languished in a London prison for six years. He was then set free and sent to Dublin. On reaching that city he was again lawlessly thrown into prison, but he escaped, and reached Kerry in safety. The Mullaghmast massacre, moreover, in which 400 unarmed clansmen of Leix and Offaly, invited to a peaceful conference, were ruthlessly slaughtered, had taken place but two years before, and had bequeathed a lesson not to be despised. The marvel is that Desmond began the struggle so late. When, in 1579, his cousin, Sir James Fitzmaurice of Desmond, raised his revolt, the Earl had discountenanced it. But his enemies were resolved to force him by their provocations to his ruin. In a letter dated from his castle at Askeaton, Desmond wrote : 'The 4th of this present month (October 1579) Sir Nicholas Maltbie, being in camp at the

Abbey of Nenaghe (Manister), sent certain of his menne to
enter into Rathmore, a manor of myne, and there murdered
the keepers, spoiled the town and castel, and took away from
thence certayn of my evidence, and other writings. On the
6th of the same, he not only spoyled Rath-Keally (Rathkeale),
a town of mine, but also tyrannously burned both houses
and corn. On the 7th of the same month the said Sir
Nicholas encamped within the Abbey of Asketyn (Askeaton),
and there most maliciously defaced the ould monuments of
my ancestors.'

Not till then had the Earl drawn his sword. He then
fought, not to dethrone the Queen, but in defence of Faith,
liberty, lands, and life. Desmond's slowness to engage in
this war proceeded from no lack of spirit. In his early
days, at the battle of Affane, he had engaged, with a very
inferior force, a large body of men under Ormond. He fell
wounded, and was made prisoner. His enemies, while
carrying him off the field, exclaimed, 'Where now is the
great Earl of Desmond?' He answered, 'Where but where
he ought to be? On the necks of the Butlers.'

The Irish were passionately attached to the 'Great Earl,'
owing, no doubt, in part to his sympathy with the poor in
their sufferings. In a letter to Lord Burleigh he denounces
those authorities who compelled a poor man to carry for
five, eight, or ten miles on his back as many sheeves as the
'horse-boies' demand of him; and if he goes not a 'good
pace, though the poor soul be over-burdened, he is all the
way beaten outt of all measure.' What Desmond lacked
was readiness and generalship. He was a sleepy old war-
horse overtaken by wolves.

Dominicus O'Daly, a Gael, but not the less passionately
attached to the great Irish Norman, of whom he boasted
himself a clansman, illustrates in every line of his history *The Rise, Increase, and Exit of the Geraldines*, the
affection with which the race once 'alien' had come to
be regarded in Ireland. He begins his record thus :—
'Florence claimed this beauteous plant for her own; and
well might she glory in it, for "its branches stretched
forth unto the sea, and its boughs unto the river." That
tree was the noble race of the Geraldines, which, under the

shadow of Tuscan banners, penetrated regions whither Roman cohorts did not dare to venture.' He ends thus :— 'Four hundred and fifty years had its branches extended over the four provinces of Ireland. Not fewer than fifty lords and chieftains paid them tribute, and were ever ready to march under their banners. Beside the palatinate of Kerry, the country for 120 miles in length and 50 in breadth was theirs. The people paid submission to them throughout all their holdings : they had 100 castles and strongholds, numerous seaports, lands that were fair to the eye, and rich in fruits : the mountains were theirs, together with the woods: theirs were the rocky coasts and the sweet blue lakes which teemed with fish. Yea, this fairest of lands did they win by the sword and govern by their laws. Loved by their own, dreaded by their enemies, they were the delight of princes and the patrons of gifted youth. O but they were a great and glorious race ! '[1]

Page 112. *Florence MacCarthy's Farewell.*

There is a striking description of Florence MacCarthy in the *Pacata Hibernia.* He 'was contented (*tandem aliquando*) to repair to the President, lying at Moyallo, bringing some fourty horse in his company ; and himself in the middest of his troope (like the great Turke among his janissaries) drew towards the house, the nine and twentieth of October, like Saul, higher by the head and shoulders than any of his followers.'—P. 170. The moral indignation constantly expressed by the author of the *Pacata Hibernia* at Florence MacCarthy's method of countermining the far darker intrigues of the Lord President, recorded in that work, with intrigues of his own, is curious. Before the period he describes, Florence had been for many years detained in England, sometimes in prison, sometimes on parole. While in that country he seems to have captivated all who approached him, and acquired that remarkable knowledge and those varied accomplishments which, at a later time, rendered the yew-woods of Loch Lene as formidable to strange feet as the fastnesses of Ulster. In 1601 he was again

---

[1] *Rise, Increase, and Exit of the Geraldines*, p. 118.

shamelessly arrested when visiting the President, under the 'Queen's protection,' and sent to the Tower, where he passed the rest of his life. See the singularly interesting *Life and Letters of Florence MacCarthy Reagh*, compiled from unpublished documents in the State Paper Office, by a clansman of his ancient sept, Daniel MacCarthy, Esq. (Longmans.)

> Page 115.   *My Prince, my chief, my child on whom*
> *So early fell the dungeon's doom.*

Red Hugh O'Donnell, when but a boy of fifteen, was already celebrated for his beauty, his courage, and his skill in warlike accomplishments. To prevent him from assuming the headship of Tirconnell the following device was resorted to by Sir John Perrot, Lord President of Munster. During the summer of 1587 Red Hugh, with Mac Swyne *of the battle-axes*, O'Gallagher of Ballyshannon, and some other Irish chiefs, had gone to a monastery of Carmelites situated on the western shore of Lough Swilly, and facing the mountains of Inishowen, the church of which had long been a famous place of pilgrimage. One day a ship, in appearance a merchant vessel, sailed up the bay, cast anchor opposite Rathmullan, and offered for sale her cargo of Spanish wine. Young Red Hugh was among those who went on board during the night. The next morning he and his companions found themselves secured under hatches. He was thrown into prison in Dublin, where he languished for three years and three months. At the end of that time he made his escape, and, flying to the south, took refuge with Felim O'Toole, who was forced to surrender him. 'He remained again in irons,' says the chronicle, 'until the feast of Christmas, 1592, when it seemed to the Son of the Virgin time for him to escape.' Once more he fled, accompanied by two sons of Shane O'Neill, to the mountains of Wicklow, then covered with snow. After wandering about for three days and nights, O'Donnell and one of his companions (the other had perished) were found by some of O'Byrne's clansmen beneath the shelter of a cliff, benumbed and almost dead from hunger; for during those three days their food had consisted of grass and forest leaves. On the restoration of his strength O'Donnell succeeded, with the assistance of O'Neill, in making his way to his native mountains. From that moment the two great northern princes of Tirconnell and Tyrone, renouncing the ancient rivalries of their several Houses, entered into that common alliance against the invader, the effects of which were irresistible until the reverse at Kinsale.

Page 118. *She whose marriage couch.*

The celebrated picture of an Irish artist, Mr. Maclise, has well illustrated Eva's doom. After the capture of Waterford the king of Leinster led forth his daughter and married her to Strongbow.

Page 118. *Catch that death-shriek.*

The manuscript Irish Annals of Queen Elizabeth's reign record this event:—'At a feast wherein the Earl (Sussex) entertained that chieftain, and at the end of their good cheer, O'Neill with his wife were seized; the friends who attended were put to the sword before their faces; Phelim, with his wife and brother, were conveyed to Dublin, where they were cut up in quarters.' See also the *Four Masters*, and Leland's *History*, vol. ii. p. 257.

Page 119. *Sing the base assassin's steel*
By Sussex hired to slay O'Neill.

The intended victim was Shane O'Neill, Prince of Tyrone, against whom the Queen supported the pretensions of his illegitimate brother Matthew, Baron of Dungannon, and of his sons. A letter from Sussex to Elizabeth, which is preserved in the State Paper Office, thus concludes:—'In fine I brake with him to kill Shane, and bound myself by my oath to see him have a hundred marks of land. He seemed desirous to serve your Highness and to have the land; but fearful to do it, doubting his escape after. I told him the ways he might do it, and how to escape after with safety, which he offered and promised to do.'

Page 119. *Whom thy country and thy sire.*

The illegitimacy of Elizabeth rests not more on Catholic authority than on that of Archbishop Cranmer, and an Act of Parliament never repealed even in her own reign :— ' Cranmer, "having previously invoked the name of Christ, and having God alone before his eyes," pronounced definitively that the marriage formerly contracted, solemnised, and consummated between Henry and Anne Boleyn was, and *always had been, null and void.* The whole process was afterwards laid before the members of the Convocation and the Houses of Parliament. The former presumed not to dissent from the decision of the metropolitan; the latter were willing that in such a case their ignorance should be guided by the learning of the clergy. By both the divorce was approved and confirmed.'—LINGARD's *Hist.* vol. v. p. 36. As for the Queen's *Parliamentary* title, that was not likely to meet with unquestioned respect in Ireland. ' In the Lower House a majority had been secured by the expedient of sending to the sheriffs a list of Court candidates, out of whom the members were to be chosen.'—LINGARD, vol. vi. p. 5. The Court *named five candidates for the shires, and three for the boroughs!*

Page 119. *Trampling that Faith whose borrow'd garb.*

Not only had Elizabeth repeatedly asserted herself to be a Catholic in her sister's reign, but for some time after her own accession she wore the same mask. ' She continued to assist and occasionally to communicate at mass : she buried her sister with all the solemnities of the Catholic ritual ; and she ordered a solemn dirge, and a mass of requiem for the soul of the Emperor Charles V.'—LINGARD. Her coronation was conducted with all the ceremonial of the Catholic Pontifical, and at it she received the Sacrament under one kind.

The following contemporaneous sketch of Elizabeth's last year is not commonly known :—' Sir John Harrington, her godson, who visited the Court about seven months after the death of Essex, has described in a private letter the state

in which he found the Queen. She was altered in her
features and reduced to a skeleton. Her food was nothing
but manchet bread and succory pottage. . . . For her protection she had ordered a sword to be placed by her table,
which she often took in her hand, and thrust with violence
into the tapestry of her chamber. About a year later he
returned to her presence. "I found her," he says, "in a
most pitiable state. She bade the archbishop ask me if I
had seen Tyrone. I replied with reverence that I had seen
him with the Lord Deputy. She looked up with much
choler and grief in her countenance, and said, ' O, now it
mindeth me that you was one who saw this man elsewhere,'
and hereat she dropped a tear and smote her bosom. She
held in her hand a golden cup, which she often put to her
lips; but, in truth, her heart seemed too full to need any
more filling." . . . At length she obstinately refused to return to her bed: and sat both day and night on a stool
bolstered up with cushions, having her finger in her mouth,
and her eyes fixed on the floor, seldom condescending to
speak, and rejecting every offer of nourishment. The bishops
and the lords of the council advised and entreated in vain.
For them all, with the exception of the Lord Admiral, she
expressed the most profound contempt. He was of her own
blood; from him she consented to accept a basin of broth;
but when he urged her to return to her bed, she replied
that if he had seen what she saw there he would never make
the request. To Cecil, who asked if she had seen spirits,
she answered that it was an idle question beneath her
notice. He insisted that she must go to bed, if only to
satisfy her people. "Must!" she exclaimed; "is *must* a
word to be addressed to princes? Little man, little man,
thy father, if he had been alive, durst not have used that
word; but thou art grown presumptuous because thou
knowest that I shall die." Ordering the others to depart,
she called the Lord Admiral to her, saying in a piteous tone,
" My lord, I am tied with an iron collar about my neck."
He sought to console her, but she replied, "No, I am tied,
and the case is altered with me." '—LINGARD, vol. vi. pp.
315, 316. Edit. 1854.

No name except that of Cromwell is encircled with such

gloomy associations in Irish history as that of Elizabeth. Yet it would not be just to charge upon her all that was done by her servants in Ireland. She was not 'without some misgivings as to the injustice with which her Irish subjects were treated; and she was once so touched by the picture presented to her of their sufferings that she exclaimed, "Ah, how I fear lest it be objected to us, as it was to Tiberius by Bato, concerning the Dalmatian commotions, 'You it is that are in fault, who have committed your flocks, not to shepherds, but to wolves.'"'[1] The Queen had no more devoted adherent in Ireland than Ormond, of whose consanguinity with her she was justly proud; but on some unworthy service being demanded of him by Lord Burleigh, he wrote thus in reply:—'My lord, I will never use treachery to any man: for it would both touch her Highness' honour and my own credit too much; and whosoever gave the Queen advice thus to write is fitter for such base service than I am. Saving my duty to her Majesty, I would I might have revenge by my sword of any man that thus persuadeth the Queen to write to me.' Elizabeth expressed detestation of the massacre of the Spaniards at 'the Golden Fort' after their surrender, as historians affirm: and a letter addressed to her by a brave and upright officer in her Irish army, denouncing a massacre committed by her representatives, could hardly have been written except in the belief that such acts would be odious to her.

Page 121. *The Sugane Earl.*

This title, which means 'the Earl of Straw,' was absurdly used by his enemies to discredit a man whose father, though pushed aside by the 'great Earl of Desmond,' was, notwithstanding, the elder brother. The mode by which Sir George Carew, President of Munster, contrived to separate the 'Sugane' Earl of Desmond from his allies is narrated in the *Pacata Hibernia,* the work of Stafford, Sir George Carew's Secretary, pp. 65, 91, 97, 193. Dublin, 1810. The principal

---

[1] *Illustrated Hist. of Ireland,* by M. F. C. Cusack, p. 386. In two despatches she expressed her displeasure at the attempt to poison Shane O'Neil.

allies of the Sugane Earl were Dermond O'Connor and Redmond Burke. The latter was induced to betray the Earl by the expectation delusively held out to him that in this case his pretensions to the Barony of Leitrim would be recognised. Dermond had married the Lady Margaret, sister of the young Earl of Desmond, who had been from his child-hood detained by Elizabeth as a prisoner in the Tower, but whom she had sent back to Ireland in order to divide the adherents of the Sugane Earl. Sir George Carew formed a plot. The pretext by which Dermond was to be apparently justified in surrendering his chief, the Sugane Earl, consisted in a letter supplied by the President, by which it was to be made to appear that the Earl himself had been the traitor, and was in secret league with the President for the destruc-tion of his own allies. Of this letter Stafford remarks: 'Forasmuch as the contents thereof doe manifest the inven-tion, I have thought not unfit to bee inserted in the present relation.'

Another plot against the Sugane Earl is related in the *Pacata Hibernia* with an equal unconsciousness that it contained anything unfit to be divulged. A man of the name of Nugent, who had been servant of Sir Thomas Norris, deserted the English cause for the Irish, and, having subsequently quarrelled with his new friends, delivered himself up with a view of receiving the Royal protection. 'Answer was made that forsomuch as his crimes and offences had been extraordinary, he could not hope to be reconciled unto the State, except he would deserve it by extraordinary service.'—P. 67. Nugent offered to assassinate, or, as he called it, to 'ruine,' either the Sugane Earl or his brother, John Fitz-Thomas. 'The President having contrived a plot for James Fitz-Thomas (as is before shown) gave him in charge to undertake John, his brother.'—P. 68. Eventually the Sugane Earl was delivered up by the 'White Knight,' while concealed in a cave. This event and the capture of Florence MacCarthy nearly at the same time, and just before the arrival of their Spanish succours, were soon after con-summated by the defeat at Kinsale.

Page 142. *The Intercession.*

The Irishman has a special reason, besides those common to all Christians, for execrating the memory of those who, during a short period subsequent to the Ulster rising of 1641, dishonoured their country by murders inflicted upon the unarmed and defenceless. Terribly were those crimes of individuals revenged upon Ireland. The Puritan party at once, in the interest alike of sectarian hatred, of policy, and of cupidity, turned the facts placed at their disposal, in themselves disgraceful enough, into a legend of atrocity which, propagated by such writers as Temple and Borlase, is still, though often refuted, reproduced whenever a demand for such statements has sprung up. According to the legend these deplorable murders constituted a carefully planned massacre : they were unprovoked, and uncondemned by the leaders at the Irish side : they continued long, and extended largely over Ireland ; and, lastly, the number of the victims was according to some 30,000, and according to others 300,000 ! Against every one of those misrepresentations there is the clearest historical evidence, while in their favour the evidence rests chiefly on those 'reports' so justly stigmatised by Edmund Burke, the reports of witnesses who deposed that they had seen the ghosts of the murdered walking on a river, and raising spectral hands to heaven ! We have fortunately sounder contemporary evidence. 'The Rev. Dr. Warner, an English Protestant clergyman, in his *History of the Rebellion in Ireland*, took great pains to ascertain the truth out of " authentic documents," and the result of his minute enquiry was, " that the number of persons killed *out of war*, not at the beginning only, but in the course of the two first years of the rebellion, amounted altogether to 2,109 ; on the report of other Protestants, 1,619 more ; and, on the report of some of the rebels themselves, a further number of 300; the whole making 4,028 ;" besides 8,000 killed by ill usage. . . . This account, he tells us, was corroborated by a letter which he copied out of the Council books at Dublin, and which was written ten years after the beginning of the rebellion, from the Parliament commissioners in Ireland to the English Parliament.'[1] The commissioners expressly

[1] Haverty's *Hist. of Ireland*, p. 523.

say in this letter, that it then appeared that besides 848 families, the number of victims who perished was 6,062. These estimates are in harmony with the statement of Carte, that the whole number of *English* in Ulster at the time could not have exceeded 20,000, of whom a large proportion certainly escaped injury.

Equally untrue are the other allegations referred to. The murders did not rise out of any premeditated design. They took place, not at the first outbreak of the rising, but when those who had flung themselves into it were infuriated by the loss of some of their earlier advantages, and by the massacre of the Irish at Island Maghee.[1] Those murders were never sanctioned by the leaders at the Irish side, with the partial exception of Sir Phelim O'Neil. All acts of violence, whether against life or property, were officially denounced by solemn assemblies of the leaders, civil and ecclesiastical, and forbidden in repeated proclamations, especially by the great Ulster leader, Owen Roe O'Neil, who at once on his landing in Donegal (June 1642) expressed his horror at them, and sent the remaining prisoners in safety to Dundalk. 'The leading men among the Irish have this to say for themselves, that they were all along so far from favouring any of the murderers, that, not only their agents, soon after the King's Restoration, but even in their remonstrance, presented by the Lord Viscount Gormanstown and Sir Robert Talbot, on March 19, 1642, the nobility and gentry of the nation desired that the murders, *on both sides committed*, should be strictly examined, and the authors of them punished according to the utmost severity of the law; which proposal certainly their adversaries could never have rejected, but that they were conscious to themselves of being deeper in the mire than they would have the world believe.'—LORD CASTLEHAVEN'S *Memoirs*, p. 21, Edit. 1815.

Page 150. *Let Charles the Confederates win or lose them.*

Men at once patriotic and loyal have seldom been placed between alternatives so cruel as were the Confederates

[1] See the *Collection of some of the Massacres and Murders committed on the Irish in Ireland since the 23rd of October*, 1641, appended to Clarendon's *Vindication of the Earl of Ormond*, and to Curry's *Review of the Civil Wars*, p. 623.

of Kilkenny. The event by no means enables us to deter-
mine to which of the two policies there advocated the pre-
ference should have been given, that of conditional or that
of unconditional adherence to Charles, since neither policy
was, or indeed could have been, consistently maintained.
Those most disinterestedly loyal to Charles were doubtless
those most loyal to their Country and their Religion likewise ;—they, therefore, demanded the repeal of the Penal
Laws. It had been repeatedly proved that in the mouth of
Charles, insidiously charged as he was with 'Popery,' vague
promises to the Catholics availed nothing. Early in his
reign they had granted him large sums in return for his
'graces,' *i.e.* the temporary suspension of Penal Laws, with a
promise to abrogate them. That promise had ever been
broken : and the Puritans denounced, as complicity with
idolatry, even the intention of relinquishing persecution. On
the one hand, it was certain that their victory meant the
destruction of Ireland : on the other, it was next to certain
that if Charles recovered a nominal sovereignty to be enjoyed
at their pleasure (and he had his dealings with them as well
as with their intended victims), being at the same time
bound by no public engagement to the Catholics, his course
would be that which his son adopted on the Restoration.

The Confederates could not trust Charles because he was
not free. Before the Ulster rising he had yielded Strafford
to death, the one great man at his side, and had practically
become the servant of a Parliament bent on his destruction.
Early in 1641 he had commanded Parsons and Borlase,
nominally his Lords Justices, to proclaim to his Irish subjects
that the Royal engagements contracted with them should be
fulfilled. They disobeyed him ; but for which disobedience
Charles used to say that the Ulster rising would never have
taken place. Ormond was equally bent, until too late, on
frustrating the King's kindlier intentions towards the Irish
Catholics. At a great crisis Charles had expressly given
him authority to concede the abrogation of the Penal
Statutes. He concealed that permission from the Confederates, and a priceless opportunity was lost. Had the full
union which took place later been cemented on that occa-
sion, Ireland would have been the King's in a month ; and

Montrose would have had four times as many Irish soldiers beside him as shared his triumphs under the gallant Mac Donnell. Later, Lord Glamorgan had been sent by the King to make the same concession, but to make it secretly. The terms were accepted and acted on by both parties ; but an accident having divulged the treaty, the royal envoy was imprisoned by Ormond and disavowed by his master. The Confederates could not have trusted Charles.

Whatever course they had taken the fate of Ireland was probably sealed from the day of the first decisive Puritan success. Had the Parliamentary war been one for liberty only, Ireland would have had nothing to fear. In that case statesmen must have seen that the Covenanters' grievance, an Anglican Liturgy obtruded upon a Protestant Church, was a small matter compared with the Irish grievance—the Faith of a nation branded as high treason. ' Ship-money ' would hardly have outweighed the confiscation of Ulster, and that second intended confiscation, when, as Burke expressed it, 'the war of chicane succeeded to the war of arms,' and when Strafford's ' project was nothing less than to subvert the title to every estate in every part of Connaught, and to establish a new plantation through this whole province.' [1] But the struggle for liberty was at that time but a body of which Puritanism was the soul. The Scotch Covenanters had been the prop of the English Parliament. The Puritans had resolved to extirpate Catholicism in Ireland—dealing first, however, with the Monarchy and the Church of England. At the Ulster rising the Parliament had raised vast sums from ' the Adventurers ' on the credit of the destined Irish confiscations. That fund was created for the reduction of Ireland ; but it was employed in the war against the King. The Puritan policy was neither to put down the Irish revolt speedily, nor to prevent it from spreading. Hume affirms that the Lords Justices of Ireland were ' willing to foment the rebellion in a view of profiting by the multiplied forfeitures.' Elsewhere he states that ' by disposing beforehand of all the Irish forfeitures, they (the English Parliament) rendered all men of property desperate, and seemed to threaten an *utter extirpation of the natives.*'

[1] Leland's *Hist. of Ireland*, vol. iii.

Clarendon affirms that the sufferings inflicted by the Puritans upon the Irish, chiefly, it is true, at a later period, were exceeded only by those endured by the Jews at the hands of Titus during the siege of Jerusalem.   Many writers with no Irish leanings have indignantly recorded the arts, and above all the cruelties, exercised against loyalists, by which the Lords of the Pale were *compelled* to rise in defence of their lands, as well as of their Religion and Freedom.   But they rose in the interests of Charles, not less than in their own. Their victory would, supposing the penal laws cancelled, have been his also.

The same arts, united with the vacillating weakness of Charles, complicated the whole career of the Confederates. They made their mistakes; but in justice to them it is to be remembered that when thwarting his ostensible representatives, they were often in entire accord with his secret agents; and, again, that in dealing with the insincere it is difficult to be consistent.

The two men who in that dreadful struggle might have preserved Ireland for Charles, and Charles for Ireland, were Ormond and Inchiquin.   The former was Charles's most faithful friend except Clanrickard (a Catholic), and his most ill-starred adviser.   The latter returned to the King's cause after his military genius had ruined it in southern Ireland. He returned also to the Catholic Faith.   Both Ormond and Inchiquin had been early captured by Queen Elizabeth's celebrated ' Court of Wards,' and reared in a religion opposed to that of their parents and their ancestors.

Page 154.   *My sons by adoption ;   mail'd knights of the Pale.*

On the hill of Crofty, in Meath, the most important men of the Pale met—Lords Fingal, Gormanstown, Slane, Louth, Dunsany, Trimbleston, Netterville, Sir Patrick Barnewell, Sir Christopher Bellew, and many besides.   A body of the Ulster leaders, headed by Roger O'More, appeared in sight. The Lords of the Pale rode to meet them, and Lord Gormanstown demanded 'for what reason they came armed into the Pale ?'   O'More replied ' that the ground of their coming thither, and of their taking up arms, was for the liberty of their consciences, the maintenance of his Majesty's prerogative, in which they understood he was abridged, and the making the subjects of this kingdom as free as those of England.' Lord Gormanstown answered, 'Seeing these be your true ends, we will likewise join with you therein.'

Page 154. *Your moanings, my sons, and your wailings, my daughters.*

At the end of the Cromwellian war, the population of Ireland was reduced from more than 1,400,000 to 800,000. A law was passed banishing all Catholics to the west of the Shannon. More than half of the land of the country was confiscated. Sir William Petty ends his statement thus :— 'So there were lost 689,000 souls ; for whose blood some one should answer both to God and the King ! '

Page 164. *The Lady turned beggar.*

This lady was the widow of Lord Roche, a Royalist. In her old age she used to be seen begging in the streets of Cork.

The feelings of the Irish towards Charles II. are nowhere more vigorously illustrated than in the works of an eminent prelate of his time, Dr. Nicholas French, Bishop of Ferns. The following passage is from the preface to his *Bleeding Iphigenia* :—' Courteous reader, the author of this preface hath drawn another Iphigenia of the body of a noble, ancient Catholic Nation, clad all in red robes, not to be now offered up as a victim, but as already sacrificed, not to a profane deity, but to the living God, for holy religion.'

The Bishop thus addresses Charles II. :—' Give freedom, great King, to a poor priest to speak truth to your Majesty : it is no new thing that good priests speak to kings ; and God Himself saith He will curse the blessings of those priests that will not speak truth and give glory to His holy Name.' In another tract he thus describes the policy sanctioned by that King :—' These are verities not to be doubted of, which after ages will hardly admit, seeing the like was never before recorded in annals or mentioned in any history; for since the creation of Adam to this day (and perhaps our posterity to the world's end may be as far to seek) wè cannot produce another example of the like measure extended to a Christian people, under the government of a most Christian Prince. The most bloody tyrants of former ages, even those monsters of nature who seemed to be born for no other end than the desolation of mankind, did never extirpate their old friends to make room for their reconciled enemies; so that it must be a very difficult matter to persuade those who are not eye-witnesses of the fact, that the royal authority of our gracious King, which here in England maintains the peer in his splendour and dignity, the commoner in his birthright and liberty, which protects the weak from the oppression of the mighty, secures the nobility from the insolence of the people, and by which equal and impartial justice is indifferently distributed to all the inhabitants of this great and flourishing realm, should at the same time be made use of in his kingdom of Ireland to condemn innocents before they are heard, to destroy so many thousand widows and orphans, to confirm unlawful and usurped possessions, to violate the public faith, to punish virtue, to countenance vice, to hold loyalty a crime, and treason worthy of reward.'

If this be plain speaking, the 'Advice of the Bishop to the Irish People' is not less marked by moderation :—'If justice shall be done you, and cause of joy come from the King's good pleasure and determination, praise God and the King for that happiness, and pray to God for his long and prosperous reigne. But if this shall not be done (God permitting things to goe on as they doe either for punishing our and our fathers' sins, or for trying our patience in this world), let His holy Name be ever blessed. Bear patiently your poverty, and you shall find poverty a great blessing.'

Another tract of Dr. French's, 'The Unkinde Desertor of Loyall Men and True Friends,' is an impassioned invective against the Duke of Ormond's conduct subsequently to the Restoration, and derives a singular pathos from the fact that to the writer it had apparently seemed an impossibility that a son of the House of Ormond could ever take a course hostile to Ireland. A friend, he tells us, earnestly dissuaded him from publishing his work, and 'suggested that regard should be had of Ormond's noble Catholic ancestors, and especially of his grandfather, Walter, Earl of Ormond,[1] and of his own pious parents, and of his brother, Mr. Richard Butler—a chevaliere of great devotion, and yet valiant in the face of his enemy—and of his sisters, all of them virtuous Catholic ladies.'

Page 167. *The Irish slave in Barbadoes.*

'Sir William Petty, writing in 1672, states that 6,000 boys and women were thus sold as slaves to the undertakers of the American islands. . . . When the Rev. John Grace visited those islands in 1666, he found that there were as yet no fewer than 12,000 Irish scattered amongst them, and that they were treated as slaves.'—*Historical Sketch of the Persecutions suffered by the Catholics of Ireland under the Rule of Cromwell and the Puritans.* By the Rev. PATRICK FRANCIS MORAN (now Bishop of Ossory). J. Duffy, Dublin.

Page 174. *But against you we drew not that knife ye had drawn.*

Some important mistakes made by Lord Macaulay respecting the conduct of the Irish Parliament in the time of James II., especially as regards the Act of Settlement, are effectually refuted in an article on his History in the *Dublin Review.* In the days of Queen Mary the Corporation of Dublin hired seventy houses for English Protestants flying from persecution, and entertained the refugees for a year and a half, as is recorded by Harris, O'Driscoll, and others.

Page 188. *Beyond Marsiglia's valley.*

The battle of Marsiglia, fought by the French under Catinat against the Duke of Savoy and Prince Eugene, close to the Waldensian Alps, in the year 1693, was decided by the valour of the 6,000 Irish who fought on the French side.

[1] On account of his piety styled ' Walter of the Beads.'

Page 188.   *Long-leaguered Barcelona.*

The French had lost 10,000 men in vain attempts to take Barcelona : at last the Irish regiments of Dillon dislodged the Spaniards from the neighbouring hills, and the capture of the city followed.

Page 189.   *The valleys echoed ' Fontenoy.'*

'Gentlemen of Ireland,' said the French King at the critical moment, 'there stand your enemies ! ' The charge of the Irish Brigade gained the battle of Fontenoy. 'Accursed,' exclaimed King George, on hearing of this battle, 'be the laws that deprive me of such soldiers ! ' The Irish Brigade at Fontenoy consisted of the regiments of Clare, Lally, Dillon, Berwick, Roth, and Buckley, with FitzJames's Cavalry. It was commanded by OBrien, Lord Clare. As the Brigade charged up the hill its war-cry was, ' Remember Limerick and the Sassanach faith '—an allusion to the violated treaty.

Page 195.   *Like those slow aloes seldom flowering.*

A species of aloe is said to flower only once a century.

Page 196.   *To weep a Troy than theirs more holy.*

Fiesole boasted that it had been founded by a remnant escaped from Troy.

Page 218.   *Saint Columba's Farewell.*

This is a translation from an ancient Irish poem. It need hardly be said that three other poems, at pages 177, 179, 180, are, in a large part, versified from the ' Lamentations.'

Page 224.   *Where the Theban King in his blindness sat.*

Œdipus.   See Sophocles' *Œdipus Coloneus.*

Page 231. *A Deliverer stepp'd from the camp of her foes.*

Grattan, the noblest of Ireland's patriots during that crisis with which her new era began, belonged to her latest race, and was the first fully to understand the *amende* owed by that race to Ireland. He knew that the Irish Constitution of 1782, if it did not represent a people as well as a class, was but a name; and therefore he insisted on Parliamentary Reform and Catholic Emancipation.

Page 288. *Which smiled to meet Catullus' homeward smile.*

'Peninsularum, Sirmio, insularumque ocelle.'—CATULLUS.

Page 289. *Sows the slow olive for a race unborn.*

Quoted from Landor's *Gebir*.

Page 295. *Vinum dæmonum.*

This expression, used by one of the Fathers in speaking of poetry, is perhaps most applicable to that seductive species of poetry which embodies great aspirations at war with great truths:—poetry which enters the region of the spiritual, but yet does not acknowledge, and therefore sets itself up as a rival to, religion. The plea of 'invincible ignorance,' that is, of an ignorance relating to Revealed Truths, and not proceeding from an adverse Will (as Faith proceeds from a Good Will, and on that account is meritorious), *may* be applicable even in the case of errors the most deplorable. The ordinary 'latitudinarian' theory is obliged to abandon such cases as beyond its limit of hope, notwithstanding the violence which it is also compelled to offer to any fixed standard of Faith.

Page 301. *Whereon Colonna mourn'd alone,*
An eagle widow'd in her nest.

Vittoria Colonna, the widow of the Marquis of Pescara, to whom Michael Angelo addressed his most remarkable poems.

Page 323. *Lit from above, yet fuell'd from below.*

An analogous thought by which this line was probably suggested is doubtless familiar to the readers of poetry. It occurs in Mr. Patmore's beautiful poem of *The Angel in the House.* It is there applied to love, not poetry.

LONDON : PRINTED BY
SPOTTISWOODE AND CO., NEW-STREET SQUARE
AND PARLIAMENT STREET

www.ingramcontent.com/pod-product-compliance
Lightning Source LLC
Chambersburg PA
CBHW032300280326
41932CB00009B/643